9/11
The
Conspiracy
Theories

About the author

David Gardner is an experienced writer and journalist, currently working as an editor for *Newsweek*. He also worked for the *Daily Mail* as a crime writer and senior foreign correspondent, filing dispatches from war-torn Beirut, covering the first Gulf War – he was the first British print journalist into Baghdad – and travelling around the world on assignments for the award-winning newspaper. He moved to California as the *Mail*'s Los Angeles correspondent, which saw him cover four presidential elections and all the biggest US stories of the past two decades and worked until recently as the London *Evening Standard*'s US correspondent. He has written several books, including *The Last of the Hitlers* (2001), an account of how he discovered the descendants of the German dictator, and *Legends: Murder, Lies and Cover-Ups* (John Blake Publishing, 2016), in which he investigated some of the most famous celebrity deaths in recent history, including those of President John F. Kennedy, Marilyn Monroe and Diana, Princess of Wales. He has also written two novels. He divides his time between the UK and LA.

9/11

The Conspiracy Theories

The truth and what's been hidden from us

David Gardner

JB

First published in the UK by John Blake Publishing
an imprint of Bonnier Books UK
4th Floor, Victoria House
Bloomsbury Square
London WC1B 4DA
England
Owned by Bonnier Books
Sveavägen 56, Stockholm, Sweden

www.facebook.com/johnblakebooks
twitter.com/jblakebooks

First published in paperback in 2021

Paperback ISBN: 978-1-78946-425-2
Ebook ISBN: 978-1-78946-426-9
Audio book ISBN: 978-1-78946-427-6

British Library Cataloguing-in-Publication Data:

A catalogue record for this book is available from the British Library.

Design by www.envydesign.co.uk

Printed and bound in Great Britain by Clays Ltd, Elcograf S.p.A

1 3 5 7 9 10 8 6 4 2

Text copyright © David Gardner 2021

John Blake Publishing is an imprint of Bonnier Books UK
www.bonnierbooks.co.uk

To my wife, Michelle, my partner in life and love, and our three children, Mickey, Jazmin and Savannah.

Acknowledgements

I'd like to give special thanks to Toby Buchan and Ciara Lloyd at John Blake Publishing. It is the second book I have worked on with Toby and he is a superb editor and an absolute gentleman to work with. The scale of 9/11 was such that it divides many of our lives to before and after the catastrophic assault on New York and Washington DC. With that in mind, this project has brought back memories of the time I spent working with Tim Miles in our US News and Features office on Spring and Lafayette in Soho, New York when the Twin Towers were still standing strong, as were we. Our time there with Tim and his wife, Wendy Henry, were some of our happiest. Dating back to my *Daily Mail* years in London, I would also like to acknowledge two other old colleagues, Dave Williams and Paul Henderson, who have remained close friends to this day.

During my research for this book, I was caught by surprise at how little the 9/11 survivors and families who lost loved ones still know about the events surrounding that terrible morning, and I am very appreciative of the time and care that

Mark Rossini, Kristen Breitweiser, Matt Campbell and Tim Frolich, in particular, took to help me understand their long and painful journeys to try and get to the truth. Any author writing about 9/11 should take a moment to remember those who died, and I would ask you to do the same now.

Contents

Introduction

Even at a time when news is flashed around the world in moments, there are few events that stop us in our tracks. If people once remembered where they were when JFK was assassinated, then 9/11 engraved itself into the consciousness of later generations so indelibly that the simple date is enough to elicit the same deep sense of shock and outrage we felt so strongly twenty years ago.

We remember the burning towers; bodies falling like rag dolls from the sky, the immense buildings, those monuments to America's pride, collapsing into rubble. We saw what happened on 11 September 2001. Some were there and lived to tell the tale. We all watched it on television.

But why did it happen, and how? These are questions that have still not been answered satisfactorily all these years later.

Like many people, I have visited One World Trade Center, the $25 billion complex that sits uncomfortably on the site of the Twin Towers in downtown Manhattan as a cross between a bustling tourist destination and a solemn memorial. What remains of the rubble is scrubbed and on display in a museum filled with photographs that reflect the fading snapshots in our minds. We can read how history remembers that terrible morning, but if you were to ask the survivors, or, indeed, the families of the nearly 3,000 people who died, if they know what led to the attacks I can guarantee you that most of them would not be able to tell you the full story. The US government will certainly not tell you.

This explains why so many conspiracy theories have sprung up attempting to explain the events leading up to 9/11. There are rabbit holes here that are certain to infuriate most right-minded people, let alone those who lost their loved ones.

When a President of the United States publicly doubts the election results of the world's defining democracy, and when people can seriously question whether an atrocity on the scale of the Sandy Hook school shootings that left twenty children dead even happened at all, then it is little wonder that people bristle at the term 'conspiracy theory'. There are certainly people who promote preposterous ideas for their own nefarious or deluded ends about everything from the Holocaust to the moon landings.

But history is also littered with brave souls who dared to stand up and speak out, sometimes at great danger to themselves. Indeed, what do you call a conspiracy theory that proves to be correct? I guess you'd call that the truth.

Some of the so-called conspiracy theories stemming from 9/11 are not just the lunatic ramblings of the fantasist fringe; some are serious issues raised by serious people. The idea that the Twin Towers were felled not by the fires from the planes, but by controlled demolitions from explosives planted in advance, may sound far-fetched, but a group comprising literally thousands of architects and engineers points to detailed scientific evidence supporting exactly that idea.

Similarly, it really does not make sense that the American military, the most powerful and advanced in the world, did not manage to get a jet fighter within miles of the doomed airliners in the one hour and seventeen minutes from when American Airlines Flight 11 first hit the North Tower of the World Trade Center, to United Airlines Flight 93's crash landing in the fields of Shanksville, Pennsylvania. In these pages, however, you will see the minute-to-minute chaos that left America's skies disastrously vulnerable as the terrorists closed on their targets. Human error is an ever-present reminder of our fallibility, but deception and self-interest have always been close to the surface in politics and espionage, and the people who control those worlds are often selective in what they choose to disclose to the public. They will argue that it is not in our best interests to know the truth about sensitive issues, when it is more likely that our knowing is not in their best interests.

The US authorities have misled the public about 9/11, of that I have no doubt. Worse, they have deceived the families of those who lost loved ones in a purposeful, unforgivable campaign of lies and misinformation.

You may think you know what happened the morning the world stood still to watch in horror as New York and Washington DC came under attack. You may even trust that, in the case of such an immense event in America's history, those in power would do the right thing. You would be wrong.

From the secret arrival of the first al-Qaeda terror teams in California in January 2000, watched and monitored by the CIA, to the secret military project that identified four of the leading 9/11 hijackers, including ringleader Mohamed Atta, eighteen months before the attacks, and through to the failure to prevent the hijackings and to the cover-ups in the aftermath of America's nightmare, I have connected the dots with the help of inside sources and thousands of formerly classified documents to highlight examples showing exactly how the catastrophic airborne attacks could have been prevented.

The conspiracy theories are all here. Some are utterly debunked. Others, with careful examination, bear closer scrutiny. You will read the stories of decent, caring, intelligent people who absolutely reject the US government's account of 9/11.

This is the version of 9/11 that many intelligence agents closely involved in the investigation believe but are afraid to make public. After all this time, there is still too much at stake. A brave few who have come forward have been targeted by the authorities.

Most importantly, this is the account of 9/11 that the commission set up by President George W. Bush in the aftermath of the attacks patently failed to tell.

For the first time, twenty years after 9/11, this book explains what really happened – the real story behind the attacks on New York and Washington DC. ... and the truth that has been hidden from us.

DAVID GARDNER
England and LA, 2021

Chapter One

The Gambler

**Manchester, England,
March 2000**

Niaz Khan was at rock bottom when, in March 2000, he stumbled out of a casino in Oldham, near Manchester, with gambling debts of more than £9,000. With a wife and family to support and only his paltry income from waiting tables at a curry restaurant, he was at the end of his tether.

It was the moment that the two men who had been watching him for weeks were waiting for. As his troubles mounted, Khan had been increasingly drawn to a local mosque where the radical imam spoke in glowing terms about Osama bin Laden and the virtues of jihadism. The martyrdom he espoused was particularly attractive to a man who had gambled his future on the toss of a dice.

The strangers introduced themselves outside the casino and told Khan they could make his gambling debts disappear.

They knew the Taliban. If Khan was prepared to go to a camp in Pakistan and agree to take part in 'a mission' then they would ensure that his debts would be paid. All he had to do was say yes and everything would be taken care of.

'First they say, "We can help you,"' recalls Khan. 'I say, "How can you help me?"'

They then persuaded him to sit in their car and he says they asked him if he'd heard of bin Laden.

The Burnley-born waiter, then twenty-seven, decided he had nothing to lose by taking up their offer to fly to Lahore, Pakistan, where he would start training for his mission. He shouldn't tell his family where he was going. He should just go.

On 22 March 2000, Khan picked up his ticket from a travel agency as instructed and flew out that same day. On arrival, he was given £3,000 and told to wait for more instructions at a Lahore hotel. Bin Laden's men picked him up a short while later, blindfolded him and took him to a safe house at a camp across the border in Afghanistan, about a forty-minute drive from his hotel. It was only here that he discovered what was expected of him.

He learned how to hijack planes, how to smuggle weapons on board, how to force his way into a cockpit and how to terrorise and kill. There was no coming back from this mission, he was told. It was a one-way flight to martyrdom.

Khan spent a week training to be a hijacker, looking at photos of the inside layouts of airliners, watching Hollywood action movies featuring hijackings and even using a mock cockpit of a Boeing 767 aircraft.

'You will be making plans to hijack a plane in America, in the United States,' Khan says he was told by his al-Qaeda mentor.

The instructions were detailed. It was a how-to in hijacking. For instance, he was told it was better that the first person he hit during the takeover was with a knife rather than a gun to make a more shocking impact on the passengers and crew. 'The first person to hit was the crew in the face or neck, so when you cut there would be blood everywhere and the people who watch would be scared,' Khan said in a deposition. 'They told me you would be leaving, and to pack to go to America, because we need you to be in America. They asked me, "Are you ready for this? Are you scared? Are you ready to do a suicide?" I said, "Yeah, no problem."'

He said he was told about the hardships Osama bin Laden had faced fighting the jihadist cause and asked repeatedly if he was prepared to die.

Khan's departure was just as sudden as his arrival. He was told to pack his bags after about a week and to travel to John F. Kennedy International Airport in New York via a circuitous route through London and Switzerland.

Once at JFK, on 2 April 2000, he was supposed to make contact with a taxi driver wearing a distinctive white cap whose name was 'Babu Khan'. The plan, he was now told, was that he would meet up with five or six other recruits in the United States, a number of whom would be trained pilots. Together, they would hijack a plane using 'pen guns' and explosives provided to them by jihadists employed in the airport's duty-free service.

The hijacking was set for some time between 7 and 21 April. But Khan's resolve was crumbling. By the time he arrived in America, he was already questioning whether he could go through with the suicide mission and, instead of meeting his terrorist accomplices, he travelled to Atlantic City and gambled away all the money his al-Qaeda bosses had given him.

Terrified he would be hunted down by the terror group, Khan called the police in Atlantic City, saying he feared for his life and offering to tell all about the hijack plot. The Federal Bureau of Investigation was quickly notified and agents from the Newark, New Jersey, office interviewed the scared – and broke – Briton on 7 April.

Initially, the agents in Newark were sceptical, but Khan passed two lie-detector tests. Enquiries in Pakistan appeared to tie in with his story. He offered to work with the agency to expose the terrorists involved. 'Of course, I was ready to do this,' he said later.

The problem was that, while the Newark agents came to believe Khan, their FBI bosses in Washington and New York thought he was making the whole thing up. The decision was taken to fly Khan back to England and hand him over to the British authorities. But according to the FBI, 'the British had no interest in this case from the start'.

'The case agent stated that he would have liked to continue the operation once Khan was back in England, and to try to use Khan as a potential asset. However, according to the case agent, the British were not interested, and the CIA was scared off by Khan's possible suicidal tendencies,' said a classified FBI report.

Because Khan was a British citizen, the FBI felt that MI5 should handle any undercover operation. In fact, MI5 agents spent just forty-five minutes with Khan at Heathrow before letting him go.

The case file on Khan had also been sent to the Central Intelligence Agency. The roles of the two US agencies are clearly defined and bound by law; the FBI is responsible for domestic operations and the CIA for foreign intelligence gathering. But while the FBI had been upfront about Khan with the CIA, that trust had not been reciprocated. The CIA already knew, in April 2000, that two other potential al-Qaeda hijackers were in the United States and had known that for three months, but they had illegally withheld that information from the FBI, the agency that should have taken over the investigation.

The reason for that betrayal of trust has never been revealed … until now.

If the FBI had known two al-Qaeda agents were already on American soil when Khan exposed the plane hijack plot, there is a very real chance that they would have arrested the terrorists and foiled the plot long before 2,977 people lost their lives on 11 September 2001. But the CIA had a motive for keeping Nawaf al-Hazmi and Khalid al-Mihdhar's presence and movements in the US to themselves.

It is the great unsaid secret of 9/11 that explains why successive American presidents and their administrations have actively prevented the families who lost their loved ones and the survivors of the worst terror attack in US history from learning the truth. It explains why the intelligence services from the United States, Saudi Arabia and Britain kept key details of the 9/11 investigation secret for twenty years. And it explains why the CIA and MI5 wanted nothing to do with Niaz Khan's offer to go undercover with the al-Qaeda hijackers.

The only explanation is that the CIA was already running an illegal operation using Hazmi and Mihdhar, which they believed gave them the inside track on Osama bin Laden's plans. They would consider Khan, the twentieth hijacker working as a double agent, a liability, a loose cannon who had gone from suicidal gambler to devoted jihadist and back to hopeless gambler in a matter of a fortnight. He could have ruined everything.

As it turned out, the CIA operation was irreparably flawed anyway. What could have been the biggest undercover success in US history was undeniably the absolute worst. It began with a gamble on 'turning' a terrorist to get an inside source to spill secrets from the heart of the world's most feared terrorist group, but crashed and burned as the recruitment operation went horribly awry. Only when the hijacked planes were slamming into the World Trade Center and the Pentagon did

America's spy chiefs realise the scale and the consequences of their failure.

How did the CIA get it so wrong and how high did the knowledge about its off-the-books operation go? The look on President George W. Bush's face, when he learned in a Florida primary school classroom that hijacked planes had hit the World Trade Center on a bright, cloudless September morning two decades ago, tells its own story.

It is both astonishing and shameful that so many of those who lost so much on 9/11 are still trying to discover the full facts about that fateful day, and it is disgraceful that the people in power we trust to protect and to lead us still obfuscate the truth.

The 9/11 families have long complained that nobody has connected the dots for them to satisfactorily explain the lead-up to the attacks on New York and Washington. It partly explains why so many of them – more than 6,000 family members of those who were killed and survivors of the attacks – are still involved in two lawsuits, the biggest in US history, seeking to prove Saudi Arabia's complicity in the plot. This is no conspiracy theory; it's a serious legal complaint that has already changed the law in America, making it possible to sue a foreign power through the US courts.

It's easy to forget, too, that fifteen of the nineteen hijackers were from Saudi Arabia.

But the House of Saud didn't want 9/11 to happen any more than the Americans. The Saudis weren't in league with Osama bin Laden and al-Qaeda; they were working with the CIA and the Bush administration. As you will read, the real story is how their joint operation, carried out with the aid of MI5, went so disastrously wrong.

There are some ludicrous theories that have gathered support in the years since 9/11. The so-called 'no planers' allege a *Wag the Dog* CGI conspiracy by the US government and the media. They claim the attacks never happened and have harassed relatives of the dead by claiming they're in on the scam.

It's almost as hard to make a case that a secretive cabal at the very heart of the Bush administration masterminded the hijackings to ignite an oil war in the Middle East. But have no doubt that America's dependency on oil and its historic relationship with the Saudis did have a fundamental bearing on 9/11 and, especially, on attempts to cover up the truth about what really happened. The interests of Israel and Saudi Arabia rank way above any others in Washington, as successive administrations have proved. The UK's 'special relationship' doesn't even compare.

But if we can establish a case that the US government is orchestrating a deception to hide the truth about 9/11 from the public – including the very families who lost loved ones – then what can we believe about the official narrative concerning that terrible day and the days and months leading up to it?

Chapter Two

The Advance Party

**Los Angeles, California,
15 January 2000**

Nawaf al-Hazmi and Khalid al-Mihdhar, both Saudis, had travelled to an al-Qaeda camp in Afghanistan for a crash course in terrorist hijacking. Like Niaz Khan, they had been shown old Hollywood movies with hijacking scenes and taught how to kill with maximum bloodletting for maximum impact on aircraft passengers. They, too, were told that they were volunteering for a one-way skyjacking mission to the United States.

But both men had a couple of major obstacles to overcome; they couldn't speak any English and hadn't a clue how to fly a plane. Their al-Qaeda trainers showed them how to read using phone books and to say simple English phrases. They also practised with flight simulators and poured over airline timetables to check flights that would be in the air at the same time.

It was difficult to believe, even for their terrorist teachers, that the pair's slippery grasp of the language and lack of any real understanding of Western culture would be enough for them to succeed. They struggled with the basics.

Unlike the ultimately unreliable Khan, however, they had proved their mettle by fighting with the mujahideen in Bosnia and with the Taliban in Afghanistan in the 1990s. They also already had US visas and, most importantly, they were hand-picked by Osama bin Laden as the first of the hijackers.

The idea of sabotaging America's most treasured landmarks was hardly new. In June 1942, eight men were dropped offshore by German submarines in Long Island, New York, and Jacksonville, Florida, with enough explosives for a sustained two-year campaign of terror in New York to weaken Washington's resolve in the Second World War. Within a few days, the Nazi plot was in tatters after the group's leader confessed all to the FBI, and six of the saboteurs went to the electric chair.

Wartime FBI chief J. Edgar Hoover portrayed the arrests of the saboteurs as a triumph for the bureau, despite the fact that the leader of the group, George Dasch, wasn't believed when he first phoned the agency out of the blue to tell them all. Hoover took the credit and tried to have Dasch, the whistleblower, executed as a spy (he was released and deported to Germany in 1948 but never pardoned). Truth, again, was the first casualty of politics.

Islamic insurgents got even closer on 26 February 1993 when terrorist Ramzi Yousef masterminded a truck bomb attack below the North Tower of the World Trade Center. The North Tower was supposed to collapse into the South Tower and kill thousands in the process. That didn't happen, but six people did die and more than a thousand were injured.

Bin Laden was impatient to achieve what the Nazis and the 1993 bombing had failed to do and bring the United States to a standstill with a debilitating strike to its heart. A member of one of Saudi Arabia's richest non-royal families, the world's most wanted man and leader of al-Qaeda, the Islamic extremist group he founded in 1988, had long looked towards the United States as the debauched ringmaster of the capitalistic West he abhorred, and as the prime target for his war of terror. Once considered a dilettante propagandist, despite forgoing his wealthy Saudi roots to fight the Soviets in Afghanistan, bin Laden wanted the world to sit up and take notice.

In Khalid Sheikh Mohammed, his veteran jihadist lieutenant, bin Laden had someone with the dark vision to bring him out of the shadows to fulfil the Western world's worst nightmares. KSM, as he was known, was Yousef's uncle and had bankrolled his nephew's 1993 attempt to topple the Twin Towers. Now he had an even more ambitious plan to wreak havoc.

At a meeting in Kandahar, Afghanistan, in 1999, KSM outlined his plot to use aircraft as weapons. Bin Laden favoured the White House and the Pentagon as targets; KSM preferred the World Trade Center and the US Capitol. On one thing they were agreed – the plan was worth pursuing.

Bin Laden handed over the planning and the recruitment for the attacks to KSM with the one proviso that Hazmi and Mihdhar, his Bosnia protégés, should be sent to America as soon as possible to form a bridgehead for the rest of the team. They were to train as pilots and to act as leaders on the ground.

With his wandering, restless eyes, always searching the corner of the room, and with what appeared to be a knife scar resting across one cheek, Mihdhar was the more devout of the two and spoke better English. He differed from his travelling partner – and from the other hijackers who would follow – in that he was not only married to Hoda al-Hada, the sister of a friend in Yemen, but he also had two daughters and his wife was pregnant with a third child. His in-laws were jihadists with close ties to bin Laden. Nevertheless, his family marked him out as different from the others; he had a lot to lose.

Hazmi, gentler and open-faced, was comparatively outgoing and more interested in making friends. The son of a grocer from Mecca, he told friends that the long scar on his forearm was the result of his father's attempt to kill him when he was a child. Bin Laden offered him a family and a cause, and he dreamed of one day becoming famous, even if infamy was his only option.

After their training and haphazard English lessons in the autumn of 1999 at the Mes Aynak camp in Afghanistan, Hazmi and Mihdhar flew to Kuala Lumpur, Malaysia, on 4 and 5 January 2000 to take part in a three-day terror summit at a condo overlooking a Jack Nicklaus-designed golf course, owned by a US-educated al-Qaeda associate. Nine jihadists attended the meeting where blueprints were agreed for a planned attack later that same year on the USS *Cole* warship and a coordinated number of aeroplane hijackings, although the date had not yet been set for the terrorist showstopper.

On 8 January, the two friends flew on to Bangkok, ostensibly to pump up their profiles as globe-trotting tourists, but also to collect $36,000 in cash to start their new lives in America. Then, on 15 January, they arrived in Los Angeles International Airport.

They could still barely speak English, but bin Laden was confident that his first goal had been achieved; he had two committed, tried and tested jihadists in the United States without arousing any suspicion.

While that was certainly true of the FBI, the law-enforcement arm of the US security services with the responsibility for domestic operations, the CIA was very much aware of Hazmi and Mihdhar's presence in California. They had monitored the men's movements in Kuala Lumpur, liaising with the local intelligence networks, covertly photographing them on a number of occasions and tracking them through Bangkok to Los Angeles.

Both men had been pinpointed in late 1999 because of terror fears surrounding the new millennium. Leave across the States was cancelled for the US security services, and the counterterrorism agencies were on high alert with twice-daily briefings made to FBI Director Louis Freeh, CIA Director George Tenet and National Security Agency Director Michael Hayden. Among the communications from a bugged 'hot' phone number in Yemen that operated as a switchboard for the al-Qaeda network was one indicating that an 'operational cadre' of suspects was travelling to Kuala Lumpur in early January. 'Khalid' and 'Nawaf' were among the names of those supposedly on their way to Malaysia.

The al-Qaeda switchboard was at the Yemeni home of Mihdhar's father-in-law, Ahmad Mohammad Ali al-Hada, the patriarch of one of Yemen's most feared terrorist clans. Hada was said to have fought against the Soviets in Afghanistan alongside bin Laden and was photographed sitting next to him at a banquet in 1999. In other words, his terrorist credentials were in no doubt.

'Michelle' – codename for a CIA desk officer working in the Bin Laden unit at the agency's headquarters in Langley, Virginia – identified the two men as Khalid al-Mihdhar and Nawaf al-Hazmi, linking them to al-Qaeda and to the 1998 bombings in Kenya and Tanzania that first propelled bin Laden into the limelight. Up to fifty people worked at the intelligence unit, which was unusual in that it targeted an individual rather than a country. Even before 9/11, bin Laden was considered that dangerous.

The nefarious decision was quickly taken by the CIA to break into Mihdhar's hotel room in Dubai, where he had stopped en route to Malaysia. Without him knowing, a photo was snapped of the Saudi's passport – it contained a valid multiple-entry US visa with New York listed as his intended destination.

Among the other known terror suspects captured in the Kuala Lumpur surveillance photographs were Ramzi bin al-Shibh, a 9/11 plotter who failed to get a US visa to join his co-conspirators, Tawfiq bin Atash, known as 'Khallad', who was bin Laden's bodyguard and a key figure behind the attack on USS *Cole* in October 2000, and Fahd al-Quso, who was supposed to have filmed the suicide attack on the *Cole* and served as one of bin Laden's paymasters.

So, the CIA knew who they were dealing with and they knew where they were heading. By telling the FBI or the State Department, both men could have been prevented from ever entering the United States or could have been targeted for arrest if they landed on American soil.

They were, undoubtedly, a huge threat, but they were left to run.

Rather than risk the FBI pushing for arrests and prosecutions, the CIA hid behind a 'wall' between the services so that they could keep their intelligence sources up and running.

The legal wall was a long-standing rule barring the FBI's criminal investigators and the CIA's intelligence operators from sharing information with each other. It was supposed to solve the dilemma the agencies faced when one was tasked to uncover evidence to bring suspects to justice and the other focused exclusively on collecting intelligence.

In pushing for prosecutions, the FBI could effectively wreck some intelligence-gathering efforts. If incriminating information was simply withheld from the prosecutors – hidden behind a virtual 'wall' – there would be no pressure to intervene in ongoing operations. The 'wall' extended to FBI agents working with the CIA on shared intelligence. They, too, would have to withhold information from their superiors.

The lack of cooperation in this case would prove to be disastrous.

But for now, the CIA had a quandary. They knew two al-Qaeda terrorists were in California; they may have even known something about their mission. They were already violating the law by not telling the FBI what they knew, and by getting physically involved in a domestic operation, they would be in even deeper trouble if it all went pear-shaped.

What if a foreign intelligence service with its own tentacles into al-Qaeda partnered in a joint operation, known only to a few very senior officials, with the goal of taking bin Laden's terrorist group down once and for all?

Saudi Arabia's spy network, the Mabahith, had traditionally close ties with the CIA that dated way back before the first Gulf War and a history of secretly sharing information about al-Qaeda that belied its support for the kind of Islamic fundamentalism that promoted extremist views.

The FBI may have been kept out of the loop regarding the terrorist summit in Kuala Lumpur, but the CIA did tell the Saudis – and it was they who confirmed Mihdhar and Hazmi were members of al-Qaeda. The Saudis had been monitoring the movements of both men since arresting them in 1997 for attempting to bring weapons into the kingdom and knew them to be committed followers of bin Laden.

The tongue-tied terrorists would need help embedding themselves in America, lots of it. They had to find places to live, buy food, drive cars … learn to fly. And yet, by law, the CIA's hands were tied. Once it became a domestic operation, they had an obligation to hand it over to the FBI or, at the very least, to inform its sister agency.

The CIA did neither.

But when they arrived at LAX on 15 January 2000, Hazmi and Mihdhar were not left to their own devices. They had a helping hand from Saudi intelligence.

Chapter Three

The Spy

San Diego, California,
1 February 2000

Omar al-Bayoumi didn't waste any time in making Hazmi and Mihdhar welcome in California. He met the newcomers in a supposedly random lunchtime encounter at the Mediterranean Gourmet Restaurant on Venice Boulevard in Los Angeles on 1 February 2000 and, three days later, he was helping them apply for an apartment neighbouring his own, one block west of the Islamic Center in San Diego.

Nothing was too much for Bayoumi's new friends. He co-signed for them at the Parkwood Apartments in San Diego, allowing them to use his address as their previous residence, loaned them $1,500 for their first month's deposit and organised a dinner to introduce them to the local community.

Only the meeting wasn't random and Bayoumi was not who he seemed.

Mihdhar and Hazmi had spent two weeks in Los Angeles, barely able to speak the language and with little idea how to settle into a strange new world. They had attended the King Fahad Mosque in Culver City where Fahad al-Thumairy, an accredited Saudi Arabian diplomat, served as an imam.

It really wasn't going very well. It wasn't so much that the two men stood out, more that they felt lost and overwhelmed in an unfamiliar city where everything was always moving at a hundred miles per hour.

So, when a friendly middle-aged Saudi Arabian man dropped his newspaper as he walked past their table in the Mediterranean Gourmet and struck up a conversation in Arabic, it must have seemed like good fortune. He spoke about the beautiful weather in San Diego, a two-hour drive down the coast, how much more he liked it than the hustle and bustle of LA, and how happy he would be to help out his fellow Muslims and get them settled in the city.

The fortuitous lunch encounter would later be portrayed by some FBI agents as being set up by 'friends' of al-Qaeda within the Saudi regime as part of a sanctioned welcoming party to help the hijackers settle in the United States. The 9/11 Commission concluded there was no support network in place for the terrorist interlopers, not from the Saudis or anyone else. Officially, the FBI agreed, although some senior agents had serious reservations. A brief look at the circumstances around the terrorists' first weeks in the United States makes it abundantly clear they were getting help.

The truth is that it was Hazmi and Mihdhar who were the dupes. The CIA, via the Mabahith, already had eyes on the al-Qaeda duo. It was Bayoumi's job to befriend them and take them under his wing.

Fahad al-Thumairy was certainly aware Mihdhar and Hazmi had turned up in LA and he almost certainly knew who they were. As a representative of Saudi Arabia's Ministry of Islamic Affairs, he was head of the mosque where the two men headed soon after arriving on the West Coast. He even helped them with somewhere to stay in those early days, sending them to a moderately priced hotel close to the mosque.

On 1 February, Bayoumi told a friend that he was heading up to LA from his San Diego home to meet with some 'very important visitors'. A married man with four children, the gregarious, popular Saudi, then forty-two years old, described himself as a student but never seemed to want for money and nobody knew where he went to school. He would often be seen videotaping events at the Islamic Center on San Diego's Balboa Avenue and was known to have well-connected friends in Saudi Arabia.

It was whispered that he was a spy.

That February morning, Bayoumi drove up to the non-public gate at the Saudi consulate on Sawtelle Boulevard in Los Angeles and was buzzed through to park in the interior parking garage. He went up to meet Thumairy in his private office, where he was given the names of a couple of places where he might find Mihdhar and Hazmi that lunchtime.

Having followed the two terrorists from Dubai, through to Malaysia and then Bangkok, it was inconceivable that the CIA wouldn't also have a tail on them now that they were in their own backyard. But it would make more sense for Saudi intelligence to initiate contact, both to avoid suspicion and to keep the FBI at bay.

The Culver City mosque where Thumairy was an imam was known for its anti-Western views and Bayoumi was said to be a mentor to some of the younger, more militant Muslims, despite his later claims that he was an avowed moderate. The two would-be hijackers would feel comfortable in such company. They were young and idealistic; it was only to be expected that fellow Muslims would offer a helping hand to fellow Saudis in a strange land.

Bayoumi left the consulate and went to the wrong restaurant initially, finding that it was a butcher shop, hardly the actions of a sympathiser in cahoots with the plotters. He found the men in another restaurant around the corner, a small shopfront place with a handful of seats outside, and used the dropped newspaper ploy to strike up a conversation. They said they were in the US to learn English; Bayoumi was happy to help.

It wasn't as if Bayoumi's day job as a spy was much of a mystery, either. Even members of the Islamic community in San Diego, where he was generally liked and well regarded, didn't trust Bayoumi and his ever-present video recorder.

The FBI had received more than a dozen calls about him and opened inconclusive investigations into his activities in 1998 and 1999, after the manager of the apartment complex where he was living at the time reported that he received a suspicious package with wires protruding from it from the Middle East and a maintenance worker spotted strange wires beneath his bathroom sink. The enquiries into Bayoumi were shut down after counterterrorism officers within the agency instructed the investigating agent not to interview him, because it could compromise 'a large sensitive counterterrorism investigation involving an alleged terrorist organisation'.

Money wasn't an issue, either. Bayoumi, who had lived in San Diego for about seven years, had come up with more than $400,000 from Saudi Arabia to help fund a mosque in the city a couple of years earlier. Owning and effectively running places of worship was an acknowledged way the kingdom had built influence abroad.

His pay from an aviation company with ties to the Saudi government also rose accordingly while Hazmi and Mihdhar were on his beat. Before they turned up, he claimed about $465 a month in 'allowances'. While they were in San Diego, he got a rise to $3,700 a month from March until December of 2000, by which time they had both moved on, and his money dropped to

$3,200 a month until he left the US in August 2001, one month before the 9/11 attacks.

On 4 February, Bayoumi welcomed Hazmi and Mihdhar to San Diego and helped them move into the Parkwood Apartments where he also lived with his family. Call records show that Bayoumi logged almost a hundred phone calls to Saudi government offices in the US in the first four months that Hazmi and Mihdhar were in the country.

The two newcomers weren't short of cash, either. Bayoumi took them to the Bank of America and helped them open an account with $9,900 in cash. When the cashier told them that it was too soon to give them a bank cheque so they could pay their rent and first month's deposit, Bayoumi simply wrote the $1,558 cheque for them and they paid him back the money immediately.

Four days after they moved in, Bayoumi asked a favour of his new friends. He was putting on a dinner for a sheikh from Norway who had lectured at the local mosque during Ramadan. Because the female guests would be gathering at his apartment with his wife, Bayoumi asked the two men if the male guests could congregate in their bare, ground-floor garden flat, which was empty of any furniture and would be perfect to host the meal of a whole baked lamb, albeit the diners would all have to sit on the floor.

Although Hazmi and Mihdhar didn't sit down with the two dozen guests and remained largely in a back room, perhaps unwilling to socialise with so many strangers so soon, they did relax and chat as the evening went on. Bayoumi's video recorder captured the evening on film. Some of the guests insisted they did not want to be taped.

The two new renters worked out at the apartment complex's gym and would joke with each other, pushing and shoving, but clammed up as shy students of English at the local community college. They didn't watch TV, rarely went out and ate their meals cross-legged on the floor, telling the few people they knew that they were Bedouins, from a nomadic Arab tribe.

They had a phone put in the flat, and if they were hiding at the time, it was in plain sight – Hazmi's name was in the 2000 San Diego phonebook. Both used their real names to rent the flat, get driving licences and, of course, to enter the country. If you knew who you were looking for, they certainly weren't hard to find.

It may be that the al-Qaeda men were also becoming suspicious of Bayoumi. Hazmi told a fellow Saudi college student that he believed the older man was a spy and had been following them when they met up at the Mediterranean Gourmet restaurant in LA. Bayoumi, while claiming he did nothing but offer common courtesies to the two fellow Saudis, later told members of the 9/11 Commission that Hazmi's description of him as a spy 'hurt me very much'.

The hijackers, however, were not altogether happy with their new home, complaining that the Parkwood Apartments were too expensive. Perhaps they also thought the flat was too close to a man they thought was spying on them.

Their next move would be just as intriguing. There are two conflicting stories of how the future hijackers came to be living in the home of an FBI informant. One says that they were introduced to their new landlord by Bayoumi and the other, according to the informant himself, Abdussattar Shaikh, says that they answered his ad on a bulletin board at the mosque. Either way, the pair moved out of the Parkwood Apartments in May 2000 and moved in with Shaikh.

By this time, Hazmi and Mihdhar were clearly trying to distance themselves from Bayoumi, perhaps worried about his motives in keeping such a close eye on them and their movements.

Where better to monitor the movements of Mihdhar and Hazmi than from the home of a trusted and reliable stalwart of the San Diego Muslim community, who had been leading a double life as an FBI 'asset', feeding the agency with information and tidbits about anything and anyone he deemed suspicious?

This is where the operation gets murkier. It is ludicrous to think that two of the hijackers could live in the house of an FBI informant for months – and even, as we shall see later, meet another two of the hijackers – without sounding an alarm. But it seems Shaikh never told his FBI handler in Los Angeles about any suspicions he may have had about his two new lodgers. The Saudis, both from a 'friendly' country, did nothing to arouse any untoward suspicion during their time in the informant's home and, perhaps other than some tittle-tattle, Shaikh didn't say anything that could raise an alarm with the agency. Besides, the FBI had no reason to ponder the movements of Mihdhar and Hazmi. They didn't know they were in America.

For the CIA and the Mabahith, however, Shaikh was the right man in exactly the right place because they did know the two men were in San Diego and they wanted to know everything about them.

It's not that the FBI wouldn't have been interested. Under former CIA Director Louis Freeh, the agency had grown its overseas operations, expanding its foreign legal attaché offices from nineteen to forty-four. It had also made counterterrorism a separate division in 1999 and launched a unit to focus exclusively on Osama bin Laden.

The reach of the FBI investigation into al-Qaeda on the West Coast in the 1990s was never disclosed to the 9/11 Commission or any other official inquiries in the wake of the New York and Washington attacks. One focus of the probe was the San Diego Islamic community, which probably explained why the agency took a pass on interviewing Bayoumi at a time when they wouldn't have wanted to make any waves that might suggest Muslims in the area were being targeted.

In the handwringing that came after 11 September, the intelligence services bemoaned their apparent inability to get a decent source inside al-Qaeda, but even before Hazmi and Mihdhar turned up on the scene, the FBI had a high-up source inside the terror group. At the urging of his FBI handler, the 'asset' met directly in 1993 with bin Laden, who told him he was looking to finance attacks in the US.

The informant also provided information that thwarted a planned al-Qaeda attack on a British cruise ship and on a Masonic lodge in Los Angeles.

The US-based source, groomed by top FBI counterterrorism agent Bassem Youssef, was linked to the 'Blind Sheik', Omar Abdel-Rahman, found guilty in 1995 of conspiring with the perpetrators of the 1993 World Trade Center bombing, and was described as being 'very in tight' with the al-Qaeda leadership; he flew out to meet bin Laden.

Youssef reportedly flipped the asset by collaborating with his wife from an arranged marriage to get him deported – and then offering him repatriation to the States in return for his cooperation in providing information about bin Laden and terror cells operating in California.

An official document from 1994 disclosed 'the FBI identified and supported an investigative effort which uncovered a large terrorist group operating out of the Los Angeles and San Diego areas'.

'I quickly developed a scenario to gain the source's trust, and in a short period of time, I gained the source's trust,' Youssef wrote in a court deposition. 'During the relatively short recruitment period, it became evident this source was in a unique position to know and provide highly valuable information, not just about the main subject but regarding two very active, thriving IG terror cells,' he added, using the initials for Islamic Group, an al-Qaeda affiliate headed up by the Blind Sheik.

Intriguingly, the movements of the asset and his whereabouts since 1994 have remained a closely guarded secret and his role in al-Qaeda in the lead-up to 9/11 has never been disclosed.

The CIA, on the other hand, had no decent sources inside al-Qaeda at this point. When he was appointed head of the CIA's Counterterrorist Center in June 1999, Cofer Black was said to have been aghast that the agency hadn't infiltrated bin Laden's group and was 'determined to do something about it'. This was the catalyst for the disastrous intelligence operation that remains the biggest untold secret of 9/11.

Back in San Diego, awaiting further instructions, Mihdhar and Hazmi had a tricky assignment that would turn out to be trickier than they expected. They had to learn to fly.

One flying club in San Diego sent them packing after one lesson because of their poor English and neither man impressed instructor Rick Garza when they turned up at his Sorbi's Flying Club at Montgomery Field in Mesa, a short distance from where they were living in San Diego.

They were told to read chapters one to three of their flight textbooks after their first lesson but only managed to reach page one. They didn't want to learn on Garza's small Cessna 172 training plane. 'They asked me if they could fly Boeings,' he said.

The bungling aviators couldn't grasp simple flight operations, such as radio communications and left and right turns.

'It was like *Dumb and Dumber*,' Garza told the *San Diego Union-Tribune* later. 'That's when I sat them down and said, "Sorry guys, I can't continue with you. My recommendation is to go to a school and learn English." They pleaded with me and begged me. They offered to pay me more money. I felt bad I had to turn them down, but I felt very firm in my decision. I was doing the right thing. They were going to be dangerous if I continued.'

They tried one more flight school but eventually gave up.

To Mihdhar and Hazmi, Abdussattar Shaikh's comfortable two-storey home on a bluff in Lemon Grove on the east side of San Diego would have been a vast improvement on their bare-bones apartment where they slept on blankets on the floor. It was also much cheaper – $300 a month to share a bedroom rather than $1,000 for the flat.

Dr Shaikh, as he liked to be called, was a retired English educator from India and a leader at the local mosque. A paid asset for the San Diego FBI office, his handler was an agent named Steven Butler, and he had been recruited in 1994, at about the time the FBI was working the mystery source close to bin Laden and the California terror cells.

It was Shaikh who helped the Saudis buy a car and a computer and even tried, unsuccessfully, to hook Hazmi up with a Mexican bride on the Internet. The car, a 1988 four-door navy-blue Toyota Corolla with well over 100,000 miles on the clock, would be the clue that led investigators back to Lemon Grove. Registered to its new owner, Nawaf al-Hazmi, at the San Diego address, it was abandoned at Dulles International Airport, near Washington DC, on the morning of 11 September 2001, before he and Mihdhar met the flight that they would hijack and crash into the Pentagon.

'If I had any hint, I would have tipped off the authorities,'

Shaikh told the *Washington Post* in the days after 9/11 – and before he was revealed as an FBI snitch. He gave the kind of answers one might expect of a clueless landlord, saying they were quiet, devout, unassuming young men who gave him no reason to suspect them of any wrongdoing.

Credit-card records appeared to suggest the pair were not as devout as they seemed. They had been regular visitors at Cheetahs and Dancers, both San Diego strip clubs.

The FBI was quick to release a rare statement clearing Shaikh of any involvement in 9/11. After his role as an informant was made public and he became altogether more reticent about being questioned, the feds explained that he had only given his lodgers' first names to his handler and hadn't thought to tell any more. They were Saudis, he claimed, and Saudi Arabia was a friendly ally to the US.

Attempts to interview Shaikh by the 9/11 Commission, Congress's Joint Intelligence Committee Inquiry and the US Office of Inspector General were rebuffed by the FBI, who also tried to prevent Butler from speaking. The agent, who was hung out to dry by his superiors, insisted on speaking to congressional investigators, but his testimony was behind closed doors and he retired shortly afterwards.

Neither the FBI agent nor his informant could therefore answer questions about the other men seen visiting Hazmi and Mihdhar in San Diego.

Neighbours of Shaikh in Lemon Grove were certain that Mohamed Atta, the leader of the al-Qaeda hijackers, was a frequent visitor to the house between August and early December in 2000. Wearing Western clothes and driving a red car, he was polite and friendly and made no attempt to hide from the locals. He even helped a neighbour with some gardening.

Marna Adair, who lived just fifty feet from Shaikh's house

and had a clear view of his driveway, said she was 'positive' she saw Atta and confidently identified him in photographs shown to her by FBI agents in the wake of the attacks. Another neighbour, Deborah Fortner, was equally certain. 'He was the one that was scary. He's got these piercing eyes. That's something you never forget about him,' she said.

On 9 June 2000, Mihdhar flew to Yemen to visit his wife, following the birth of his first child, leaving Hazmi on his own in San Diego. Bored of life so far away from his family and impatient for action, he had left without permission and only bin Laden's intervention prevented him from being kicked off the hijacking operation altogether.

Biding his time, Hazmi got a job at a petrol station and let slip that he would soon become famous. The boast from an immigrant with few prospects and little ambition outside finding himself an instant wife was taken with a grain of salt. He had as good as given up trying to learn English, but on 8 December 2000 a 'longtime friend from Saudi Arabia' arrived to pick him up.

Hani Hanjour had travelled from Dubai via Paris and Cincinnati. The fourth hijacker was now in San Diego and he already knew how to fly a plane.

Chapter Four

The Dropped Cable

Alec Station, CIA Headquarters, Langley, Virginia,
5 January 2000

Every morning, agents working at Alec Station, the CIA section specifically set up to handle the threat from al-Qaeda at the spy agency's nondescript headquarters a short hop from Washington DC in Langley, Virginia, would arrive to a raft of cables in their queues. Some would require action, many were just for information, but they provided an extraordinary real-time record of clandestine activities around the world.

As one of two FBI agents seconded to the station, it was Doug Miller's job to sift through the never-ending flow of cables to find anything of interest to his own bosses, especially if there was a suggestion of a domestic end to an operation.

At his desk early on the morning of 5 January 2000, Miller was reading through his queues when he came upon exactly the kind of message that he was looking for. The very fact that he was there among fifty or so CIA analysts was an attempt to try and combat the bitter rivalry between the agencies that caused damaging divisions in the past. By seconding FBI and CIA agents to each other's units, the idea was that a better working relationship would be fostered. The FBI could see what the

CIA was up to, and vice versa. Sometimes, the sheer numbers of cables would be like drinking water from a fire hydrant, but this one stood out.

The cable – sent to Alec Station and, tellingly, Riyadh Station in Saudi Arabia – included a photo of Mihdhar's passport. It described his involvement in the terror summit in Malaysia and the fact that surveillance photos had been taken. Most importantly for Miller, it revealed that Mihdhar had a three-month, multiple-entry US visa and appeared to be heading to New York.

This was gold dust for the FBI and Miller quickly set about writing a Central Intelligence Report (CIR) with copies to the FBI's offices in Washington DC and New York and his fellow FBI special agent at Alec Station, Mark Rossini. With his CIR, Miller included two CIA cables detailing Mihdhar's movements and sent them into an electronic queue to await approval from the CIA before they went out.

Two days later, the CIR was still not approved. The only contact from the CIA was to tell Miller to 'hold off for now'.

Frustrated, Miller went to Rossini, the senior agent, and asked him to help move the message along.

Rossini, a popular, sharply dressed agent with a shock of black hair, was handpicked by John O'Neill, the hard-charging head of the FBI's Joint Terrorism Task Force in New York, to be his 'eyes and ears' at Langley and was treated with some suspicion, at least initially, by his new colleagues at the CIA.

He was quickly struck by the differences in the two agencies. 'Even in the early 2000s, they were way far more advanced than any other agency as far as electronics and computers and communications were concerned. I marvelled at how they communicated to each other on a constant and immediate basis,' he said.

'And everything was so freewheeling. You could be flying to another country that night based upon your chief's directive. In comparison, the bureau was so bureaucratic and slow. But there's a reason for that, because everything we did ended up in court and nothing that they do does; there's just no consideration of that proper record-keeping which a defence attorney could pick apart, let alone our own internal Inspection Division.'

It was a dynamic that would have considerable bearing on what happened to Miller's CIR. 'Doug's CIR comes to me first,' remembered Rossini. 'I kick it out the door and then it goes to this individual's queue sheet. And it sits there for two days. And in the CIA, two minutes is a long time.

'So, Doug comes to me and asks if I can see what's holding it up and I tell him, "Yeah, no problem."' But when Rossini asked for an explanation, he is shut down by one of the CIA's bin Laden specialists and told the information about Mihdhar is of no interest to the FBI.

'She gets up out of her chair, puts her hand on her hip and waves her finger at me and says that she has information that the next al-Qaeda attack is going to happen in South East Asia. And she says to me, "It's not a matter for the FBI. If we want the FBI to know about it, we will tell them. You are not to say anything."'

Rossini asked about the US visa. What happens if Mihdhar comes to America? 'She said, "Well, no, that's just a diversion to throw us off. If they come here, it has nothing to do with the attack or South East Asia. It's just a diversion."

'The problem was that we knew the rules. You have no reason to believe that they won't do the right thing and tell the FBI when necessary. She was kind of, okay, well, that's how it is. Very matter of fact.

'So, then I go back to Doug and I say, "Well, she said to me, it's a CIA matter. It's their case, you know. There's nothing we can do about it."

'And he shook his head. He says, "Well, they must have a very good reason, but I just don't get it."'

As a career investigator, Rossini said there's usually one defining moment that determines whether or not a crime will happen. If a getaway driver doesn't turn up on time, the bank robber gets caught; if the pen runs out of ink, the Wall Street fraudster can't write the incriminating cheque. The CIA's decision to prevent the FBI from seeing Doug Miller's CIR about Khalid al-Mihdhar was, he believed, the defining moment of 9/11.

'I know a lot of people say, "Well, I would have defied the CIA and gotten the message to the FBI." The reality is that you wouldn't, because at that moment in time they may have visas, but you don't know if they're coming or not. It wasn't like we knew what was going to happen, and you have to abide the rules of being a detailee to another agency.'

The hardened former FBI man ruffled his hands through his hair, trying to hold back the deep-seated emotions that can still overwhelm him every time he thinks about what happened and how close he was to making a difference.

Hindsight is an easy thing, but he accepted, 'That's the moment 9/11 would have been stopped. That's it. That's the moment you keep going back to in your head.'

The obvious question that Rossini has asked over and over again is why. In the inevitable inquests held since the withheld cable's existence became public knowledge, the CIA has insisted it simply fell through the cracks.

'You can't tell me with a straight face that it fell through the cracks,' said Rossini. 'Don't give me that bullshit that the CIA was overwhelmed and didn't get a chance to address it and send it. It's a simple thing, quick, boom, done. There had to be a good reason to hide it.'

Neither FBI men were ever told anything more about Mihdhar, although Rossini did check to find out that there were never any al-Qaeda attacks or attempted attacks in South East Asia, nor was there any cable traffic about such a mission. The CIA's basis for believing an attack would happen in South East Asia was because bin Laden's brother-in-law, Mohammed Jamal Khalifa (bin Laden's emissary there), was actively distributing funds to various al-Qaeda-affiliated terror groups in the region.

Rossini was convinced that one key reason the bureau was frozen out was because the Alec Station chiefs knew that John O'Neill, the FBI's counterterrorism boss in New York, would have insisted on taking over the operation targeting Mihdhar. They also knew he was close to then US Attorney General Janet Reno.

'Perhaps the most pathetic and emotionally cringing part, is that they, the management of the CIA, Alec Station and the CIA's Counterterrorist Center (CTC), did not want the FBI, in the persona of Special Agent in Charge John P. O'Neill, Jr, to interfere in their effort, and or the unilateral effort of the Mabahith, which the CIA would have had to have given permission for to operate in the USA. Permission they had no legal authority to do,' he said.

'This recruitment effort/operation failed miserably and resulted in the tragic attacks. Neither O'Neill nor the FBI would have allowed such an operation to take place in the USA without the FBI's management of it and approval from the Attorney General. The fear on the part of the CIA was that the FBI/O'Neill could not be controlled nor could be dissuaded from potentially making arrests and shutting down the operation when they saw fit, and thus causing the Saudi's "embarrassment".' Tragically, O'Neill retired from the bureau just three weeks before 9/11 to become chief of security at the World Trade Center. He was killed in the attacks.

'His last day was Friday the 24th,' recalled Rossini. 'My fortieth birthday was Tuesday, August 21. I had a party at a restaurant in New York on the Lower East Side the night of Friday the 24th. He swung by, had a drink and worked the room as he usually did. He was in a very good mood. He stayed for a bit, and then gave me a kiss and hug, as was our usual way of greeting and departing, and said as he left, "I'll see you next time you are in NY." I never saw him again.'

Rossini is in no doubt things would have turned out very differently had the FBI been informed about Mihdhar and Hazmi. 'Of course, John O'Neill would have taken over the case,' he said. 'He wouldn't care what the CIA said – he would have told them, "I'm in charge and when and if I feel like arresting these people, I will."

'The CIA knew they couldn't ever win that battle with John. He had Janet Reno's ear and she would've sided with the FBI. And Bill Clinton wouldn't have gotten involved. They knew that and that's what it was all about.'

Rossini – and he is far from alone among current and former FBI investigators – was convinced that the CIA targeted Mihdhar as the perfect double agent. There would certainly have been a detailed psychological profile drawn up on Mihdhar to determine his potential as a source and countless hours spent on a chess-game strategy to make the best moves to try to recruit him. The fact that he left the US on 9 June 2000 to attend the birth of his third child and attend his wife's birthday in Yemen was enough of a clue that he still had a lot to live for. He had failed to learn how to fly and quickly became disillusioned with life in America, missing his family and the familiar comforts of home. He had roots, unlike Hazmi and the other hijackers. There were enough angles to work with.

An approach may have been made any time after Mihdhar left California. After all, he wasn't any of the FBI's business if he was out of the country and could certainly have been linked with some of the possible threats that were being flagged up.

'The logical choice would have been to monitor him, try and get close to him to see what's going on,' said Rossini. 'And again, I can't prove it, but logic and the circumstantial evidence certainly supports it.'

Mihdhar flew back to Yemen and flew on later to Afghanistan, perhaps to meet up with bin Laden. At some point, he loses his passport and gets a replacement issued in Jeddah, Saudi Arabia. Unknown to him, the Saudis imprinted a chip in the passport, signifying his ties to al-Qaeda. Still, he was being watched.

Mihdhar also goes to the US consulate in Jeddah for a new visa. Are we supposed to believe the visa was renewed without the CIA's knowledge? There is even a suggestion that the consular affairs officer in Jeddah was actually a CIA agent in cover status, who issued the visa to all the Saudi hijackers.

He spent some time in Mecca, pondering his future, perhaps.

Any calls he made from his father-in-law's house, where he was living with his family, were also bugged. It was an FBI lead that identified the al-Qaeda 'switchboard' at the house in Yemen – the number was learned from an interview with British-born Saudi terrorist Mohamed Rashed Daoud Al-Owhali, who was jailed for life for his part in the 1998 US Embassy bombings in Kenya and Tanzania – but only the CIA and the Mabahith would have understood Mihdhar's significance, and they would not have shared that significance with the FBI.

Another former FBI agent, Jack Cloonan, who was with the FBI's Bin Laden unit between 1996 and 2002, told the makers of a French documentary, *The Roads to Terror*: 'My theory is that if you tell us about these two guys in the United States sixteen or eighteen months before the attacks on 9/11, are those people we might be interested in? Of course. What could we have done in sixteen or eighteen months? First of all, we can put them under surveillance. First of all, we can probably get their phones wiretapped; I think we can make an argument that they are agents of a foreign power.

'Secondly, we can compromise their computers; we could look at every chat room that they went to, every Internet café, every wire transfer that they made. We would have all this information. Do you think we would be in the middle of the conspiracy for 9/11? I think you could make a very strong argument that we would have been in at least one part of it.'

Rossini remains haunted by the lost opportunity to do the right thing.

'If we had been following them from San Diego, from LA airport on, we would have taken them down way, way before that. And again, how do you wilfully, purposefully, not tell the FBI about something that is clearly in their jurisdiction?

'Mihdhar was followed halfway around the globe using other intelligence services. You go through the trouble of requesting foreign intelligence services to set up their own surveillance teams to photograph him and follow him and get tape and get recordings on it. That doesn't rise to the level of telling the FBI that this guy has the potential to travel to the USA, and then after you learn in March 2000 that Mihdhar did travel to America in January 2000, along with Nawaf al-Hazmi, you still don't tell the FBI that two terrorists are on American soil? In March 2000, a cable is sent from either Kuala Lumpur or

Bangkok station addressed to CIA HQ, Alec Station, CTC, CIA stations in New York and Los Angeles, that Mihdhar and his travel companion Hazmi did arrive in Los Angeles in January 2000.

'It doesn't pass the smell test. I shouldn't accept it. And neither should you. And that's what my quest has been all about to get to the heart as to why Doug's memo was not passed on. I've always said this; let's say I never was born, Doug never was born. We were never there. They had an obligation to pass this information to the FBI as they have done other things in the past.'

In order to prove or disprove this, Rossini said that 'every single cable from the CIA to the FBI in the year preceding 5 January 2000 and the year after needs to be examined and let a court and jury decide each cable's relevance or importance and you tell me what cable among them all could be as important as one that clearly shows terrorists have plans to or, at a minimum, have the ability to travel to the USA. Then, of course, you have the March 2000 cable that clearly states they arrived. What could be more important than that?

'We need to know honestly and truthfully why Doug's memo was not sent and there you will have your answer … you'll have your answer. And I've been trying to prove it for a long time. And, you know, I kept my mouth quiet about it for a long time, but what is on my mind and my thoughts almost caused me to have a nervous breakdown.

'A few years ago, a member of the Joint Terrorism Task Force reached out to me via another person who knew me. I arranged to meet this individual for breakfast and the first thing he says to me is, "Hey, I want to let you know that you were right. I've gone over everything. I've read everything that you have written. It's the only thing that makes sense. You're right. You're absolutely correct."

'He is not the only person that has said it to me over the years. I was so happy about that. A lot of my colleagues that I talk to still obviously – once in the intel community, always in that community – and they all said, "You know, you're right. But what are you going to do?" Kind of like a resignation that it's above our level, or pay grade as is more common, and there's nothing we can do about it. It's out of our hands.'

Rossini was unable to leave it alone. The deception and ensuing cover-up were eating away at him. He decided he had to speak out, insisting it was 'foolish' to pretend that 9/11 could not have been waylaid if the FBI knew about Mihdhar from the start. He spoke to author James Bamford for his book about America's National Security Agency, *The Shadow Factory*, which was published in January 2008.

'Yes … without question,' he added. 'The cell would have been disrupted and perhaps the FBI and the CIA and the Mabahith could have worked together and developed one of the cell members as a source, but we will never know.

'I still think about it every day. Yeah, I think about it. The fact that I didn't mention this at the time has caused a great disturbance in my life. And, the fact that I wasn't honest when I was interviewed by an intelligence congressional inquiry or the CIA, because I was just told not to talk to them. And the fact that I went along with that sort of cover-up mentality. And this wilful, purposeful, keeping the FBI out of it. And the fact that I know how simple it was to put it right?

'It torments me every day, it really does.'

But while Rossini and Miller were forced to sit on their hands and Mihdhar's progress around the world was being watched by intelligence agents hungry for access inside al-Qaeda, a deeply flawed spokesman for the jihadist movement was drawing attention from the FBI back home in America …

Chapter Five

The American Imam

San Diego, California,
4 February 2000

The FBI was investigating Anwar al-Awlaki at the beginning of February 2000 over his links to Osama bin Laden. The spindly soccer-loving cleric was the young preacher at the Al-Ribat Al-Islami Mosque in La Mesa in the palm tree-covered hills about nine miles east of downtown San Diego.

Born in La Cruces, New Mexico, the charismatic Awlaki had spent much of his upbringing in his parents' native Yemen but returned to the United States to attend university in Colorado and had been increasingly drawn into the more extreme fringes of his religion.

It was a curious mix of cultures – the puritanism of his fundamentalist faith and the edgier freedoms of America in the 1990s – that would lead to Awlaki's double life as an al-Qaeda operative and a spy for the US intelligence services.

Before February 2000, he was seen by the FBI as an informant with the potential and enough interesting friends to get the inside track on bin Laden's ambitions within the US.

The previous month, he had met with the asset groomed by FBI agent Bassem Youssef, who had been out to visit bin

Laden and handed the agency the secrets of the terror group's networks in California. He had also met with Ziyad Khaleel, former vice president of the Denver Islamic Society, who had helped get bin Laden a satellite phone, essential for the nomadic terror boss to remain in touch while he was on the move.

Khaleel, a US citizen living in Missouri, was known as bin Laden's 'procurement agent'. He bought the phone in America for $7,500 and sent it to al-Qaeda's unofficial press officer in London who, in turn, forwarded it on to bin Laden in Afghanistan.

The sale and the progress of the sat phone was monitored by the CIA, showing who the calls were made to – more than 238 to the UK – and encrypted to reveal what was said. Tens of thousands of pages of transcripts provided a treasure trove of information about bin Laden and his associates. Dozens of calls went to the home of Mihdhar's father-in-law in Yemen, the al-Qaeda communications hub, which was, again, intercepted and monitored by the CIA from Langley.

Although Khaleel's activities were well known to the intelligence services, he was allowed to continue buying phone equipment and computers for bin Laden and to raise money through charity fronts for al-Qaeda, Hamas and other terrorist-related causes.

It wasn't until 29 December 1999 that US agents arrested Khaleel while he was visiting Jordan. If he hadn't already been an informant, he was quick to spill al-Qaeda's secrets once he was held behind bars. Inexplicably, he was then released and allowed to return to the United States.

Khaleel's contact with Awlaki had first alerted counter-terrorism agents to the cleric, although it is possible that his jihadist-tinged teachings at a Denver mosque may have also led to complaints from some mosque members who were uncomfortable with his influence on their youngsters. The FBI opened an investigation into Awlaki in June 1999 to look into reports that he had been contacted by an agent representing bin Laden.

At age twenty-five, Awlaki had moved from Colorado to San Diego, determined to make his mark, and he quickly made some interesting acquaintances. On 4 February 2000 – the day the future hijackers Hazmi and Mihdhar arrived in the city – he almost certainly spoke to them on the phone four times.

The calls were from Awlaki to Bayoumi's phone number, but an FBI source told the 9/11 Commission he was 98 per cent certain that Hazmi and Mihdhar were using their new friend's phone at the time. As the pair's new spiritual adviser, Awlaki would have regular behind-closed-doors meetings with them at the mosque.

'He was meeting with al-Hazmi and al-Mihdhar in the ante room off of the Al-Ribat mosque. Just the three of them,' said Ray Fournier, a former state department official who investigated Awlaki.

'It stands to reason that when three people get together and two of them end up being hijackers that end up in the Pentagon, they're obviously discussing how they're going to stay on track. He's absolving them of their sins. He's making sure that their cover within Western culture is being maintained. He's making sure they're going to stay operational.'

So, the jihadist cleric, with strong links to two known and active al-Qaeda operatives in the US, was now in everyday contact with two men who were known to have attended a terrorist summit in Malaysia before arriving, days earlier, in California. What did the FBI do? It closed down its investigation into Awlaki in March 2000.

Had the FBI been informed about Mihdhar and Hazmi's arrival in California, their close relationship with the San Diego cleric would have been a huge breakthrough and a key conduit to keep surveillance on the would-be terrorists. They could have used Awlaki as an informer or just kept watch on all three to see where their terrorist connections took them. As it was, the names Khalid al-Mihdhar and Nawaf al-Hazmi meant nothing to the feds, so they cut Awlaki loose.

For the watching CIA or, more likely, the Mabahith, it wasn't like they needed to search far to find the leverage to 'turn' Awlaki. The man who preached passionately about virtues and values wasn't quite the clean-living family man he pretended to be.

Just as Mihdhar and Hazmi had a penchant for strippers, their 'spiritual adviser' had a taste for prostitutes. Twice, he was arrested in red light areas of San Diego trying to pick up ladies of the night. By then, he was married to a cousin from Yemen and had two young children. His night-time proclivities, together with tip-offs to the bureau that he had been vice president of a 'front organisation to funnel money to terrorists', would be plenty of ammunition to help persuade him that his family life – and his continued freedom – depended on his cooperation with the authorities.

The FBI may have shut down its probe into Awlaki in March 2000. But the CIA just moved it undercover, and, in all likelihood, now he was working for them.

These were not coincidences happening in vacuums in different parts of the States; they were banging noisily into one another in the eighth largest city in the country.

The 9/11 Commission ruled that the interwoven relationships in San Diego and the West Coast in 2000 and the late 1990s had little or no bearing on what happened on 11 September

2001. That's simply not true; it is just one of a series of attempts to gloss over the truth.

As we shall see, Awlaki still plays a telling role in the lead-up to 9/11 and its aftermath, but none of the leading characters here lived to tell tales. All of the players would end up dead, some of them in mysterious circumstances. Anwar al-Awlaki would become the first US citizen since the Civil War to be hunted down and killed without trial by his own government. But by the time that happened, it would be way, way too late.

For now, it was time to leave California behind. Awlaki was moving on to a bigger mosque with a bigger flock in Virginia ... and he was taking the hijackers with him.

Chapter Six

The Bin Ladens
Next Door

Falls Church, Virginia,
4 April 2001

With Khalid al-Mihdhar out of the picture back home in Yemen, Nawaf al-Hazmi had hooked up with Hani Hanjour in December 2000 and the pair left San Diego to take flying lessons in San Francisco and Mesa, Arizona.

Hanjour had been back and forth from his native Saudi Arabia to the US since 1991 and spoke English well, and he had put the time in to get a private and a commercial flying licence; however he still wasn't very good. Hazmi, as already noted, was even worse.

Still, the two men had the cash, and they knew what they wanted – to learn to fly Boeing 747 passenger jets. Like the other al-Qaeda 'sleeper' operatives learning to fly in Florida at around the same time, Hanjour and Hazmi showed little interest in take-offs and landings; they were only really concerned with what happened in the air.

Hazmi was eventually deemed a lost cause as a potential pilot. He was asked by one instructor to draw a sketch of a plane and he put the wings back to front, so they faced the wrong way. Hanjour limped through, despite being warned by several instructors that he should give up.

On 4 April 2001, the two men arrived in Falls Church, Virginia, a stone's throw from the capital, Washington DC, and went straight to the Dar al-Hijra mosque. Who should be there but Anwar al-Awlaki, newly installed as the imam of one of the biggest mosques in the region, with services attended by a regular flock of between four and five hundred worshippers.

According to the 9/11 Commission, this was all a total coincidence. Two terrorists move halfway across the country to a mosque run by their 'spiritual adviser', where the pattern runs much as it did in San Diego. Awlaki sets them up with a 'friend' to help them find accommodation and anything else they need in Falls Church. It also means he can keep a close eye on what they are doing and report back to his contacts in the US and/or Saudi intelligence services.

Remember, too, that the Saudis retain a keen interest in the affairs of America's mosques, both in terms of finances and personnel. The Mabahith was waiting. Just as Bayoumi was on hand in San Diego to offer a helping hand to the al-Qaeda newcomers, so Awlaki was conveniently positioned to make them feel at home in Falls Church.

If Awlaki left San Diego because he was worried his use of prostitutes would agitate his conservative congregation in San Diego, that certainly didn't mean he was going to stop paying for sex. It wasn't long after he arrived in the upscale Virginia commuter suburb in January 2001 that he was back to his old tricks.

The FBI later interviewed a number of Washington prostitutes who told them Awlaki would regularly shell out $300 and $400 a time to either have sexual intercourse or receive oral sex. Awlaki would tell them he was an Indian computer engineer who had recently moved east from California. One woman said he would watch her from the bed with all the lights on, as she danced suggestively and stimulated herself while he would masturbate without touching her. She added that he told her he didn't like shaving his beard. Another prostitute said he 'looked like Osama bin Laden' when he arrived at her hotel room for a 5 p.m. appointment, arranged through an online escort service.

One of the swords the intelligence services could hang over Awlaki's head was the possibility that he could face prosecution for violating the US Travel Act by crossing state lines from Virginia into Washington DC to pay for the services of prostitutes. It would have been a relatively minor charge against a man suspected of consorting with the most wanted terrorist in the world, but it would certainly have damaged his reputation at the Falls Church mosque and tainted his growing stature as a spokesman for the Islamic community in the United States.

There is another reason why Awlaki and the hijackers may have chosen Falls Church – two of bin Laden's nephews worked there at the time and had already come to the notice of the FBI. The feds opened a probe in 1996 into Abdullah bin Laden's involvement with the World Assembly of Muslim Youth (WAMY) amid claims – denied by the organisation – that it was linked to terrorism. Federal agents, who opened the inquiry in February 2001, complained they were forced to shut it down after several months and before they had completed the investigation.

Abdullah bin Laden, who lived with his brother, Omar, in Falls Church, worked at the WAMY headquarters at 5613 Leesburg Pike, just a few blocks up from where Hanjour and Hazmi lived at 5913 Leesburg Pike. Another coincidence?

The Good Samaritan tasked this time to take care of the terrorists was Jordanian computer technician Eyad al-Rababah, who claimed he met the pair after a service at the mosque and they told him they were looking for somewhere to live. The added bonus was that he was known for illegally providing illegal aliens with Virginia driving licences, a scam for which he would later be deported back to Jordan.

Rababah's final job for the newcomers was to help them find a new place to live. They had been instructed to move on. He went to Hanjour and Hazmi's rented house in mid-May to find another two Saudi men living with them – Majed Moqed and Ahmed al-Ghamdi. The terror team was nearly complete.

Hazmi's rabble-rouser brother, Salem, turned up in New Jersey on 29 June 2001 on a 'Visa Express' scheme and met up with his sibling and the others at a flat in Paterson, New Jersey. He apparently had a history of boozing and petty theft during his teen years in his native Mecca and had fought with Nawaf in Afghanistan and Chechnya but, again, there is no record that the authorities were aware he was in the US. That doesn't mean they didn't know.

On 4 July 2001, Khalid al-Mihdhar returned to America, arriving at JFK airport in New York, chastened by his al-Qaeda bosses and committed to going through with the mission. On his visa, he said his planned destination was the Marriott World Trade Center Hotel.

Now all five terrorists – Hanjour, the pilot, and his four 'muscle men' – were in America and ready to hijack a plane and fly it into the Pentagon, the target their team had been designated.

Ghamdi split from the others and joined up with the crew bound for United Airlines Flight 175. His close contact with the Pentagon plotters, just as we saw with Atta's trips to San

Diego, defy the myth that the terrorists stuck to their own little cells. They were in touch, they met … and if one group was disrupted, the entire plot could have been broken up.

All were travelling under their real names with a slipstream of terrorist associations, but the FBI had been kept out of the loop … and the CIA had dropped the ball.

Alarm bells about an impending attack on the US homeland – even warnings about planes being used as weapons – were ringing loudly all the way to the White House, but the al-Qaeda team moving inexorably east from California to Virginia had either been forgotten about or lost once they left Falls Church.

They had been allowed to run and now they had run out of control.

In August 2001, Awlaki stopped to see an old neighbour, Lincoln Higgie, in San Diego and told him he was on his way to Dubai.

Mr Higgie recalled telling Awlaki to visit him again if he was ever in the area.

'I don't think you'll be seeing me,' Awlaki told him. 'I won't be coming back to San Diego again. Later on, you'll find out why.'

For now, at least, Awlaki was untouchable, and that remained the case in the days, weeks and even years after 9/11.

Initially, as the world attempted to come to terms with the events of that terrible day, Awlaki appeared to be the voice of reason, seeking answers along with everyone else and representing an Islamic community that was facing a violent backlash.

The man who would later claim that 'jihad is becoming as American as apple pie and as British as afternoon tea' was outraged at America's response to the attacks, calling it a 'war on Muslims'. But publicly he condemned the hijackings, insisting in one sermon: 'We came here to build, not to destroy. We are the bridge between Americans and one billion Muslims worldwide.'

It soon became clear to the hordes of 9/11 investigators from all reaches of law enforcement, who were initially kept in the dark about the full story behind the Pentagon hijackers, that Awlaki's background appeared suspicious, to say the least. He was interviewed four times by the FBI in the days after the attacks and some agents were absolutely convinced that he knew more than he was telling them. But the word came from on high to back off. He was even invited to speak as a 'moderate Muslim' at a Pentagon outreach event just months after 9/11, and he lunched in the Secretary's Office of the Army General Counsel.

Every time an enterprising official came up with a way to put the screws to Awlaki, it was quashed. His use of prostitutes, which continued after 9/11, was not considered enough to bring charges, neither was another investigator's plan to arrest him on passport fraud, based on a lie he gave when entering the country that he was born in Yemen, in order to claim an overseas student grant. The arrest warrant was issued, but later rescinded.

Were his intelligence handlers putting pressure on Awlaki? Was he trying to make up for leading America into the biggest intelligence disaster in US history?

After returning from a trip abroad in 2002, Awlaki made a 'sudden and unexplained appearance' at the Falls Church home of cleric Ali al-Timimi, who later wondered if he was working for the FBI to entrap him into admitting recruiting young Muslims to join the fight against coalition forces in Afghanistan. Timimi was imprisoned for life in 2005 for supporting jihad against the US, but lawyers for the US-born scholar and former cancer researcher argued on appeal that the government was hiding Awlaki's role as a longtime FBI informant.

When Awlaki visited Timimi at his Virginia home in October 2002, he 'encouraged him to recruit and actually raised issues of possible terrorist acts', according to his lawyer, Jonathan Turley, who suggested the cleric was working as an FBI 'asset'. According to court papers, Timimi 'has long believed that this visit could not have happened without the government's knowledge or facilitation despite the government's assertion that its investigation of him only began in February 2003'.

Ruling on the request, which still hasn't been settled, US District Court Judge Leonie Brinkema said that part of the answer was so highly classified that only she was allowed to see it.

In court papers, Timimi's lawyers insisted the Department of Justice possesses 'considerable undisclosed material information' on Awlaki. The law 'does not entitle any defendant to the disclosure of the extent and nature of the government's investigative tools or tactics simply because he suspects that materials are in the government's possession that might prove interesting to him,' wrote prosecutor Gordon Kromberg in response.

The very fact that Awlaki was allowed back in the US in 2002 raised serious question marks about the 'Teflon terrorist'. Arriving at JFK airport in New York on 10 October 2002, on a flight from Yemen via Saudi Arabia, Awlaki was immediately arrested on a warrant filed in Colorado over the passport technicality that he listed Yemen, rather than New Mexico, as his place of birth. It was effectively a holding charge to enable the FBI Joint Terrorism Task Force in San Diego to quiz him over his ties to the hijackers Hazmi and Mihdhar.

Despite the outstanding warrant, to the fury of the San

Diego agents, Awlaki was released within hours that same day on the orders of FBI Director Robert Mueller. The Colorado warrant was also suddenly withdrawn, although the move to vacate wasn't actually approved until the following day.

A week earlier, Mueller had written a 'secret memo' referencing a National Security investigation by the FBI Washington Field Office. The subject of the message – which was fully redacted when it was released after a Freedom of Information request – was 'Anwar Aulaqi; IT-UBL/Al-Qaeda'.

A later message from the Washington Field Office to the counterterrorism unit, again using the initials UBL for Usama bin Laden and an alternative spelling of Awlaki's name, was titled 'Anwar Nasser Aulaqi, IT-UBL/AlQaeda, OO:WFO' and refers to the term 'asset reporting'.

Awlaki was allowed back into the US despite being on the FBI-managed terrorist watchlist, which should have listed him on a law-enforcement computer database as a 'terrorist organisation member – approach with caution' and prohibited him from boarding a flight to America.

It soon became clear that the intelligence agents who were in touch with Awlaki knew he was on the flight to New York and had plans to smooth his entry if there were any complications. By this time, the 'wall' that had divided the security services by forcing intelligence and evidence-gatherers apart had been torn down in the wake of 9/11. Sharing of information – more pertinently, the lack of sharing of information – was still a huge problem, however.

The San Diego counterterrorism agents who wanted to interview Awlaki were incensed at Washington's decision to let him go. That anger was only intensified when the cleric's role was discovered in the Fort Hood mass shooting in Texas in 2009, when former US Army major Nidal Hasan shot dead thirteen people and injured more than thirty others. Hasan had been a member of Awlaki's Falls Church mosque and in close email contact with the imam in the run-up to the worst attack on a military base in American history.

Awlaki was also linked to Umar Farouk Abdulmutallab, the so-called 'Underwear Bomber', who tried unsuccessfully to detonate explosives hidden in his pants on a Christmas Day flight in 2009.

'To date,' Virginia Congressman Frank Wolf wrote to Mueller regarding the decision to grant Awlaki entry in 2002, 'this action and the timeline of these events has never been adequately explained.'

Soon after his meeting with Timimi, Awlaki left the US for good, moving to Britain for a while, lecturing youth groups on jihad, before returning to Yemen permanently. While there, he was arrested and spent some time in prison, when he says he was visited by FBI agents.

At least outwardly, Awlaki's jihadism had hardened, although those who knew him well would argue that he was never the moderate propagandist he had been painted.

In April 2010, President Barack Obama agreed to include Awlaki's name on a CIA 'kill list'. One can only assume Awlaki had outgrown his usefulness and he spent his final years hiding in southeast Yemen.

Awlaki was killed in a drone attack on 30 September 2011. The truth about his role in the 11 September attacks a decade earlier died with him, but he did leave one last clue to his recruitment as a double agent.

In his final column for the al-Qaeda newspaper *Inspire*, Awlaki confirmed that he had indeed been approached by the US intelligence services to spy for them. He wrote: 'I was visited by two men who introduced themselves as officials with the US government (they did not specify which government organisation they belonged to) and that they are interested in my cooperation with them. When I asked what cooperation did they expect, they responded by saying that they are interested in having me liaise with them concerning the Muslim community in San Diego.'

Interestingly, he didn't say what happened next.

Chapter Seven

The Twentieth Hijacker

Phoenix, Arizona,
10 July 2001

Kenneth Williams worked in the FBI's counterterrorism unit in Phoenix for eleven years and had been around long enough to know that something was up. On 10 July 2001, he was worried enough about it to send a detailed memo to his superiors in New York and Washington. What he didn't realise was that he would be stepping on sensitive toes and that his report, like almost every other lead in the hunt for the hijackers, would be crushed from on high.

While investigating local links with al-Muhjiroun, a Sunni Muslim fundamentalist group based in the UK with strong ties to bin Laden, Williams noticed that there was an 'inordinate' number of young Muslims from the Middle East at flight training schools in Arizona. He said there were at least ten individuals from Pakistan, India, Kenya, Algeria, the United Arab Emirates and Saudi Arabia. Some had been interviewed and appeared to be radicals with extreme anti-American views. He put two and two together and made four, not that anyone else would see that everything added up to a world of trouble.

In his eight-page warning, Williams worried that bin Laden

had placed operatives in flight training schools and aviation colleges around the world in a 'coordinated effort' to put them in place 'in the future to conduct terror activity against civil aviation targets'. He wanted the FBI to create a list to monitor any potential Islamic extremists signing on for flight training anywhere in the US, a suggestion that was ignored. Williams's note was described as 'speculative and not very significant'.

None of the ten people listed by Williams was among the hijackers, but at least two of the students were thought to have known Hani Hanjour, the much-travelled wannabe pilot who crashed American Airlines Flight 77 into the Pentagon. One of them, Saudi Arabian Faisal al-Salmi, was convicted in 2002 of lying to the FBI after he repeatedly denied knowing Hanjour when they both used a flight simulator at a Phoenix flight school.

It was possible at this point that the so-called 'Phoenix Memo' may have been waylaid because of systemic failures within the bureau or simply because it was considered to be too much of a long-shot hunch by a low-ranking agent from the boondocks of Arizona.

But a memo by another special agent, this time addressed to FBI Director Robert Mueller, would suggest there was more to the dismissal of Williams's warning than anyone had realised at the time. It concerned the arrest of Zacarias Moussaoui, a French citizen who was detained by the FBI in Minnesota almost a month later on 16 August 2001 and who was the summation of all Special Agent Kenneth Williams's worst fears.

Moussaoui had signed up as a student at the Pan Am International Flight Academy in Eagan, Minnesota, under trainer Clarence 'Clancy' Prevost, a retired Northwest Airlines pilot. It didn't take long for Prevost to become suspicious about the genial Frenchman who paid for most of the $8,300 course in $100 bills and insisted he wanted to learn how to fly a 747 airliner without bothering with a licence to fly a small plane.

Moussaoui's dream was to learn to fly from Heathrow Airport in London to John F. Kennedy Airport in New York, despite only having less than fifty hours flying time on a single-engine, propeller plane. It was like going straight from an L-plate in a Honda automatic to the starting grid at Le Mans. 'We don't know anything about this guy, and we're teaching him how to throw the switches on a 747,' Prevost – who later got $5 million reward money for turning in the terrorist – told his bosses.

The FBI was alerted, and Moussaoui was held on immigration charges for overstaying his visa. It later emerged that he had also trained at the Airman Flight School in Oklahoma, where Mohamed Atta and Marwan al-Shehhi – pilots of the planes that hit the North and South Towers of the World Trade Center – had been students.

In his possession when he was arrested were two knives, a laptop, 747 flight manuals and a computer disc with information about crop dusting. Worried that his flight training had a more sinister intent, FBI officials in Minnesota repeatedly requested permission to search his laptop and his apartment, but were turned down flat, over and over again. One agent who interviewed Moussaoui wrote in his notes that the suspect could be interested in flying a plane into the World Trade Center. Still, requests to check his computer for clues were knocked back.

It wasn't until after 9/11 that it was revealed just how determined the hierarchy in the FBI was to keep the Moussaoui investigation on the back burner. Then veteran agent Coleen Rowley, special counsel for the FBI's Minneapolis office, broke ranks to suggest in an impassioned fifteen-page letter to Mueller that it was possible the 9/11 plot could have been discovered in time had the Minnesota office been allowed to carry out its enquiries.

'The fact is that key FBI [headquarters] personnel whose jobs it was to assist and coordinate with field division agents on terrorism investigations and the obtaining and use of [classified search warrants] continued to almost inexplicably throw up roadblocks and undermine Minneapolis's by-now desperate efforts,' she wrote. 'When, in a desperate eleventh-hour measure to bypass the FBI [headquarters] roadblock, the Minneapolis division [notified] the CIA's Counter Terrorism Center, FBI [headquarters] personnel actually chastised the Minneapolis agents for making the direct notification without their approval!

'Although I agree that it's very doubtful that the full scope of the [9/11] tragedy could have been prevented, it's at least possible we could have gotten lucky and uncovered one or two more of the terrorists in flight training prior to September 11th, just as Moussaoui was discovered, after making contact with his flight instructors,' she added.

After 9/11, Mueller would admit that more should have been done to support the agents in Minneapolis and Phoenix who had suspicions about an al-Qaeda plot to fly planes into buildings. By then, he couldn't really argue anything else. His own agents, frustrated at their treatment at every turn, were asking questions of their own organisation ... and they weren't getting any answers.

Agents who had dedicated their careers to the pursuit of the truth were being stymied by their bosses and the government they served with such distinction without anything resembling a viable explanation. There were inexplicable gaps, vast chasms clear to anybody who cared enough to look, in the official 9/11 narrative. If anyone dared to question, they were shut down.

The result was that, despite the flurry of arrests made as much for public relations purposes as anything else in the immediate aftermath of the 11 September attacks, Moussaoui was the only successful prosecution. Most of the other Muslims who had been rounded up were either let go or deported because of immigration violations.

Zacarias Moussaoui was sentenced to six life sentences and sent to Colorado's fortress ADX Supermax prison for being the so-called 'Twentieth Hijacker' who was supposed to have been on board Flight 93, the only plane with four rather than five hijackers. Or perhaps he was the substitute waiting on the bench in case anyone pulled out. Or maybe he was being lined up for a second wave of attacks. Nobody really knew.

Bin Laden issued a statement in 2006 denying Moussaoui was ever supposed to have anything to do with the mission. In truth, his role, whatever it should have been, was relatively minor – a tip of a much bigger iceberg.

Either way, twenty years later, he was still the only person to have been convicted in connection with the murders of 2,977 people on 9/11.

You could ask yourself why it has taken so long for terrorists with real substance in the al-Qaeda network and intimate involvement in the attacks to face justice in a public court of law. That would include Osama bin Laden, who was shot dead by US Navy SEALs at his Pakistani hideaway in 2011 rather than taken for trial.

Then there is Khalid Sheikh Mohammed, the so-called 'architect of 9/11', who was arrested in Pakistan in 2003 and who has been held at Guantanamo Bay in Cuba for years. As we will see, his prosecution has been so glacial that a jury wasn't assembled for the military trial until 2021. There was time, however, for the CIA to waterboard him 183 times. You could also include Abu Zubaydah, bin Laden's counter-intelligence officer and another 9/11 planner, who has been in US custody since 2002 and at Guantanamo since 2006. He was waterboarded 83 times.

There's an obvious answer as to why these men have been kept in cold storage for so long and the families of the victims have been deprived of the small measure of closure their punishments would bring.

Successive US administrations – Bush, Obama and Trump – were afraid that the damning truth about what really happened in the lead-up to 11 September would finally become known. They have prevaricated in the hope that time would lessen the sense of betrayal many families would feel about the actions that led directly to the deaths of their loved ones.

They were wrong. If anything, the pain of injustice hurts even more.

Chapter Eight

The Moonlight Flit

Sarasota, Florida,
27 August 2001

There was food on the table and the fridge was full, clothes in the closets, two recently re-registered cars in the garage and a brand-new PT Cruiser in the driveway. The pool was still on, the house was full of furniture and the safe in the bedroom was empty, its door wide open.

Initially, neighbours in the upscale Prestancia gated community in Sarasota, Florida, thought little of the hasty departure at Escondito Circle. It was only after the events of 11 September, two weeks later, that they began to wonder why the Saudi Arabian family that lived there left so suddenly.

The FBI finally came to call, prompted by the postman who was suspicious about of the amount of mail that was piling up and the lack of a forwarding address. It didn't take long for the feds to discover that three of the hijackers – ringleader Mohamed Atta, Marwan al-Shehhi and Ziad Samir Jarrah – had learned to fly at the nearby Florida Flight Training Center and Huffman Aviation. Phone and security gate records also appeared to show that Atta and maybe his accomplices could have been in contact with the family who had left so suddenly.

Atta and Shehhi piloted the planes that crashed into the World Trade Center and Jarrah flew Flight 93, the Washington DC-diverted airliner that crash-landed in Pennsylvania.

The three pilots had arrived in the US from Hamburg the previous summer with the immediate purpose of getting their flying licences. Unlike Mihdhar and Hazmi, who had both fought with the mujahideen in Bosnia, they didn't have a jihadist past to trip them up and had been more careful with their travel. As a result, it seems they slipped into the US quietly via different routes from Europe, undetected by the security services.

But there was mingling between the groups that would flag up at least some of the hijackers. Atta, the hood-eyed Egyptian, for one, was seen socialising with the San Diego cell and Hanjour spent some time in Florida.

US agents had apparently been trailing Atta while he was still in Hamburg between January and May of 2000, failing to tell their German counterparts, after which he was spotted buying large amounts of chemicals in Frankfurt that could have been used in making explosives, but it seems the trail had gone cold.

If the CIA and their intelligence partners were initially just watching the West Coast crew, it would quickly become clear that it was imperative to keep eyes on what was going on in Florida as well. Just as in California, any approach would need to be very carefully choreographed. With most of the group hailing from Saudi Arabia, the perfect cover would, once again, be an acquaintance struck up with other Saudis living in the US.

The house at Escondito Circle belonged to a wealthy businessman, with strong links to the Saudi royal family, and his American-born wife, and, at least until their departure, it was occupied for nearly a decade by their daughter, her husband and their two children.

The scion of the family, a father of five, moved in some high-flying circles and had five expensive homes in London, Saudi Arabia and the US. Photographs from the early 2000s showed him meeting with former British Prime Minister John Major, the late Pakistan Prime Minister Benazir Bhutto and President George W. Bush. The photo with Bush is signed 'Best Wishes, George Bush'.

His wide-ranging business interests have reportedly included companies with ties both to the US intelligence community and to the bin Laden family. With his wife, he was a regular visitor to his daughter and son-in-law's 3,300-square-foot mansion.

Visitor logs and surveillance cameras capturing the licence plates of visitors to the gated community also appear to show that the hijackers – including Atta – were visitors in the months before the Saudis left.

The Saudi family strongly denied having any connections with the hijackers or supporting them in any way, claiming the hurry to leave was solely because of a new job offer. Nevertheless, local FBI agents were no doubt intrigued to learn about these suspicious connections in the chaotic days after 9/11 as the agency scrambled to make sense of what had happened. In a 2002 memo, one agent wrote that there were 'many connections' between the family that fled and the hijackers.

Ten years later, the FBI would rubbish its own agent's findings, denying there was any evidence of a link with the wealthy Saudis, who moved on to live in London and Riyadh. The episode barely rated a mention in the 9/11 Commission Report published in 2004 and the FBI stomped on any attempt to force it to disclose the details of its investigation into the family.

The impression they have sought to give is that it was a footnote, unworthy of spending hard-pressed resources. The reality is that FBI reports on the probe number an astonishing 80,266 classified pages in twenty-seven boxes at its Tampa Field Office, hardly an insignificant inquiry, and it refuses to reveal the full contents to this day, despite being reprimanded by a judge who ruled the secrecy illegal. Lawyers for the agency continue to use the old chestnut that they will endanger national security and disclose secret sources and techniques if they make the documents public.

If the file consists solely of the post-9/11 investigation, there is no good reason for the secrecy from the FBI and the US Department of Justice, even if it does point a finger of blame at the Saudis. The only explanation for the obfuscation two decades later is that the probe's scope was far broader than anything that has been revealed up to now. It seems quite possible that members of the family were working at the behest of the Saudi intelligence services. If that was indeed the case, then the Saudis, in turn, must have been working with the Americans. There is just no way the White House, because that is who we are talking about here, would cover up for a country found to have willingly aided and abetted bin Laden's troops to strike at the heart of the most powerful nation on earth. They would, however, keep the Saudis' actions under wraps if they were complicit with the US in a catastrophic intelligence failure that could have cost almost 3,000 lives.

'The FBI kept its investigation secret for a decade. It didn't inform Congress's Joint Inquiry into the attacks, which I co-chaired. Nor did the FBI tell the subsequent 9/11 Commission about it,' wrote Bob Graham, a former Florida governor and chairman of the Senate Intelligence Committee that held inquiries into 9/11.

The former Democratic senator is convinced that 'someone may have tipped off' the family about the impending attacks.

When an independent investigative publication called the *Florida Bulldog* discovered the connection, the FBI claimed at first that it had no reports detailing the investigation, then it admitted to a handful and finally to more than 80,000 pages, but only after the *Bulldog* filed a Freedom of Information suit against the authorities.

The 9/11 Review Commission, set up in 2014 to look into any new information about the attacks, agreed with the FBI that the story was a dead end.

The panel took note of the FBI report, suggesting that there were 'many connections' between the Saudi family and the hijackers, but insisted: 'The FBI told the Review Commission that the communication was "poorly written" and wholly unsubstantiated. When questioned later by others in the FBI, the special agent who wrote [it] was unable to provide any basis for the contents of the document or explain why he wrote it as he did.'

Thomas Julin, the attorney who filed the Freedom of Information lawsuit against the FBI, told the *Miami Herald*: 'The report provides no plausible explanation for the contradiction between the FBI's current claim that it found nothing and its 2002 memo finding "many connections" between the family and the 9/11 terrorists.'

As we shall see, Bob Graham's contention that the family was tipped off and urged to leave the country as soon as possible may have been correct, but not because the Saudis had pre-knowledge about 9/11. The reality may well have been that the US intelligence services had lost the terrorists in their midst and realised in horror that what promised to be the biggest 'gotcha' in their history was now shaping up to be the biggest cock-up.

Chapter Nine

The Worst Nightmare

Sarasota, Florida,
11 September 2001

Caught like a deer in the headlights in a classroom full of primary schoolchildren, President George W. Bush was desperately trying to marshal his thoughts as he tried to work out what had gone wrong. Just moments earlier, at 9.05 a.m. on 11 September 2001, White House Chief of Staff Andy Card had whispered in his ear, 'A second plane has hit the second tower. America is under attack.'

The president later explained his hesitation, squirming in his tiny chair at the Emma E. Booker Elementary School in Sarasota, Florida, as an attempt to portray calmness in a crisis. Going into the routine photo op to support his administration's 'No Child Left Behind' education initiative, Bush knew that a plane had crashed into the World Trade Center, although at that point it wasn't known if it was an accident.

But it is certain that among the many thoughts going through his head, as he tried to hold it together for the cameras after learning it was a terrorist attack, was the simple question: How was this allowed to happen?

His intelligence chiefs had assured him they were on top of

the threat from Osama bin Laden and al-Qaeda. Bush had been told about the threat from the air, about a hijacking plot. It was all being handled.

On Monday, 6 August – just thirty-six days before 9/11 – Bush had received a memo in his daily White House briefing entitled: 'Bin Laden Determined to Strike Within the United States'.

Days later, CIA Director George Tenet visited him in person at his ranch in Crawford, Texas, to tell him more about the al-Qaeda operation. Tenet had asked to meet in private, away from the prying ears at the daily briefings, to keep him updated on the spy network that was meant to keep them one step ahead of the terrorists.

The daily briefing note is detailed and eerily predicts what was to come, mentioning bin Laden's preparations for hijackings and potential targets in New York. Here is the full memo.

Bin Ladin Determined To Strike in US

Clandestine, foreign government, and media reports indicate Bin Ladin since 1997 has wanted to conduct terrorist attacks in the US. Bin Ladin implied in US television interviews in 1997 and 1998 that his followers would follow the example of World Trade Center bomber Ramzi Yousef and 'bring the fighting to America.'

After US missile strikes on his base in Afghanistan in 1998, Bin Ladin told followers he wanted to retaliate in Washington, according to a [redacted] service.

An Egyptian Islamic Jihad (EIJ) operative told an [redacted] service at the same time that Bin Ladin was planning to exploit the operative's access to the US to mount a terrorist strike.

The millennium plotting in Canada in 1999 may

have been part of Bin Ladin's first serious attempt to implement a terrorist strike in the US. Convicted plotter Ahmed Ressam has told the FBI that he conceived the idea to attack Los Angeles International Airport himself, but that Bin Ladin lieutenant Abu Zubaydah encouraged him and helped facilitate the operation. Ressam also said that in 1998 Abu Zubaydah was planning his own US attack.

Ressam says Bin Ladin was aware of the Los Angeles operation.

Although Bin Ladin has not succeeded, his attacks against the US Embassies in Kenya and Tanzania in 1998 demonstrate that he prepares operations years in advance and is not deterred by setbacks. Bin Ladin associates surveilled our Embassies in Nairobi and Dar es Salaam as early as 1993, and some members of the Nairobi cell planning the bombings were arrested and deported in 1997.

Al-Qa'ida members – including some who are US citizens – have resided in or traveled to the US for years, and the group apparently maintains a support structure that could aid attacks. Two al-Qa'ida members found guilty in the conspiracy to bomb our embassies in East Africa were US citizens, and a senior EIJ member lived in California in the mid-1990s.

A clandestine source said in 1998 that a Bin Ladin cell in New York was recruiting Muslim-American youth for attacks.

We have not been able to corroborate some of the more sensational threat reporting, such as that from a [redacted] service in 1998 saying that Bin Ladin wanted to hijack a US aircraft to gain the release of

> *'Blind Shaykh' Umar 'Abd al-Rahman and other US-held extremists.*
>
> *Nevertheless, FBI information since that time indicates patterns of suspicious activity in this country consistent with preparations for hijackings or other types of attacks, including recent surveillance of federal buildings in New York.*
>
> *The FBI is conducting approximately 70 full field investigations throughout the US that it considers Bin Ladin-related. CIA and the FBI are investigating a call to our Embassy in the UAE in May saying that a group of Bin Ladin supporters was in the US planning attacks with explosives.*

The problem was that, by this time, the CIA's bin Laden operation was fast unravelling. The recruitment attempt had failed and any source or sources inside al-Qaeda had disappeared along with bin Laden himself. All the signs around the globe pointed to an imminent attack. And worse, much worse, the US agents and their Saudi counterparts had lost touch with the would-be hijackers.

Whether it was down to operational failures or they had been double-crossed, it was still unclear. Either way, the warning memo didn't appear to bother Bush overmuch; he went bass fishing and didn't deem it serious enough to call a meeting to discuss the concerns.

Less than a month earlier, on 10 July 2001, National Security Advisor Condoleezza Rice got a call from CIA Director George Tenet asking for an urgent meeting to tell her of his fears about an impending al-Qaeda attack.

It was probably just before the panic call that Tenet was made aware of the plan to recruit Mihdhar and how it had gone awry.

But Rice and, consequently, Bush were not told anything about Mihdhar. They certainly were not informed he had first come to the US in January 2000 with Hazmi and that the information had been withheld from the FBI. That would have opened a can of worms the CIA did not want to deal with, at a point when they did not realise just how bad it was going to get.

Finally, eighteen months after Mihdhar first flew to LA following the Kuala Lumpur terrorist summit, the decision was taken by the CIA to officially tell the FBI that Mihdhar was in the United States. The call was made to the FBI's New York office on 22 August, but, even then, the CIA maintained the intelligence 'wall' meant they could not share all they knew about Mihdhar and insisted inquiries to find the suspect should be for intelligence purposes only and not to arrest and charge him. In other words, find him but keep your hands off.

They knew Mihdhar arrived in California in January 2000, left that summer and returned to the US on Saudi Airlines Flight 53 on 4 July 2001. They were also told, belatedly, that Hazmi was in the country – and that they had both been in Kuala Lumpur before coming to the States.

The bid to recruit Mihdhar had clearly failed. Not only that, he had shaken off his American and Saudi suitors at a critical time, just as the drums were beating the loudest.

News of Mihdhar's presence in the US now spread across the FBI and not just by Miller and Rossini, who had been ordered to keep it to themselves. On 24 August, the names of Khalid al-Mihdhar and Nawaf al-Hazmi were finally added to the State Department's terrorist watchlist. But that list only worked for international flights … and the hijackers were already closing in on New York and Washington DC.

Using a credit card in his own name, Mihdhar booked a plane ticket on 25 August to travel on 11 September. Two days later, Hazmi bought tickets for himself and his brother, Salem, on the same flight. Sixteen other men with Arabic-sounding names, most of them from Saudi Arabia and all of them linked by association, also booked domestic plane tickets around that time – between 25 August and 5 September – to fly on four flights departing early on that same morning of 11 September.

Still, the intelligence services were not willing to tell all they knew. As a result, one rookie FBI agent was given the job to find Mihdhar as his first task in the intelligence section. There was no urgency or priority given to a search that didn't even begin until 4 September because the agent had to finish another job. And time was fast running out.

On 29 August 2001, an FBI agent who had been heavily involved in the investigation into the al-Qaeda attack on the USS *Cole* asked his bosses at headquarters to allow the New York office to throw its full weight behind the search to find Mihdhar. He was rebuffed, with the National Security Law Unit advising that the 'wall' prohibited full-scale FBI intervention.

In the email exchange, the agent left his superiors in no doubt that he thought the decision was unconscionable. The email from FBI headquarters read: 'A criminal agent CAN NOT be present at the interview. This case, in its entirety, is based on [intelligence]. If at such time as information is developed indicating the existence of a substantial federal crime, that information will be passed over the wall according to the proper procedures and turned over for follow-up criminal investigation.' [Emphasis in original.]

This is the emailed response from the New York agent: 'Whatever has happened to this – someday someone will die – and wall or not – the public will not understand why we were not more effective and throwing every resource we had at certain "problems". Let's hope the [FBI's] National Security

Law Unit will stand behind their decisions then, especially since the biggest threat to us now, UBL, is getting the most "protection".'

The US immigration authorities told investigators later that they believe they might have been able to locate Mihdhar and Hazmi in late August through the extensive Immigration and Nationalization Service (INS) database system, had they been asked. (The INS was replaced in 2003 by the Department of Homeland Security in a shake-up following 9/11.) The Bureau of Diplomatic Security at the State Department also said it might have been able to track them down. Neither was asked.

In July 2001, Omar al-Bayoumi, the Saudi who had been so useful to the first two hijackers in San Diego, left the US and moved to England. The Saudi Arabian family in Florida left in a hurry at the end of August.

On 31 October, Prince Turki al-Faisal, the head of Saudi Arabia's spy network, the GID, since 1979, suddenly resigned.

Something was badly wrong. Privately, some investigators believe Mabahith agents learned more about Mihdhar's possible involvement in the 9/11 plot and tipped off their CIA partners. It explained the sudden departures in the weeks before the attacks.

Some investigators believe the reason the intelligence services were caught by surprise was as simple as a diary mix-up. The Americans had misunderstood the intelligence tip-off about the timing for the attacks, confusing the traditional date order in the US and the rest of the world – 9/11/2001 and 11/9/2001 – and expecting the plot to go ahead on 9 November 2001. Hard to believe, but the biggest waves start from the smallest of ripples.

After thinking for nearly eighteen months that they were one step ahead of al-Qaeda, the CIA was now one catastrophic step behind. They would only find out where they had been in that vital missing, final fortnight after planes had been flown into the Twin Towers, the Pentagon and a lonely field in Pennsylvania.

In their detailed and meticulously researched book, *The Watchdogs Didn't Bark*, authors John Duffy and Ray Nowosielski quoted Colonel Larry Wilkerson, Colin Powell's former chief of staff, as recalling he heard Tenet's words immediately after seeing the passenger manifests on the hijacked planes.

'Oh, God,' he said. 'It's all of them.'

George Bush and Condoleezza Rice would later insist there was no good information pointing to the possibility of airborne terror attacks before 9/11, but Sibel Edmonds, a former FBI translator with high-level clearance, says she spent more than three hours in a behind-closed-doors session with 9/11 Commission investigators, describing data available in the spring and summer of 2001 that suggested that not only were terrorists in the US but also that they were prepared and ready to launch an attack using aircraft as weapons.

Edmonds claimed that, while working for the FBI, she uncovered a warning about 9/11 sent to the agency in April 2001 by a top Iranian informant who was previously head of the country's SAVAK intelligence network. In her self-published book, *Classified Woman*, she claims the unnamed informant told two agents from the Washington Field Office: 'Listen, I was recently contacted by two extremely reliable and long-term sources, one in Afghanistan, the other in Pakistan's border region with Afghanistan. In the past, these guys had provided me with inside information and intelligence that was extremely hard to come by, considering the tightly based networks and groups that they were able to enter and penetrate. They notified me that an active mujahideen group led by bin Laden had issued an order to attack certain targets in the United States and were planning the attack as we spoke.

'According to my guys,' the source continued, 'Bin Laden's group is planning a massive terrorist attack in the United States. The order has been issued. They are targeting major cities, big metropolitan cities: they think four or five cities; New York, Chicago, Washington DC, possibly Los Angeles or Las Vegas. They will use airplanes to carry out the attacks. They said that some of the individuals involved in carrying this out are already in the United States. They are here in the US living among us, and I believe some in US government already know about all of this.'

She claimed the informant told the two agents that the time frame was 'very soon' and 'within the next two or three months'. He added that it was his bet that the terrorists were planning to plant bombs on aircraft and 'then have them blown up over the populated cities'. Despite the urgency of the message, Edmonds claimed that the agents filed details to their superiors but heard nothing back, and any investigation was quashed.

The informant came back in June 2001, asking about the response to his information. 'I've been thinking about this, trying to make more sense out of it myself,' he told the agents, according to the translator. 'The source mumbled something about tall buildings. Maybe they will blow up a plane over some tall buildings? I don't know ... perhaps the FBI can get more specifics from the Pakistanis; ISI [Inter-Services Intelligence]? Have they tried? After all, they are your guys; and they know all about this.'

Edmonds insists in her book that the White House and the security agencies were made aware of the Iranian intelligence insider's warning. After the 9/11 attacks, she claimed the agents who interviewed the informant and passed on his concerns were told to forget the warnings and the conversations about them ever happened. She said they were told: 'No one should ever mention a word about this, period. Never!'

When she broke ranks, Edmonds was gagged by the Bush administration on the grounds that she was breaching 'state secrets privilege'.

The Turkish-American translator, who speaks Azerbaijani, Farsi, Turkish and English, told the *Independent* in the UK: 'I gave [the 9/11 Commission] details of specific investigation files, the specific dates, specific target information, specific managers in charge of the investigation. I gave them everything so that they could go back and follow up. This is not hearsay. These are things that are documented. These things can be established very easily.

'There was general information about the time frame, about methods to be used, but not specifically about how they would be used – and about people being in place and who was ordering these sorts of terror attacks. There were other cities that were mentioned. Major cities with skyscrapers.

'President Bush said they had no specific information about 11 September and that is accurate, but only because he said 11 September,' she said. There was, however, general information about the use of airplanes and that an attack was just months away.'

In another interview, she was even more emphatic, saying: 'My translations of the 9/11 intercepts included [terrorist] money laundering, detailed and date-specific information. If they were to do real investigations, we would see several significant high-level criminal prosecutions in this country [the US] … and believe me, they will do everything to cover this up.'

Once again, here's confirmation that Bush and his intelligence services knew all about the threats posed by bin Laden and were well aware that terrorists were in the US and ready to strike. They were only told the full facts after 9/11 when it was too late to act. But, as we shall see later, the cover-up began on the day of the attacks because, had the truth become known, it may well have spelled the end for the CIA and possibly for the Bush presidency.

To better understand how and why 9/11 was allowed to happen, we need to look across the Atlantic to the story of a public schoolboy from East London who went from representing England at arm-wrestling to becoming a spy for MI6 and carrying out one of the most notorious kidnappings in the Middle East.

Chapter Ten

The Arm Wrestler Terrorist

Snaresbrook, East London, 1992

Omar Sheikh was not a nerd. He may have been the chess champion at £1,000-a-term Forest School in East London, but he was never going to be teased because he had the brawn to back up his brain. Friends remembered him knocking a teacher out cold with a punch when he was eight years old, and he would carry a suitcase full of weights around to all his classes to build up his muscles. His interest in bodybuilding led to a short-lived obsession with arm-wrestling and he forced himself into the English team via a tough initiation – taking on all comers in some of the East End's toughest pubs.

Raised in relative prosperity in Wanstead, on the grassier edge of the capital's border with Essex, the son of a successful clothes retailer, there were few clues to the notoriety he would find just a couple of years after leaving the familiar surroundings of his school in neighbouring Snaresbrook, where one of his classmates was England cricket captain Nasser Hussain.

If Sheikh was a little eccentric and an occasional handful for his teachers, his maverick tendencies were always going to be easier to accept when they came with academic ability;

he spoke five languages and his four A levels (two As, two Bs) were sufficient to win him a place at the London School of Economics reading mathematics and statistics.

From an immigrant family determined to make its mark in British society – his sister would study medicine at Oxford and his brother took law at Cambridge – Sheikh was a sociopath determined to follow his own path.

His commitment to his Islamic faith had grown during a short-lived move with his family back to Pakistan as a teenager and it flourished in his first year as a student at LSE. His rough edges as a youngster also sharpened with a greater tendency to violence.

Around this time, according to no less a source than former Pakistan President Pervez Musharraf, Sheikh was recruited by MI6, Britain's foreign intelligence service, shortly before he dropped out of LSE and went to drive aid convoys for an Islamic charity in war-torn Bosnia.

By now, acquaintances were describing him as 'psychopathic', and it wasn't long before his association with Britain's gentleman spy network was either replaced or aligned with an intelligence service that had an altogether more brutal and Machiavellian reputation for duplicity, Pakistan's Inter-Services Intelligence (ISI).

Despite representing philosophies that were poles apart, the CIA and the ISI worked closely together against the Soviets in Afghanistan, sharing information and resources to support, of all people, Osama bin Laden's nascent al-Qaeda and the Taliban, paying millions a year to train mujahideen groups in the 1980s. The rebels in this Cold War by proxy were also supported by covert actions by MI6 and by Saudi Arabia's Mabahith.

It was into this unholy alliance that Sheikh found himself

in the years before 9/11. In 1994, two years out of Forest School, he was already bound for his first jihadist mission after spending a month at a terrorist training camp in Afghanistan. By all accounts, he was a natural.

Sent to kidnap Western tourists in India and hold them to ransom as a way of putting a spotlight on the conflict over Kashmir, he used his familiarity with London to lure three British travellers – Paul Rideout, twenty-six years old, Myles Croston, twenty-eight, and Rhys Partridge, twenty-seven – and an American, Béla Nuss, forty-three, into a trap.

His first foray into terrorism was unsuccessful and short-lived; he was arrested after the Indian police tracked down the kidnap gang. He was shot in the shoulder in an unsuccessful attempt to get away and spent five years in Delhi's notorious Tihar Prisons.

But Sheikh's connections had already brought him to the attention of the hierarchy in both al-Qaeda and the ISI, who, according to the *Washington Post*, paid the legal fees for his trial.

When a Pakistani terror group hijacked an Air India flight from Nepal to New Delhi in 1999, they demanded that four of the most wanted terrorists in Indian jails should be set free in return for the release of their 154 hostages. One of the four was Omar Sheikh.

There were rumours at the time that MI6 wanted to repatriate him to Britain, promising immunity from prosecution in return for his insight into the plans of his terrorist masters. Instead, he flew back into the arms of bin Laden. At a Kandahar hotel, he reportedly spent several days huddled with Taliban chief Mohammed Omar and bin Laden, who was so charmed that he called him 'my special son'.

Returning to Pakistan, he was bought a house by the ISI

in an upscale Lahore neighbourhood and apparently lived in some style. Suggesting his continued allegiance to MI6, he was allowed back into Britain to see his family in 2000 and 2001, despite his much-publicised terrorist activities.

Western security chiefs have long been convinced that 9/11 could only have come about with the tacit involvement and support of a national intelligence agency. Sheikh's actions in the months before the attacks suggest that agency was Pakistan's ISI.

The 9/11 Commission says it never found definitive proof of where the hijackers were getting their money. Mustafa al-Hawsawi, who was handed over to the CIA from the ISI in March 2003 and has been painted as the plot's financial mastermind at Guantanamo Bay, where he remains, was dismissed as a minor player right from his first interrogation.

The conduit between the ISI and the hijackers in America was Omar Sheikh, who had carved out a niche in al-Qaeda by setting up an encrypted communications network and arranging money transfers to operatives around the world.

Using the alias Mustafa Muhammad Ahmad, Sheikh sent $100,000 from Pakistan to 9/11 ringleader Mohamed Atta in the US in the weeks before the attacks, a Bush administration source told CNN. After dispersing the funds to his sidekicks, Atta sent the remaining $26,300 back to Sheikh via the United Arab Emirates.

Days after the transfer came to light, the FBI asked for Sheikh to be extradited to face trial for the 1994 kidnapping, as that had involved an American tourist. When that was a no-go, Pakistan's President Musharraf had little choice but to force out General Mahmud Ahmed, the head of ISI, amid reports the US was investigating claims that he gave the order for Sheikh to wire the cash to Atta.

Using the same alias of Mustafa Muhammad Ahmad, Sheikh is also suspected of being behind a number of other payments to Atta and Marwan al-Shehhi between June 2000 and the day before 11 September.

It seems certain that Sheikh was the al-Qaeda paymaster for the 9/11 operation, and it is quite possible, bearing in mind General Ahmed's sudden resignation, that Pakistan was bankrolling it.

British intelligence reportedly sent signals in Pakistan that they were looking for Sheikh in August 2001, another sign that the word had gone out from the Americans that they feared something was afoot.

A quiet panic was triggered in intelligence agencies around the world. As we have seen, Saudis with any links to the hijackers in the States were leaving in a hurry. General Ahmed, at that time still in charge of ISI, was meeting with Mullah Omar in Afghanistan to discuss how they could protect bin Laden from the Americans.

By the beginning of September 2001, the general was in Washington DC, meeting secretly at the Pentagon and the National Security Council and with CIA boss George Tenet. He was at breakfast on Capitol Hill with the chairmen of the House and Senate Intelligence Committees, Senator Bob Graham and Congressman Porter Goss, when the first plane hit the World Trade Center. Whatever he had to tell them about Osama bin Laden had come too late.

Perhaps the person they should really have been talking to was still in Pakistan.

Was Sheikh, the East London schoolboy chess-champion, one move ahead of everyone? Is it conceivable that he was playing puppet master with the CIA and MI6 and leading them to believe they were in control? Then, when they were in way over their heads, he left them dangling at the behest of his real masters – bin Laden and his partners in Pakistan.

After 9/11, Sheikh felt bulletproof, for a while at least. He remained in his Lahore home for the most part but reportedly visited bin Laden in Afghanistan a few days after the attacks. There was little pressure from the US for him to be handed over. Similarly, after the ISI chief, mired in scandal over the $100,000 payment to Atta, stepped down, there was no official demand from America for him to tell all he knew.

When the *Wall Street Journal*'s South Asia Bureau Chief Daniel Pearl started asking too many questions about Pakistan's secret service in the aftermath of 9/11 and was investigating links between ISI and 'Shoe Bomber' Richard Reid, it was Sheikh who was chosen to charm him into a fake meeting with a source in Pakistan that resulted in his kidnapping and ultimate killing at the end of January 2002.

In early February 2002, FBI Director Robert Mueller reportedly flew to Pakistan to discuss Sheikh with Musharraf, and, although there is no record of what was said, the Briton was behind bars within days.

The ISI knew exactly who to call when the international pressure over Pearl's death became impossible to ignore and Sheikh spent more than a week secretly negotiating a deal that would ensure he could hand himself in and remain confident he would not be extradited to America. He would be sentenced to death for Pearl's murder, even though footage showing the veins on the hand that cut the journalist's throat would later suggest the actual killer was KSM, the 9/11 plot mastermind.

In the years since Pearl's death, friends have come forwards to claim that it was KSM and not Richard Reid that the reporter was investigating and that he died because he was getting too close to the truth about what really happened on 9/11.

Wherever he was, Sheikh was the catalyst for chaos. He was not executed but remained behind bars in Pakistan until his conviction was overturned in April 2020. Even then, he was re-arrested at the request of the Americans.

Whether he was working for the CIA, ISI, MI6 or all of them at once, Sheikh knows where all the bodies are buried. But you can bet the house that the considerable power of those agencies is making damned sure he will not talk. Musharraf is said to have told the US Ambassador Wendy Chamberlin that he would rather 'hang Sheikh myself than have him extradited'.

In the months after 9/11, Pakistan handed over more than 350 al-Qaeda terrorists, including KSM, to the Americans and was paid millions of dollars in return, despite a US ban on paying rewards to foreign governments. Some of them were taken to CIA 'black sites' around the world where they were tortured and interrogated. Some ended up at Guantanamo Bay; others were eventually set free.

As the twentieth anniversary of 9/11 approached, none of them had been brought to trial.

Chapter Eleven

The Flights

**Boston, Massachusetts, 7.59 a.m.,
11 September 2001**

The distinguished-looking man who took Seat 8B in the first-class compartment of American Airlines Flight 11 could easily have been taken for a professor from MIT, Harvard or any of the Boston-area colleges. Indeed, David Angell was known as 'the Dean' by his many friends in Hollywood because of his immaculate appearance and his gentlemanly, mild-mannered demeanour. The creator of the hit comedy series *Frasier* and *Wings* was flying home to Los Angeles through Boston, the location of another long-running TV show he wrote for, *Cheers*, after visiting the summer home he was building with his wife, Lynn, in Chatham, Massachusetts. Both in their early fifties, they had also been celebrating their thirtieth wedding anniversary.

It was an early flight and, with the three-hour time difference in their favour, they looked forward to being back at their home in Pasadena, about twenty minutes east of Los Angeles, by lunchtime. He would likely have given little thought to the Boeing 767-200 airliner as he checked the breakfast menu just before an on-time take-off at 7.59 a.m.

To Mohamed Atta, the brooding passenger sitting across the

first-class aisle from the Angells in Seat 8D, the plane, weighing 351,000 pounds with a full tank of 20,450 gallons of jet fuel, was a guided missile. Next to Atta in the middle two seats in first class was Abdulaziz al-Omari and up front, in seats 2A and 2B, were brothers Wail and Waleed al-Shehri. The fifth member of the gang, Satam al-Suqami, was behind in aisle seat 10B in business class. All of them, bar Atta, who was Egyptian, came from Saudi Arabia.

As we now know, David and Lynn Angell and the other seventy-four passengers on Flight 11 would never make it to their destination.

At 8.46 a.m., Flight 11 would hit the North Tower of the World Trade Center between floors 93 and 99, killing everyone aboard instantly.

Seventeen minutes later, at 9.03 a.m., United Airlines Flight 175 with fifty-one passengers, five hijackers and nine crew members aboard, ploughed into the South Tower between floors 77 and 85.

Another thirty-four minutes passed before American Airlines Flight 77, with fifty-three passengers, six crew members and five hijackers, crashed into the Pentagon at 9.37 a.m.

Then there was a further twenty-six minutes until 10.03 a.m., when United Airlines Flight 93, carrying thirty-three passengers, seven crew members and four hijackers, slammed into a field in Shanksville, Pennsylvania. Between the first plane hitting the World Trade Center and Flight 93 being forced down in Pennsylvania, there would be one hour and seventeen minutes.

In the hours, days and years that followed, loved ones have done their best to come to terms with the quirks of fate that put innocent, honourable people in the crosshairs of history that terrible morning.

In these pages, we have sought to understand the catastrophic intelligence failure that allowed the 9/11 terrorists, many of them known by the US authorities and all travelling under their own names, to board those four flights.

But many more unexplained questions about the events of 11 September still haunt the victims' families and all of us who trust our governments to keep us from harm. And they begin with the one hour and seventeen minutes when a group of nineteen terrorists, armed only with box-cutters and evil intent, ruled the skies unchallenged over the nexus of power in America.

In the following chapter, for the first time, we will see the chaos and confusion as the North American Aerospace Defense Command (NORAD) tried and failed to stop the hijackers. It is an excruciatingly raw glimpse, full of snap decisions and erroneous judgements, but then history is never kind when looking back on events in real time.

While al-Qaeda had been planning for 9/11 for years, and there is a good argument to suggest that America's intelligence services should have known what was coming, nothing had prepared the country's air-defence chiefs for what they were about to face. One of the most enduring conspiracy theories puts Vice President Dick Cheney at the forefront of a perfidious plot involving Bush, Defense Secretary Donald Rumsfeld and other Republican hawks to allow the hijackings to happen with the sole intention of triggering a war with Afghanistan and Iraq to win control of lucrative oil reserves in the Middle East and turn the balance of power towards the West.

One of the central planks of that sensational accusation is the time it took for the US administration to react to the attacks once they had begun and the failure to send even a single fighter jet to tackle the airborne threat that morning, even after the first planes had struck the Twin Towers.

After fleeing the Sarasota primary school, the president was being kept above the fray – sometimes at such a high altitude he couldn't be reached – aboard Air Force One, bound for Barksdale Air Force base in the middle of nowhere (Bossier City, northwest Louisiana) while his staff tried to work out if he was a target and consequently Bush was relatively ineffective as the nightmare was unfolding. Much was made afterwards of the tough decision that Cheney, standing in for Bush in the White House bunker, had to make to give his go-ahead to allow military jets to shoot down a passenger plane if there were suspicions it had been hijacked. The fact is that all four seized aircraft had crash-landed by the time the order was finally made and passed on to the military pilots.

That theory, which has more support than you might imagine, would certainly explain why the hijackers were given such a free pass by the US security agencies. But, reading through the transcript of the real-time drama being played out as the 9/11 plot unfolded, it seems much more likely that the chaos and confusion among those who were trying to work out how to respond stems from the simple fact that they had never handled anything like it before. Add to that, the al-Qaeda pilots knew enough to turn off the transponders that identify individual planes, making them much harder to trace.

There is no suggestion in the tapes of any 'stand down' order from Cheney to keep fighter jets grounded, as has been claimed by some sceptics who have accused the administration of complicity. You can clearly see the confusion between the civilian air controllers in the Federal Aviation Authority and the military with their outdated procedures designed to combat a Cold War threat from Russia, which threw everybody off course.

It didn't help that some officers at the Northeast Air Defense

Sector (now just the Eastern Air Defense Sector) in rural Rome, New York, thought at first – and some for quite a while – that the hijackings were being faked as part of an exercise planned for that very morning.

Despite my lack of faith in the government's 9/11 narrative, I still find it impossible to believe the president or the vice president was a party to an unconscionable plot that would take so many American lives. But as you read this fascinating transcript, provided through the Freedom of Information Act, please note that there were just two sections that were redacted from the tapes – thirty minutes of a cockpit recording from Flight 93 and a conference call between Cheney, Rumsfeld and other high-level officials.

Cheney had been literally carried from his office to the underground bunker by Secret Service agents and his account of the attempts he made to get his 'shoot down' order across sounds as chaotic as the transcripts you are about to read. They chart the real-time melee above America's skies as the hijacked planes headed inexorably towards their targets.

'At about 10:15, a uniformed military aide came into the room to tell me that a plane, believed hijacked, was eighty miles out and headed for DC,' Cheney wrote in his autobiography. 'He asked me whether our combat air patrol had authority to engage the aircraft. Did our fighter pilots have authority, in other words, to shoot down an American commercial airliner believed to have been hijacked? "Yes," I said without hesitation. A moment later he was back. "Mr Vice President, it's sixty miles out. Do they have authorisation to engage?" Again, "Yes."'

Warned one plane was just five miles from the White House, Cheney says he told his military chiefs: 'If it looks threatening, take it out.'

In the spirit of transparency, it is still hard to understand why the redacted recordings would be cut, unless somebody has something to hide.

Here, published in full, is how the morning of 11 September unfolded in real time.

AMERICAN AIRLINES FLIGHT 11

8.09 a.m. Boston flight controller Peter Zalewski passes on instructions to American Airlines Flight 11 – and then loses contact.

AA11: Check in

AA11: Boston Center, good morning, American 11 with you passing through one niner zero for two three zero.

Boston Sector: American 11, Boston Center, roger, climb, maintain level two eight zero.

8.13 a.m.

AA11: 20 Right

Boston Sector: American 11 turn 20 degrees right.

AA11: Turning right, American 11.

8.13 a.m.

AA11: Lost Contact

Boston Sector: American 11, climb, maintain flight level three five zero.

Boston Sector: American 11, climb, maintain flight level three five zero.

Boston Sector: American 11, Boston.

Boston Sector: (Indistinct) Mike Lima how do you hear?

Mike Lima: Mike Lima has you loud and clear.

Boston Sector: American 11, Boston.

Boston Sector: American one one, the American on the frequency, how do you hear me?

Athens Sector: This is Athens.

Boston Sector: This is Boston, I turned American 20 left and I was going to climb him, he will not respond to me now at all.

Athens Sector: Looks like he is turning right.

Boston Sector: Yeah, I turned him 20 right.

Athens Sector: Oh, OK.

Boston Sector: And he's only going to, I think, twenty-nine.

Athens Sector: OK.

Boston Sector: Well.

Athens Sector: That's fine.

Boston Sector: But I'm not talking to him.

Athens Sector: He's NORDO [no radio], roger.

Boston Sector: Thanks.

Boston Sector: Mike Lima descend at pilot's discretion and maintain flight level two four zero.

Mike Lima: Two four zero, will begin now, Mike Lima.

Boston Sector: American 11, Boston.

Boston Sector: American 11, if you hear Boston Center, ident.

Boston Sector: American 11 if you hear Boston Center ident please, or acknowledge.

Boston Sector: American 11, if you hear Boston Center re-contact Boston Center on one two seven point eight two, that's American 11, one two seven eight two.

Rockfield Sector: Athens, this is Rockfield, couple of things (indistinct) hey, also, are you trying to get through to company on the American 11?

Athens Sector: We are trying everything here.

Rockfield Sector: Has he really got no transponder, screw-up, or what?

Athens Sector: It appears that way.

Rockfield Sector: OK, bye.

8.19 a.m. American Airlines Flight 11 flight attendant Betty Ong uses a seatback airphone to call the AA reservations office in Cary, North Carolina, and is passed on to operations agent Nydia Gonzalez.

Betty Ong: Number 3 in the back. Um, the cockpit's not answering. Somebody's stabbed in business class, and um I think there is Mace that we can't breathe. I don't know, I think we're getting hijacked.

AAL: Which flight are you on?

Betty Ong: Flight 12.

AAL: And what seat are you in? (Silence) Ma'am, are you there?

Betty Ong: Yes.

AAL: What seat are you in? (Pause) Ma'am, what seat are you in?

Betty Ong: We just left Boston, we're up in the air.

AAL: I know.

Betty Ong: We're supposed to go to L.A. and the cockpit's not answering their phone …

AAL: OK, but what seat are you sitting in? What's the number of your seat?

Betty Ong: OK. I'm in the jump seat right now. That's 3R.

AAL: OK, are you the flight attendant? I'm sorry, did you say you're the flight attendant?

Betty Ong: Hello?

AAL: Hello, what is your name?

Betty Ong: Hi, you're gonna have to speak up. I can't hear you.

AAL: What is your name?

Betty Ong: OK, my name is Betty Ong. I'm Number 3 on Flight 11.

AAL: OK.

Betty Ong: And the cockpit is not answering their phone and there's somebody stabbed in business class and there's, we can't breathe in business class. Somebody's got Mace or something.

AAL: Can you describe the person, that you said someone is what in business class?

Betty Ong: I'm, I'm sitting in the back, somebody's coming back from business. If you can hold on for one second, they're coming back. (Inaudible) Anyone know who stabbed who?

Background: (Inaudible) I don't know, but Karen and Bobby got stabbed.

Betty Ong: Our, our Number 1 got stabbed. Our purser is stabbed. Ah, nobody knows who stabbed who and we can't even get up to business class right now because nobody can breathe. Our Number 1 is, is stabbed right now. And our Number 5. Our first-class passenger that, ah first ah class galley flight attendant and our purser has been stabbed and we can't get to the cockpit, the door won't open. Hello?

AAL: Yeah, I'm taking it down, all the information. We're also, you know, of course, recording this. Uhm, at this point?

Nydia Gonzalez: This is operations. What flight number are we talking about?

AAL: Flight 12.

Nydia Gonzalez: Flight 12, OK.

Betty Ong: No, we're on Flight 11 right now. This is Flight 11.

AAL: This is Flight 11. I'm sorry, Nadine.

Betty Ong: Boston to Los Angeles.

AAL: Yes.

Betty Ong: Our Number 1 has been stabbed, and our 5 has been stabbed. Can anybody get up to the cockpit? Can anybody get up to the cockpit? We can't even get into the cockpit. We don't know who's up there.

AAL: Well if they were shrewd, they would keep the door closed, and …

Betty Ong: I'm sorry?

AAL: Would they not maintain a sterile cockpit?

Betty Ong: I think the guys are up there. They might have gone there – jammed their way up there, or something. Nobody can call the cockpit. We can't even get inside.

(Silence)

Betty Ong: Is anybody still there?

AAL: Yes, we're still here.

Betty Ong: OK. I'm staying on the line as well.

AAL: OK.

Nydia Gonzalez: Hi, who is calling reservations? Is this one of the flight attendants, or who? Who are you, hon?

AAL: She gave her name as Betty Ong.

Betty Ong: Yeah, I'm Number 3. I'm Number 3 on this flight, and we're the firsts–

Nydia Gonzalez: You're Number 3 on this flight?

Betty Ong: Yes and I have …

Nydia Gonzalez: And this is Flight 11? From where to where?

Betty Ong: Flight 11.

Nydia Gonzalez: Have you guys called anyone else?

Betty Ong: No. Somebody's calling medical and we can't get a doc …

8.21 a.m. Nydia Gonzalez relays details from her call with Betty Ong to the American Airlines emergency centre.

AAL: American Airlines Emergency line, please state your emergency.

Nydia Gonzalez: Hey, this is Nydia at American Airlines calling. I am monitoring a call in which Flight 11, the flight attendant is advising our reps that the pilot, everyone's been stabbed.

AAL: Flight 11?

Gonzalez: Yeah.

Gonzalez: They can't get into the cockpit is what I'm hearing.

AAL: OK. Who is this I'm talking to?

Gonzalez: Excuse me, this is Nydia at American Airlines at the Raleigh Reservation Center, I'm the operations specialist on duty.

AAL: And, I'm sorry what was your name again?

Gonzalez: Nydia.

AAL: Nydia, and what's your last name? Gonzalez: Gonzalez, G-O-N-Z-A-L-E-Z.

AAL: Raleigh reservations, OK.

Gonzalez: I've got the flight attendant on the line with one of our agents.

AAL: OK, and she's calling how?

Gonzalez: Through reservations. I can go in on the line and ask the flight attendant questions.

AAL: OK, uh, uh, I'm assuming they've declared an emergency, let me get ATC [Air Traffic Control] on the line here, stand by.

Gonzalez: Gotten any contact with anybody? I'm on with security, OK Betty? You are doing a great job just stay calm, OK. We are, absolutely.

AAL: OK, we're contacting the flight crew now, we're alc–, we're also contacting ATC.

Gonzalez: OK.

AAL: Anything else from the flight attendant?

Gonzalez: Uh, so far what I've gotten, the Number 5 flight attendant's been stabbed, but she seems to be breathing, the Number 1 seems to be stabbed pretty badly, she's lying down on the floor, they don't know whether she is conscious or not. The other flight attendants are in the back, umm, and that's as far as I know. It seems like the passengers in coach might not be aware of what's going on right now.

AAL: These two passengers were from first class?

Gonzalez: OK, hold on. Hey Betty, you know any information as far as the men in the cockpit with the pilots, were they from first class? They were sitting in two A and B.

AAL: OK.

Gonzalez: They are in the cockpit with the pilot.

AAL: Who's helping them, is there a doctor on board?

Gonzalez: Is there a doctor on board, Betty that's helping you guys? You don't have any doctors on board? OK. So, you've gotten all the first-class passengers out of first class?

AAL: Have they taken everyone out of first class?

Gonzalez: Yeah, she's just saying that they have, they're in coach. What's going on hunny?

Gonzalez: OK. The aircraft is erratic again, bobbing very erratically.

Gonzalez: She did say that all the first-class passengers have been moved back to coach, that first class the cabin is empty.

Gonzalez: What's going on, on your end, Craig?

AAL: Uhhh, we contacted Air Traffic Control. They are gonna handle this as a confirmed hijacking so they are moving all the traffic out of this aircraft's way.

Gonzalez: OK.

AAL: He turned his transponder off, so we don't have a definitive altitude for him. Ahhh, we are just going by, they seem to think, that they have him on a primary radar, they seem to think that he is descending.

Gonzalez: OK.

AAL: Yeah. OK, Nydia.

Gonzalez: Yes, dear I'm here.

AAL: OK. I have the dispatcher currently taking a current fuel on board.

Gonzalez: Uh huh.

AAL: And, ah, we're gonna run some profiles.

Gonzalez: OK.

AAL: To see exactly what his endurance is.

Gonzalez: OK.

AAL: Did sh–

Gonzalez: She doesn't have an idea who the other passenger might be in first. Apparently they might have sprayed something so it's, it's umm, they're having a hard time breathing or getting in that area. What's going on Betty? Betty, talk to me. Betty, are you there? Betty. (Indistinct) do you think we lost her? OK, so, we'll like, we'll stay open. We, I think we might have lost her.

AAL: OK.

8.24 a.m. A Boston controller hears hijacker Mohamed Atta talking over the radio, mistakenly believing he is talking to the passengers on American Airlines Flight 11.

Keying 2 Transmissions

(Indistinct. Microphone keyed three times)

Boston Sector: Is that American 11 trying to call?

Mohamed Atta: (Indistinct) We have some planes. Just stay quiet and we'll be OK. We are returning to the airport.

Background: Air traffic communications.

Boston Sector: And, uh, who's trying to call me, here?

Background: Air traffic communications.

Boston Sector: American 11 are you trying to call?

Atta: Nobody move, everything will be OK. If you try to make any moves, you will injure yourself and the airplane. Just stay quiet.

Unknown Boston Controller: Yeah, uh, we got him on primary.

Unknown Boston Controller: Hey, 38?

Athens Sector 38: Yes.

Unknown Boston Controller: You guys heard anything from American?

Athens Sector 38: No.

Unknown Boston Controller: OK, we think there might be somebody in the cockpit right now, taking it over.

Athens Sector 38: OK.

Unknown Boston Controller: Yeah, we just (indistinct).

Unknown Boston Controller: Call the supervisor, please.

Unknown Boston Controller: Yeah, we're already doing it.

Unknown Boston Controller: OK, I know.

Dial tone (indistinct)

Unknown Boston Controller: Ah, not right now. Go ahead 38.

Unknown Female Voice: Yeah, American 11. Ah, we suspect there is someone in the cockpit that has taken over. We have just put him in direct Watertown, Jamestown. Last we knew he was on present heading, cleared to flight level two nine zero. No one is talking to him. ARINC [Aeronautical Radio, Incorporated] has been called. We broadcasted on guard. We've tried through company.

Unknown Boston Controller: OK, thanks.

Unknown Female Voice: And 2-9-0 is not verified.

Unknown Boston Controller: OK, thanks.

Unknown Female Voice: You're welcome.

Unknown Female Voice: We've taken the American back because he appears to have turned.

Unknown Boston Controller 1: Yep, bye.

Unknown Boston Controller 2: Go ahead.

Unknown Female Voice: Yeah, I need you to look west of Albany, American 11, and put him on your scope. He is, ah, NORDO [radio failure], has been since he talked to Boston High. We assume he's at flight level two nine zero. Ah, we're not sure. We think there is someone in the cockpit with him. Ah, we've broadcasted over guard, we've gone ARINC, we've gone company, nobody is talkin' to him. We don't know where he is going, we don't know what altitude he's at.

Unknown Boston Controller 2: Thanks.

8.29 a.m. The hijacked plane moves into Cleveland aerospace.

> Boston Center: Alright, Cleveland, New York. Boston. Ah, I got a little situation with American one, one, American 11. He is a, uh, seven fifty seven, departed Boston, goin' to LAX. Ah, we don't know where the aircraft is goin'. He, ah, in, ah, supposedly goin' to LAX, was goin' westbound, we lost his, ah, frequency, and we lost his transponder, and now the aircraft is, ah, just west of Albany, headin' due south.

> Cleveland Center: Oh, my goodness. K. We have, do we have a, a data block on him, who's got the, ah …

> Boston Center: Yeah, we, it's a primary target, presently, as I said, headin' southwest bound.

> Cleveland Center: OK, uh, understand.

> Boston Center: (indistinct) right now. I'll advise the area.

> Boston Center: Last altitude observed was ah flight level two niner zero.

> Cleveland Center: 29.

> Unknown Controller: Headin' south bound?

> Boston Center: Headin' southwest bound, he's like towards Hancock, ah, right, right around there. He's southwest of Albany, by one five miles.

> Unknown Controller: You have no idea where he's goin'?

> Boston Center: No idea, sir.

> Unknown Controller: Alrighty.

> Herndon Center: You can tag him on the, ahhh, TSD [flight history].

> Unknown Controller: I've got him tagged, primary only?

> Herndon Center: You can pick him up.

> Boston Center: Primary only.

Unknown Controller: OK.

Boston Center: OK.

Herndon Center: Thank you.

8.30 a.m. Ray Howland, American Airlines operations control supervisor, and Nancy Wyatt, a supervisor at Boston Logan International Airport, try to work out what is going on.

Herndon Center: Well Boston Center claims that, uh, ah they lost radio communication with the aircraft.

Unknown: And transponder, too

Herndon Center: And the transponder. And there's also, ah, they're trackin' the primary target at this point, he was last known at ah flight level two nine zero.

Unknown: Uh, huh.

Herndon Center: And he appears to have turned, ah, south, southwest bound, and uh, also, there was some mention of some sort of a, a threat bein' made, or ah …

Unknown: He made?

Herndon Center: A threat to the cockpit, or some threat.

Unknown: Oh shit, let me get the managers involved.

Herndon Center: In the cockpit. (Indistinct) Boston is uncertain exactly what was said. I guess they are goin' to pull the tapes as quick as they can.

Unknown: Hey Tom, where can I reach you back? What number at?

Herndon Center: Um, xxx-xxx-xxxx.

Unknown: OK, alright, (indistinct) I'll call you back.

Ray Howland: (indistinct) Ray Howland.

Nancy Wyatt: Ray Howland, Nancy Wyatt, ah, Boston flight service.

Howland: Yes.

Wyatt: OK, we've got the flight attendants on the line here.

Howland: You do have them on the line?

Wyatt: From the plane, yeah.

Howland: Can you conference them in with us?

Wyatt: I have no idea how to do that, if you can help me out, uh, hold, ah, he's getting some information, here.

Wyatt: I'm gonna read his notes for you. Ah, it looks like, ah, he's Middle Eastern. Speaks no English. He was in 10B, 10 baker.

Howland: Right

Wyatt: 9D and G, speaks no speaks no English. Ah, the plane's in a rapid descent, ah …

Howland: (indistinct) Is the cockpit still …

Wyatt: Yep. OK, the flight attendants are concerned they don't know what's going on in the cockpit. Are you in con– contact with them?

Howland: No, we're not, (indistinct) we're, we're tryin' to get in contact with the cockpit.

Wyatt: OK.

Howland: Alright. We really don't want to tell her that.

Wyatt: OK. Don't, OK got it. OK there, ah, we're not sure. Ah, OK, looks like there's severe bleeding, that ah, he's keeping her on the line, there's severe bleeding, there's a slashed throat.

Wyatt: Michael, is that severe, is that slashed throat a flight attendant? (Background) Michael: No, the Cap–

(Background) Unknown: Amy, what's that?

Howland: Boston flight service has another one of the flight attendants on the phone here.

Boston flight service: You lost it?

Howland: OK, we lost the (indistinct). I really need to get on the phone with her.

Wyatt: Something's wrong. Ah, Amy, Amy Sweeney's on the phone.

Howland: Amy Sweeney? [Flight attendant on AA Flight 11]

Wyatt: Yeah she's the Number 9.

Howland: OK.

Wyatt: And he's having trouble talkin' to her, right now?

Howland: Alright. These are the two that are injured, 1 and 5.

Wyatt: She started screaming and saying something's wrong, and now he's havin' trouble.

Howland: OK.

Wyatt: (indistinct) thinks he might be disconnected. OK, we just lost, ah, the connection.

Howland: Lost the connection.

Wyatt: Yep

Howland: (Sigh)

Wyatt: Something's wrong with the airplane? They're not in the cockpit? OK. They're in the back of the plane.

Howland: They're in the back of the airplane

Wyatt: Yeah, they're in the back of the airplane, they're not, oh, the hijackers are in the cockpit. Holy …

Howland: Oh no.

Wyatt: OK, they're in the cockpit.

Howland: Hey Craig, Craig. They're saying the hi–, they're in the cockpit.

(Background) Unknown: Amy said that?

Wyatt: Listen, let's just see when the next flight to Kennedy is, just to see if he's goin' to Kennedy, so we can be ready.

8.33 a.m. Atta comes back on the radio, again apparently believing he is talking to the passengers.

> Mohamed Atta: Nobody move please. We are going back to the airport. Don't try to make any stupid moves.

8.33 a.m. Meanwhile, NORAD is trying to scramble some fighter jets.

> Dan Bueno [air traffic controller]: Hey Cape, ah, Dan Bueno callin' from Boston Center. Hey, we've got a situation with American 11, a possible hijack.
>
> Cape Approach [FAA facility at Otis Air National Guard Base at Falmouth, Cape Cod, Massachusetts]: American 11?
>
> Bueno: Yes sir, departed Boston going to LAX, right now he's out to Albany, like to scramble some fighters to go tail him.
>
> Cape Approach: Well, OK. Well, we'll talk to Otis here.
>
> Bueno: OK, and (indistinct) if you want just depart and, ah, we'll put a flight plan in for him and, ah, we'll aim him toward, ah, Hampton direct.
>
> Cape Approach: American 11 (indistinct).
>
> Bueno: OK.
>
> Cape Approach: And right now he's (indistinct) Albany.
>
> Bueno: No, no, no, no, no he's, ah, right now southwest of, he's airborne about 40, to south of Albany, primary only.
>
> Cape Approach: (indistinct) I'll talk to them right now. And who is this here? Bueno: Dan Bueno from Boston, TMU.
>
> Bueno: Correct.
>
> Cape Approach: Alright.

8.35 a.m. American Airlines Flight 11 moves into New York State, way off its planned route to LA.

Kingston Sector: Yeah, heads up for you here. I've got an American 11. He's right over Kingston right now. He's at, we think he's at flight level two nine zero. There appears to be some possible problem with him. He's departed Boston, going to ah Los Angeles. But, ah, somewhere along the way here he took a left turn and he's not talking to anyone. Hasn't talked to anybody in about 75, maybe a hundred miles. So, he's southeast bound right now, so he's going to pass just, like, over Carmel, and again, we don't have a verified altitude. We think he's at flight level two nine zero, we're tryin' to verify that now.

Kennedy Sector: You have a code on him?

Kingston Sector: Ah, no, he's flying x-ray, there, there's no code on the guy. He's flying x-ray, and we approved that, so he's a primary now, right over Kingston, flight level two nine zero, supposedly.

Kennedy Sector: Supposedly, two nine zero, and he's headed southeast bound?

Kingston Sector: Headed southeast bound, and now he's gonna go, between, ah, it looks like maybe right over Dewey's intersection. So I'm just giving you a heads up, we're not talkin' to him, no one's talked to him the last about 20 minutes.

Kennedy Sector: And what's the call sign?

Kingston Sector: American 11.

Kennedy Sector: American 11.

Kingston Sector: I'll, I'll call you when he gets a little closer to your boundary, OK?

Kennedy Sector: OK.

8.37 a.m. Boston air traffic controller Joseph Cooper calls Sergeant Jeremy Powell at NORAD's Northeast Air Defense Sector (NEADS) to flag up the hijacking.

> Cooper: Hi, Boston Center, TMU, we have, ah, a problem here, we have a hijacked aircraft headed towards New York and we need you guys to, we need someone to scramble some F-16s or something up there to help us out.
>
> Powell [Senior Director (Weapons) technician at NEADS]: Is, is this real world or exercise?
>
> Cooper: No, this is not an exercise, not a test.
>
> Powell: OK. Hey, ah, hold on one second, OK?
>
> Cooper: Yes.
>
> Powell: Hey, hey, hey, hey, hey, hey, hey, seriously, (indistinct) big time (indistinct).
>
> Powell: Sir, sir, sir.
>
> Cooper: Yes sir.
>
> Powell: Yeah, I've got an MCC [Mission Crew Commander] comin' right now to talk to you so you can handle all that.
>
> Cooper: Thank you.
>
> Powell: Alright.
>
> Major Dawne Deskins: Hi, this is Major Deskins.
>
> Cooper: Hi, Joe Cooper, Boston Center, we have a–
>
> Deskins: Yeah, Joe.
>
> Cooper: Hijacked aircraft headed towards the New York metro area. Wonderin' if you could, uh, send someone up there, some F-16s or somethin' to help us out, maybe out of–
>
> Deskins: New York metro.
>
> Cooper: Maybe out of Otis.
>
> Deskins: Do you have a mode 3 on it?

Cooper: No, no.

Deskins: A mode 3 code?

Cooper: It's just a primary target only, we lost, ah, we lost the, ah, mode, the mode C on it, so you'd have to get up in the air and we'd have to vector you towards the aircraft.

Deskins: OK, so you'd wanta control the intercept, because–

Cooper: We'd have to, yeah.

Deskins: You'd have to, right.

Cooper: Until you guys can pick him up on primary radar.

Deskins: OK. Do you have a general location as to where he is?

Cooper: We're still trackin' him right now.

Deskins: You're trackin' him.

Cooper: Yeah.

Deskins: Can you, can you give me a lat long, where he is for our SA?

Cooper: Yeah, hold on a second.

8.38 a.m. NEADS techs Stacia Rountree, Shelley Watson and Maureen Dooley try to find out what's going on from Boston military ops specialist and air traffic controller at FAA's Boston Center, Colin Scoggins.

Tech Sergeant Shelley Watson: What?

Master Sergeant Maureen 'Mo' Dooley: Whoa!

Watson: What was that?

Senior Airman Stacia Rountree: Is that real world?

Dooley: Real world hijack.

Watson: Cool.

(Background): Dial tone

Watson: Open line.

Colin Scoggins: Boston, military desk.

Watson: Yeah, Huntress calling, ah, in reference to the hijacked aircraft

Scoggins: Yes.

Watson: We're seeking to get some information from you, if we could.

Scoggins: OK, what (indistinct) you need?

Watson: We need call sign, type aircraft.

Scoggins: It's, ah, American 11

Watson: American 11.

Scoggins: Type aircraft is a, uh, seven sixty seven.

Watson: And, number of souls on board, do you know that?

Scoggins: Uh, I don't, know, hold on. Hey Dan, do we got souls on board, and all that?

Scoggins: No. We don't have any of that information.

Watson: You don't have any of that? OK.

Scoggins: We know the position about 40 miles north of Kennedy.

Watson: Forty miles north of Kennedy?

Scoggins: Right.

Watson: Do you have, ah, mode 3?

Scoggins: No we don't, he's a primary target, only.

Watson: Primary target only?

Scoggins: Yeah.

Watson: OK, and you don't know where he's coming from or destination?

Scoggins: No idea. He took off out of Boston originally heading for, ah, Los Angeles.

Watson: Boston to Los Angeles?

Scoggins: That was his original destination, yeah.

Watson: And where are they going now, do you know?

Scoggins: No idea. He's headin' towards Kennedy, looks like his speed is decreasing, I'm not exactly sure where, nobody really knows.

Watson: Are you the controlling agency? Or is New York?

Scoggins: Boston Center.

Watson: Boston Center.

Scoggins: Right now we are, he's headed right for New York Center.

Watson: And is there any military assistance requested?

Scoggins: Ah, yes. We're actually trying to get ah F-15s to ah–

Watson: (Indistinct) to get F-15s out.

Scoggins: Yeah, F15s out of Otis.

Watson: But you don't have, uh, you don't have any modes or codes on him?

Scoggins: Uh, no, right now, right now, it's just, ah, no we don't have any mode C.

Watson: Is he inbound to JFK?

Scoggins: We, we don't know. Heh–

Watson: You don't know where he is at all?

Scoggins: He's been hijacked. The pilots having a hard time talkin' to the, I mean, we don't know, we don't know where he's going, he's headin' towards Kennedy, he's, ah, like I said he's like thirty-five miles north of Kennedy now at three hundred sixty seven knots.

Watson: OK.

Scoggins: No idea where he's goin' (indistinct).

Watson: If you could please give us a call, and let us know, ah, you know any information, that would be great.

Scoggins: OK. Right now I guess we're trying to work on, I guess there's been some threats in the cockpit, ah, the pilot.

Watson: Based on what? I'm sorry.

Scoggins: Ah. We'll call you right back as soon as we know more info.

Watson: Thank you.

8.39 a.m. Battle stations. But first they've got to find the rogue passenger jet.

(Background) Weapons Position: (Indistinct).

Deskins: Hey Nasty, lookin' for assets (indistinct) lat long.

Weapons Position: Real world hijack. You got it. (Indistinct) yep. Once we, ah, once he comes into our radar, we will, we'll be takin' it, give me those slides quick.

Deskins: Four one one five north, zero seven eight four six west.

Weapons Position: (Indistinct) make sure you know what's goin' on. Real world hijack, forty mi–, forty miles north of Kennedy. Otis on battle stations. Putting Otis on battle stations.

8.39 a.m. The confusion continues as air traffic controllers from different sections speak to the radar unit responsible for flying planes safely in and out of New York.

Boston Central: Boston Center here. Can I get New York TRACON [Terminal Radar Control Facility]?

Herndon Center: You bet (indistinct) with the, ah, cockpit.

Boston Central: Yeah, for the American 11.

Herndon Center: Say it again?

Boston Center: Oh, reference American 11.

Herndon Center: Have you have you had any contact with him yet?

Boston Center: Ah, no, no contact, ah it is confirmed ah hijack, though

NY TRACON [Terminal Radar Control Facility]: TRACON.

Boston Center: OK, TRACON, hi, ah good morning, American 11, ah seven fifty seven, possible hijack.

NY TRACON: K. American 11, seven, seven five and uh (indistinct). Where's he landing?

Boston Center: Ah, right now, we don't have any idea. But ah, he was to the northwest of Albany and now he's ah down by Sparta, losing speed very rapidly, we believe he is a primary only, and uh, we believe he's in a descent, and that's why he's, ah, he's, he's slowing down.

New York Center: Everybody copy?

Herndon Center: Say that again, please.

Boston Center: We, we … looks like we lost the primary target about twenty west of Kennedy, and we had a report of an ELT [Emergency Locator Transmitter] in the area. We're gonna ah, guess we'll ah, get some Coast Guard activity up there.

Unknown: Well, we lost the track, too.

New York Center: Hey Boston, this is New York, ah what type of aircraft was the American?

Boston Center: Seven sixty seven.

ACI [Air Crash Investigation] Watch: This is the ACI watch. Say again if you lost, ah, track of the aircraft, over.

Boston Center: Boston has lost track, on our frequency

we had some threats that it was a hijack, (indistinct) the tapes …

New York Center: New York confirms that we lost track as well, and we were, ah, had report of ah ELT in the area that the track was in.

New York Center: Kennedy Tower reports, (indistinct) you serious? Kennedy Tower reports that there was a fire at the World Trade Center. And that's, ah, that's the area where we lost the airplane.

8.40 a.m. Powell puts two pilots from Otis air base in Cape Cod, Massachusetts, on battle stations and orders them to take off, despite not yet having permission from the US defence secretary.

Cape Approach: Cape Approach is on.

Jeremy Powell: Giant Killer [US Navy air traffic control call sign for the East Coast of the US].

Giant Killer: Giant Killer.

Powell: This is Huntress [NEADS call sign] placing Panta four five, four six [two F-15 fighter jets with call signs Panta 45 and Panta 46] on battle stations, I repeat battle stations, time one two four one, authenticate hotel romeo, all parties acknowledge with initials. Command Post.

Powell: Giant Killer, Tower.

Tower: (Indistinct).

Powell: Approach.

Cape Approach: Tango Juliet and say again the call sign.

Powell: Panta, papa alfa november tango alfa, four five, four six.

Approach: (Indistinct).

Powell: Juliet Papa, all parties are cleared to drop.

8.42 a.m. NORAD Mission Crew Commander (MCC)
Major Kevin Nasypany speaks to Major James 'Foxy' Fox
as they try to work out where to send the fighters.

Major Fox: I've never seen so much real world stuff
   happen during an exercise.

Unknown: (Indistinct).

Fox: Steve, lat long, forty one.

Unknown: Right.

Unknown: What was that?

(Background) Unknown: two nine zero (indistinct).

Fox: OK. Find this guy.

Major Nasypany: Yeah, forty one.

Nasypany: Yeah, we're puttin' it in.

(Background) Unknown: Fourteen forty three.

Nasypany: Fourteen forty three, look for it, right there,
   OK, mode three, fourteen forty three, last known. No,
   this is real world. OK, we're in the high chair.

Background: I've got a Z point, sir.

Nasypany: Last known position, that we got out this
   guy, was right there at the Z point, he's headed one
   nine zero at twenty-nine thousand feet, headin' down,
   so we're lookin' for somebody, you know what start
   hittin' up tracks all around that area, that Z point, OK,
   just north of ah …

Mission Crew Commander Technician: SD, scramble
   Otis.

Fox: Copy, say mission.

Fox: I don't know where I'm scramblin' these guys to, I
   need a direction, ah, destination.

Nasypany: OK, I'm going to give you the Z point. It's just
   north of, ah, New York City.

Fox: I got this lat long forty one fifteen seventy four

thirty six, or seventy three forty six.

Nasypany: Head 'em in that direction.

Fox: Copy that.

8.46 a.m. American Airlines Flight 11 crashes into the North Tower of the World Trade Center

8.46 a.m. The military is still trying to find American Airlines Flight 11.

Nasypany: OK. What, what we're doin', we're tryin' to (indistinct) locate this guy. We can't find him via IFF [Identification, Friend or Foe, a radar system to ID military aircraft]. What we're goin' to do, we gonna hit up every track within a twenty-five mile radius of the Z point that we put on the scope. Twenty nine thousand, heading one nine zero, we're just gonna do, we're gonna try to find this guy. They can't find him, then he's not in uh, there's been supposedly there's threats in the cockpit, so we're just, ah, doin' the thing.

(Off-mic conversation)

Nasypany: True. And, probably right now, with what's goin' on in the cockpit, (indistinct) probably the crazies, so, it probably needs to simmer down and we'll get some better information. I've scrambled Otis, already, per your direction. We're sendin' them in that general direction, we're sendin' them right to that Z point, and then we can, ah, we can maneuver 'em as deemed uh …

(Off-mic conversation)

Nasypany: Right, we'll, we'll work with them, make sure weapons works with them, now.

8.50 a.m. Smoke is reported to be coming from the top of the World Trade Center in Lower Manhattan, but they still can't find American Airlines Flight 11.

Unknown Pilot: Anybody know what that smoke is in lower Manhattan?

New York Center: I'm sorry, say again.

Unknown Pilot: Lot of smoke in lower Manhattan.

New York Center: A lot of smoke in lower Manhattan?

Unknown Pilot: (Indistinct) coming out of the, ah, top of the World Trade Center building, a major fire.

(Indistinct)

8.52 a.m. The penny drops, and the fighters are directed towards New York City.

Naspany: So, if we can find it, we'll intercept it. Did you did you just say somethin' hit the World Trade Center or somethin' reports? No keep on going with it.

Unknown: I talked with ID, and we had a phone call that came down to us saying that they had a possible hijack out of Boston.

Scoggins: OK.

Unknown: And uh, I just whipped around and we were just, we always watch the news, and a seven thirty seven hit the World Trade Center, and I was just curious at the same time if that was the aircraft. Last I knew they had a primary on it. Track was not squawking seventy five hundred but it was, ah–

Nasypany: Could be it.

Unknown: Under duress.

Nasypany: Send them to New York City, still, continued go.

Scoggins: Sir, hold on.

Nasypany: K, OK, who's plugged in up there? Plug in.

Scoggins: Sir, I have to have you hold on for a minute.

Unknown: OK.

Nasypany: This is what I've got so far.

Unknown: OK.

Nasypany: This is what I got. Possible news that a seven thirty seven just hit the World Trade Center, this is real world, and we're tryin' to confirm this. OK, continue takin' the fighters down to the New York City area, JFK area, as best as you can. Make sure that the FAA clears a, you a route all the way through. Just do what we gotta do, OK. Just press with it. And it looks like somebody, looks like this guy could've hit the World Trade Center.

8.53 a.m. But still confusion clouds the military response.

Major James Fox: Alright, our last actual reported position if he didn't crash into the World Trade Center is twenty miles south of JFK. So, I want you to take him down into this area, hold as needed, whatever altitude they need to go for Center to make that work, is fine with me. That's the area I want him to go and hold, right in that little gap there.

Fox (to background): Alright, this is what we're doin'; we're takin' him down into this area to hold for now. Whatever altitude Center needs for them to do that is fine. But, ah, is, the weapons team should have that. The fighters should be talkin' to Center they're goin' pass that to the fighters exactly what we want them to do.

Nasypany: Now, Foxy.

Fox: Yeah, no, no, because if he's still airborne.

Nasypany: OK, right now, if you can hand the fighters over directly to FAA.

Fox: They're still under FAA control, we're never goin' take 'em.

Nasypany: Just take 'em all the, work with them, coordinate with them as best that you can with that, take them to the area and let them handle that airspace.

UNITED AIRLINES FLIGHT 175

8.38 a.m. As the military and air traffic controllers searched for American Airlines Flight 11, another plane, United Airlines Flight 175, appears to be acting normally.

New York Center: OK, United 175, you have him at your twelve o'clock, now five, ten miles.

UA175: Affirmative we have him, uh, he looks about twenty, say about twenty nine, twenty eight thousand.

New York Center: OK, thank you.

New York Center: United 175, (indistinct) turn 30 degrees to the right, I want to keep you away from this traffic.

UA175: Thirty degrees to the right, United 175, heavy.

8.41 a.m. Until it doesn't ...

New York Sector: United one seventy five, go ahead.

UA175: Ah, we figured we'd wait to go to your center, ah, we heard a suspicious transmission, ah, on our departure out of Boston, ah, with someone, ah, uh, sounded like someone keyed the mike and said, uh, everyone, uh, stay in your seats.

New York Sector: Oh, OK, I'll pass that along over here. Hey Kingston on ninety three line.

Kingston Sector: Go ahead.

New York Sector: That United 175 just came on my frequency, and he said that he heard a suspicious, uh, transmission when they were leaving Boston.

Kingston Sector: Oh yeah?

New York Sector: Everybody stay in their seats, that's what they heard as a suspicious transmission. Now that USAIR five eight three code, the American he spotted him, was at twenty nine.

8.48 a.m. It gets worse.

New York Center: OK, this is New York Center, ah, we're watching the airplane, he is 15 west of Kennedy now, we had t– one or two confirmations that he was still at twenty nine, excuse me, one at twenty nine, one at thirty one, didn't, couldn't
see him.

New York Center: Ah, I also had conversation with American Airlines, and they've told us that they believe that, ah, one of their stewardesses was stabbed and that there are people in the cockpit who have control of the aircraft, and that's all the information they have, ah, right now.

8.51 a.m. United Airlines 175 is no longer answering.

New York Center: United one seventy five, recycle your transponder and squawk code of one four seven zero.

New York Center: United 175, New York.

New York Center: United 175, do you read New York?

New York Center: Delta 1489, do you read New York?

D1489: Delta 1489, go ahead.

New York Center: OK, just wanted to make sure you read New York, ah, United, United 175, do you read New York?

8.53 a.m. Federal Aviation Authority air traffic controller David Bottaglia is trying to work out what is happening ... and which planes may have been hijacked.

David Bottaglia: Tim?

New York Controller: Hello?

Bottaglia: Do you, ah, see that United 175 anywhere? And do me a favour, you see that target there, the thirty three twenty one code, at thirty three five climbin'? Don't know who he is, but you got the USAIR 583 if you need to descend him down you can. Nobody, we, we have a hijack, we have some problems over here right now.

New York Controller: Oh, you do?

Bottaglia: Yes. That, that may be real traffic, nobody knows, I can't get a hold of United one seventy five at all right now, and I don't where he went to.

New York Controller: Alright. OK, I'll see if I have one.

Bottaglia: Alright.

8.54 a.m. There is also concern from other flight crews as they hear a plane has crashed into the World Trade Center.

USAIR 583: Yeah, yes, ah, reports on over the radio of a commuter plane hittin' the World Trade Center. Is that, ah, seven–oh–seven six still in the air?

Bottaglia: Don't know but just stand by. Delta 2433 turn left to a heading of one seven zero, now. I have traffic, I'm not really sure if it's good, out of thirty two, might be descending, might be climbing. I'm showin' him at thirty one right now.

Bottaglia: United 175, do you read New York?

(Background) Unknown: One o'clock, ten miles turning

into your airspace, descending out of thirty three.

Bottaglia: Delta 2433, umm, can you climb to flight level three three zero, the traffic looks like he's descended back down to thirty one, now.

D2433: Yeah, we can go up.

Battaglia: OK. Climb and maintain flight level three three zero, Delta 2433.

D2433: Climbin' to thirty three, Delta 2433.

Bottaglia: I got some hand offs here. We got some incidents goin' over here. The Delta 2433 gonna be OK at thirty three?

New York Controller Unknown: (Indistinct).

Bottaglia: I've got him climbin' for traffic, if they can. United 175 that just took off out of a, thing, we might have a hijack over here, two of 'em.

New York Controller Unknown: (Indistinct).

Bottaglia: So, is Delta 2433 OK comin' back?

New York Controller Unknown: Yes, Delta thirty three.

Bottaglia: OK, and, uh, Delta 1489 is comin' to you, also.

New York Controller Unknown: OK (indistinct).

Bottaglia: Delta 1489 contact New York Center, now, on one three four point three two.

D1489: Delta 1489, three four three two.

Bottaglia: Delta 2433, thank you for your help. That, ah, United just took off and we're not really sure what he's doin'. You thought it was United seven sixty seven, though?

D2433: That's, ah, that's what it looked like.

Bottaglia: Thank you Delta 2433. Climbing at two seven zero, join J seventy five. Resume all navigation, thanks for the climb.

9.01 a.m. With two passenger jets now off the grid, the FAA's New York air traffic control tells FAA Command at Herndon, Virginia, to call in the military.

Mulligan [New York Air Traffic Control]: Check with your NOM [operations manager], do you know if any one down there has done any coordination to scramble fighter type airplanes?

Bell: (Indistinct) still think the airplane's in the air?

Mulligan: No, we have several situations goin', goin' on here. It is escalating big big time, and we need to get the military involved with us.

Bell: Why, what's goin' on?

Mulligan: Just get me somebody who has the authority to get military in the air, now.

Bell: Alright. I'll go tell 'em.

9 a.m. The controllers see a plane rapidly descending …

New York Center Unknown: Hey Joe, you see three three two one code just southwest of Newark by about fifteen, eighteen, twenty miles.

Joe: Hold on.

New York Center Unknown: Fifteen thousand, descending.

Joe: I'm looking, hold one, southwest of Newark by about fifteen twenty?

Joe: I don't see any.

New York Center Unknown: They were trackin' him, made a hard left turn, he descended pretty rapidly, and especially with just happened in there.

Joe: I got somebody that keeps coasting, but he looks like he's goin' into one of those small airports down there.

New York Center Unknown: Hold on a second. No, this guy's a big boy. This guy's a big boy 'cause he's leavin' some big contrails, I'm trying to bring him up here, get ya, there he is, right there, hold on.

(Background) Unknown: Southwest of Newark.

Joe: He's out of ninety five hundred, nine thousand now.

New York Center Unknown: Do you know who he is?

Joe: We just, we just, we don't know who he is. We're just pickin' him up now.

New York Center Unknown: Alright. Heads up man, looks like another one.

Joe: Alright.

9.02 a.m. And then it hits …

New York Center Unknown: Hey, can you look out your window right now?

New York TRACON [New York Terminal Radar Approach Control]: Yeah.

New York Center Unknown: Can you, can you see a guy at about four thousand feet, about five east of the airport right now, looks like he's–

New York TRACON: Yeah, I see him.

New York Center Unknown: Do you see that guy, look, is he descending into the building also?

New York TRACON: He's descending really quick too, yeah.

New York Center Unknown: Well, that's–

New York TRACON: Forty-five hundred feet now, he just dropped eight hundred feet in like, like one, one sweep.

New York Center Unknown: That's another situation. What kind of a plane is that, can you guys tell?

New York TRACON: I don't know. I'll read it out in a minute.

9.03 a.m. United Airlines Flight 175 crashes into the World Trade Center.

New York TRACON: Another one just hit just hit the building.

New York Center: Wow.

(Background) New York TRACON: (Indistinct). Oh my god.

New York TRACON: Another one just hit it hard.

New York Center: Another one just hit the World Trade.

New York TRACON: The whole building just, ah, came apart.

(Background) New York TRACON: (Indistinct). Oh my god!

New York Center: Holy smokes! Alright. I guess you guys are going to be busy.

New York TRACON: OK.

New York TRACON: I think an airplane just plowed into the City.

New York Center: I, yeah, they did, ah, duh, the World Trade Center hit (indistinct).

New York TRACON: No, another one, we just saw another one do it.

New York Center: Another one?

New York TRACON: Yeah.

New York Center: Holy cow, that's two, ah, one just hit (indistinct) an hour ago.

New York TRACON: Yeah, one just a moment ago.

New York Center: No shit.

Boston Center: Hey Tony, are you still there?

Herndon Center: Yes, I am, Terry.

Boston Center: Tony? I'm going to reconfirm with, ah, with downstairs, but ah, the ah, as far as the tape, but,

Bobby Jones seemed to think that the guy said that we have planes. Now I don't know if it was because of the accent, or if there's more than one. But, ah, I'm gonna, I'm gonna reconfirm that for ya, ah, and I'll get back to you real quick, OK?

Herndon Center: Appreciate it.

(Background) Unknown: And what?

Boston Center: Planes, as in plural.

9.03 a.m. As the word goes out that there are more than one hijacked plane, controllers start grounding flights.

Boston Center: Tony, it sounds like, we're talkin' to New York, that there's another one aimed at the World Trade Center.

Herndon Center: There's another aircraft?

Boston Center: A second one just hit the Trade Center.

Herndon Center: OK, yeah, we've gotta get the, we've got to alert the military real ah, ah quick on this, ah …

(Background Boston Center) Jones: Another, another airplane just crashed into the other tower.

Herndon Center: Do we know what type, Terry?

Boston Center: No. We just got that report from, ah, from New York Center.

Herndon Center: Alright, alright, we're standin' by.

Boston Center: We're gonna stop everybody, we're gonna shut, we're gonna shut Boston down, I'd suggest the same elsewhere.

Herndon Center: You're gonna do what?

Boston Center: We're shuttin' the airplanes down, we're not lettin' anyone go, right now.

Herndon Center: That's a good move.

Boston Center: We're putting a ground stop on

everything. Ah, there's a second plane that just hit the World Trade Center.

Herndon Center: Stop all departures out of the center, please.

Boston Center: Yeah, that's what we're doin'.

9.07 a.m. Incoming flights are warned to increase cockpit security.

Boston Center: Ah, is there a way, or, to try to get messages to the airborne aircraft to increase sec– ah, security to the cockpit, or somethin', the ACARS [Aircraft Communications Addressing, and Reporting System] or somethin'?

Unknown: I'd just as soon not have anyone else up there, that can–

Boston Center: We got internationals that are comin' into the vicinity. We're trying to talk to them but we don't want to, ah, scare anybody, but we want the ah, we're talkin' about possibly makin' some, ah, transmissions on frequency for these guys coming overseas to just ah, you know increase the security for cockpit operations.

Herndon Center: Yeah, Terry, we're getting a lot of traffic on this bridge, I, I copied that, let's keep doin' that, ah, contact to the Command Center, the ATA rep, see if we can get the airline company operations to contact their aircraft. I'd recommend, ah, maybe, possibility of the stuff coming in from overseas, Bangor as an alternate site, but leave that up to them.

Boston Center: Yeah, we'll leave it up to them, but we're also gonna let them know to increase the security for cockpit access.

Herndon Center: Alright, ah, that sounds like a good plan.

Boston Center: Boston. Listen, ah, both of these aircraft departed Boston, both were seven sixes, both heading to LA, and I'm lookin' out on the TSD [flight history] and I think that all departures out of Boston should have heightened cockpit security. Is there any way you can bring up every center in the country and relay that message so that they can tell the aircraft that are, ah, out there flying right now to increase the cockpit security vigilance on this day?

Herndon: I'll get the message out.

Boston Center: Thank you very much.

9.07 a.m. Major Nasypany, the NEADS mission crew commander, orders the fighter pilots circling over Long Island to Manhattan.

Major Nasypany: OK, Foxy, this is what, this is what I foresee that we probably need to do. We need to talk to FAA. We need to tell 'em if this stuff is goin' to keep on goin' we need to take those fighters put 'em over Manhattan. OK?

Fox: Sir.

Nasypany: That's the best thing, that's the best play right now. So, coordinate with FAA (background indistinct) tell em' if there's more out there, which we don't know, let's get 'em over Manhattan, at least we got some kind of play.

Nasypany: OK, this is what I got goin'. Tell Foxy to scramble Langley, send 'em in same location.

(Off-mic conversation)

Nasypany: Battle, battle stations or scramble? Battle stations only at Langley. OK, this is, ah who's up there? OK, are you listening? What I told the SD so far we need to get those fighters over Manhattan cuz' we don't know how many guys are out of Boston, could be two, could be more.

(Off-mic conversation)

Nasypany: I don't know, just in case. Not down in Whiskey one oh five where they, where FAA wants to hold them. We need to be more (indistinct) and stick 'em, you know.

(Off-mic conversation)

Nasypany: We're workin' it (indistinct). Yeah, so this is, yeah, OK? Yeah, well, we can't they're in ah FAA airspace. Well we can, we can. Yeah, they're ours. (Indistinct) they're mine.

Giant Killer: Giant Killer's on.

Powell: This is Huntress placing Quit two five, two six on battle stations, time one three one zero, authenticate charlie victor, that is Quit two five two six on battle stations all parties acknowledge with initials. Command post.

Powell: Langley.

Langley: (Indistinct).

Powell: Tower.

Tower: (Indistinct).

Powell: How about command post?

Command Post: (Indistinct).

Powell: ODC, say again?

Giant Killer: Giant Killer is out.

Powell: No, the female who was that?

Unknown: (Indistinct) needed?

Powell: No, you're cleared to drop. Giant Killer you're cleared to drop. Tower you're cleared to drop.

AMERICAN AIRLINES FLIGHT 77

8.56 a.m. And now American Airlines Flight 77 has gone incommunicado.

Indianapolis Center: Air Canada 579, Indy Center, roger.

Indianapolis Center: American 77, Indy.

Indianapolis Center: American 77, American, Indy.

Indianapolis Center: American 77, American, Indy, radio check, how do you read?

Indianapolis Center: American, ah, 77, American, radio check, how do you read?

(Dial tone)

Unknown: This is, ah, Dacos [Indianapolis Control, Dacos Radar].

Indianapolis Center: This is, ah, Henderson [Henderson Radar Sector], American 77, I don't know what happened to him. I'm trying to (background (indistinct)) plane took a turn to the south, and, and now I'm ah, I don't know what altitude he's at or what he's doin', (indistinct) headed towards Falmouth at thirty five.

Unknown: OK, just let me know.

Indianapolis Center: OK, I'll try to get a hold of him. Thanks.

Indianapolis Center: American 1023 contact Indy Center on one two three point seven seven, good day.

AA1023: Twenty three seventy seven, American 1023, good day.

Indianapolis Center: USAIR 1751 descent and maintain flight level three five zero.

USAir1751: Ah, 1751, descend to three five zero.

Indianapolis Center: (Indistinct) four nine Quebec Sierra cleared direct Spartansburg.

49QS: Cleared direct Spartansburg, forty nine Quebec Sierra.

Indianapolis Center: American 77, Indy, radio check, how do you read?

423: Indy, were you calling (indistinct) four twenty three?

Indianapolis Center: (Indistinct) four twenty three, negative.

Indianapolis Center: American, ah, 77, Indy Center, how do you read?

Indianapolis Center: American 77, new radio check, how do you read?

Indianapolis Center: US Air 1751, contact Indy Center on one three four point two two, good day.

USAir 1751: 1751, three four two two.

Indianapolis Center: 489 Quebec Sierra contact Indy Center on one three four point two two, good day.

489QS: Three four two two, 9 Quebec Sierra good day.

Indianapolis Center: US Air 12, correction, 217, cleared direct (indistinct) mountain.

USAir217: Direct (indistinct) mountain, US Air 217.

(Dial tone)

Dacos: Dacos.

Indianapolis Center: This is Henderson. Still haven't got American 77, ah, last he was at thirty five goin' to Falmouth, so I don't know where he is out there anywhere, yet, so we're still tryin' to get a hold of him, we contacted company.

Indianapolis Center: American 77, Indy.

AA2493: Center, American, ah, 2493.

Indianapolis Center: American 2493, go ahead.

AA2493: Yeah, we, ah, sent a message to dispatch to have

him come up on twenty twenty seven, is that what you want him to do?

Indianapolis Center: Yeah, we had him on west side of our airspace, and he went into coast, and don't have a track on him, and now's he not talkin' to me, so we don't know what exactly happened to him. We're trying to get a hold of him. We also contacted your company, so thanks for the help.

AA2493: Alright.

8.58 a.m. American Airlines dispatcher Jim McDonald is told air traffic control has lost American Airlines Flight 77.

American Airlines: American dispatch, Jim McDonald.

Indianapolis Center: This Indianapolis Center, we're trying to get a hold of American 77.

American Airlines: Ah, Indy, hang on one second please.

Indianapolis Center: What?

American Airlines: Hang on one second sir.

Indianapolis Center: Alright.

American Airlines: Who you tryin' to get a hold of?

Indianapolis Center: American 77.

American Airlines: OK.

Indianapolis Center: On frequency one two zero point two seven.

American Airlines: One two zero–

Indianapolis Center: Point two seven. We were talkin' to him and all of a sudden it just ah–

American Airlines: OK. Alright we'll get a hold of him for ya.

Indianapolis Center: Alright.

9.02 a.m. But McDonald doesn't have any more luck.

American Airlines: American dispatch, Jim McDonald.

Indianapolis Center: Yes, this is Indianapolis Center. We, ah, don't know if we talked to the same guy, about American 77.

American Airlines: Yeah, I (indistinct) called him, but I didn't get a reply back from them.

Indianapolis Center: We, we, ah, lost track control of the guy. He's in coast track, so we have, we don't really know where his target is and we can't get a hold of him. Ah–

American Airlines: I tried.

Indianapolis Center: You guys tried him and no response?

American Airlines: No response.

Indianapolis Center: Yeah, we have no radar contact and, ah, no communications with him, so if you guys can try him again.

American Airlines: We're doin' it.

Indianapolis Center: Alright. Thanks a lot.

American Airlines: We're doin' it. Thank you.

9.11 a.m. McDonald confirms it was American Airlines Flight 11 that hit the World Trade Center – and that he still can't contact American Airlines Flight 77.

American Airlines: American Dispatch, Jim McDonald.

Indianapolis Center: Indianapolis Center. Did you get a hold of American 77 by chance?

American Airlines: No sir, but we have an unconfirmed report that a second airplane hit the World Trade Center.

Indianapolis Center: Say again.

American Airlines: You know we lost American 11, to

a hijackin', so, American was up, ah, a Boston to Los
Angeles flight.

Indianapolis Center: It was, alright, I can't really, I can't
hear what you're sayin' there. Did you say American 11?

American Airlines: Yes. We were hijacked.

Indianapolis Center: (Indistinct).

American Airlines: It was a Boston LA flight. And 77 is
a Dulles LA flight. And, ah, we have an unconfirmed
report a second airplane just flew into the World
Trade Center.

Indianapolis Center: Thank you very much. Goodbye.

**9.16 a.m. Chaos still reigns with continuing confusion
over which planes have been hijacked.**

Ellen King [Command Center]: Are you able to confirm
anything within your airline to us?

Bill Halleck [American Airlines]: No, unfortunately, ah–

King: How about, can you tell me if we know for sure if
it was American 11 that went into the Trade Center or
not?

Halleck: We think that's who it was.

King: OK.

Halleck: And we're missin' another flight also.

King: Ah, what flight are you missing?

Halleck: 77.

King: And when is the last time you knew for sure
something about him?

Halleck: Ah, he was in, ah, wait a minute, well there's a, I
don't know how he got up there.

King: There's a data block (indistinct).

Halleck: But 77 is up there also.

King: OK.

Halleck: He's out of Dulles.

King: OK, and–

Halleck: Dulles LA, and they both, ah, apparently have been hijacked, and 11 is we're pretty sure is in there and, and, ah, 77, we were talkin' to him according to Indianapolis Center …

King: Uh huh.

Halleck: About 45 minutes ago, and, uh, in Indy Center.

King: Uh huh.

Halleck: I don't know he got to, to, ah, back to the Trade Center. I have no idea if, if that happened.

King: OK. It may not have, we have another call sign, of course we don't know for sure, any of these call signs right now, but, if we find that it's your aircraft, we'll certainly give you a call.

Halleck: So, ah, you have ah, you have two airplanes in the Trade Center?

King: Yes.

Halleck: And ah you don't know who either one of them are, for sure?

King: Yeah, that's true.

Halleck: OK.

King: If I did, I would share it with you.

Halleck: OK. Thanks (indistinct).

King: Alright. Bye, Bill.

9.31 a.m. The FBI get involved.

FAA: Boston FBI.

FBI: Go ahead FBI is on.

FAA: OK. We have two reports, preliminary information, ah, believe to be American Airlines Flight 77 and Flight 11, ah, collided with World

Trade Center. Ah, also, a preliminary report, ah, United Airlines flight 175 off radar. Ah, no further information.

FBI: OK. So that's American 77 and United 175?

FAA: That's correct.

FBI: Um, do we have their, ah, input of origin on both of those?

FAA: OK, back to FBI. It's American Flight 77, second flight is 11. Ah, those are the two aircraft believed to be involved with World Trade Center. Ah, route is reported as Dulles to Los Angeles for 77 and Boston to Los Angeles for 11. United Airlines is not, ah, believed to be involved in World Trade Center at this time.

FBI: OK. So it's American 77 and American 11?

FAA: That's, ah, that's correct.

FBI: American 11 was Boston to LA?

FAA: Ah, that's the report I've got.

FBI: OK, and the other one was Dulles to LA?

FAA: Dulles to LAX.

FAA: I've got, ah, ah, two flights here now. The second one was American Airlines 77.

FBI: OK, so it's 77 and 11?

FAA: Now a Dulles to LA. That's affirmative. The other report was regarding United 175. We had a report that it was, ah, off the radar, ah–

FAA: United Airlines was not involved.

FBI: OK, is that, ah, where was that United 175 from?

FAA: FAA Washington operations. Please be advised that calls may be monitored. Please stand by.

FAA: Ah, we're getting conflicting reports on that, ah, FBI, on the 175.

FBI: Where did it go off radar?

FAA: Stand by please. Back to FBI. I've got a report from eastern, FAA eastern region air traffic, that it dropped off radar that it dropped over Indiana.

9.18 a.m. Indianapolis Ops Manager John Thomas tells air traffic controllers that it doesn't look good for American Airlines Flight 77.

Herndon Center: Hey Indy, this is Bob, Command Center. Need you to find, tell me anything, or everything you can about American 77, where he is and if you have radar or not.

Indianapolis Center: Well, OK, I'm listenin' to my Ops Manager talk to Washington.

Herndon Center: I'm sorry.

Indianapolis Center: We lost communications and radar with him. Hang on a minute, I'm goin' to have the Ops Manager tell ya the story.

John Thomas: Hello, Command Center.

Herndon Center: Yes sir.

Thomas: This is John Thomas, Ops Manager. I think we need to let everybody know this right away, if they don't already. American 77 was over, ah, was just west of Charleston, West Virginia, at flight level three five zero, it's a heav–, heavy Boeing seven fifty two, and disappeared off our radar scope about twelve fifty six Z, a long with lost, ah, frequency. We were treating it as a lost, started to do some procedures to notify search and rescue, and what not, when–, when American Airlines told us they'd had some aircraft, or an aircraft hijacked. We now believe that aircraft may have been hijacked, although no one has, we have nothing, you know, to verify that. What with the World Trade Center we could have another loose aircraft out there somewhere.

Herndon Center: K. At the time of loss do you, ah, what altitude was he at? Flight level.

Thomas: Flight level, flight level three five zero.

Herndon Center: And he just, just lost primary, also?

Thomas: Lost all, yes lost, no primary, or ah that we could see. Course we couldn't, wouldn't necessarily be able to pick up a primary there anyway.

Herndon Center: I'm assuming then that you're, ah, doing what you can to do a primary read, re-track on him, if you can do that.

Thomas: Yes, sure.

Herndon Center: And then, ah, so at twelve fifty-six Zulu we lost front comm and radar. Any, ah, ELTs [Emergency Locator Transmitters]?

Thomas: No ELTs.

Herndon Center: Ah, um, OK, ah, any more information you get, I'd appreciate it, and I'll forward this immediately up to the NOM and everyone that's standin' up there.

Thomas: Thank you.

9.21 a.m. Reports that American Airlines Flight 11 (which has already hit the World Trade Center) is still airborne create even more confusion.

Colin Scoggins: Military, Boston Center, just had a report that American 11 is still in the air and its on its way towards heading towards Washington.

ID Tech (NEADS): K. American 11 is still in the air?

Scoggins: Yes.

ID Tech: On its way towards Washington?

Scoggins: It was another, evidently, another aircraft that hit the tower, that's the latest report that we have.

ID Tech: OK.

Scoggins: I'm gonna try and confirm an ID for you, but I would assume he's somewhere over, ah, either New Jersey or somewhere further south.

ID Tech: OK, so, American 1 isn't the hijack at all then, right?

Scoggins: No, he is a hijack.

ID Tech: He, American 11, is a hijack.

Scoggins: Yes.

ID Tech: And he's on his way towards Washington?

Scoggins: Could be a third, it could be a third aircraft.

9.21 a.m. Now the military jets are being sent to Washington.

Unknown: OK, third aircraft hijacked, heading towards Washington.

Major Nasypany (NEADS): OK, ah, American Airlines is still airborne, 11, the first guy, he's heading toward Washington. OK, I think we need to scramble Langley right now and I'm, I'm gonna take the fighters from Otis and try to chase this guy down if I can find him.

(Off-mic conversation)

Nasypany: Yeah

Nasypany: You sure?

(Off-mic conversation)

Nasypany: OK, he's heading towards Langley, or I should say Washington. American 11, the original guy, he's still airborne. We're still (indistinct) gettin' a–

(Off-mic conversation)

Nasypany: We're gettin' a position. Got a position?

(Background) Unknown: (Indistinct) got a hijack real world, gotta go.

Nasypany: OK.

Nasypany: Foxy, scramble Langley. Head 'em toward the Washington area.

Major Fox: Roger that.

Nasypany: Could be American–

Unknown: Hold on a second.

Nasypany: We're tryin' to get a code on this guy right now. We do have a tail number. It's a–

(Off-mic conversation)

Nasypany: Uh,ooh, we are, it's ah, uuuuh, what was the tail number?

Unknown: Panta four five four six.

Senior ID Tech: November three three four alpha alpha.

Nasypany: November three three four alpha alpha. If we can find him. We, we're gettin', we're tryin' to get, we're tryin' to get the modes, tryin' to get the position on this guy. So, (indistinct) then we'll run on him.

Nasypany: OK, right now what we're running with out there is two by zero by two by guns for Langley, two gan– and two, ah, two tanks. OK. Also, we have the Panta four five four six, zero by ten by two by guns, three tanks. Let me give you another head–

Unknown: Try and get into a tail chase with this American one one headed toward Washington, if we can find him.

Nasypany: Three tanks, affirmative. Plus I have, ah, more stuff available if I need it from the SOF there. Also, I have a tanker, a Maine 85.

(Off-mic conversation)

Nasypany: OK you got the tanker, I have additional tankers out of McGuire, KC10s. Team call sign, I'm not sure on the, ah, numbers, two two and two three. Two KC10s. I'm sticking 'em in ah Whiskey107. Yeah, and did you get the word that Langley got scrambled.

Unknown: Go ahead, sir.

Nasypany: Yes. They just got scrambled about, ah, two minutes ago. No, that's OK.

Unknown: FO. FO says forget the tail chase, even though we couldn't find him.

Nasypany: Yeah, great, that's great.

9.23 a.m. Scramble ... but where to?

Langley Command Post: Langley Command Post on.

Powell (NEADS): Alright, this is Huntress with an active air defense scramble for Quit two five and two six, I repeat an active air defense scramble for Quit 25, 26. Scramble immediately, time one three two four, authenticate, bravo x-ray, scramble on a heading of zero one zero, flight level two niner zero. Contact Huntress on frequency two three four decimal six and back up three six four decimal two. Do all parties acknowledge with initials, Langley Command Post?

Langley Command Post: Command Post.

Powell: Giant Killer copy?

Norfolk Approach: (Indistinct) copy.

Powell: If you have any questions give me a call me on the land line.

Langley Command Post: OK.

9.28 a.m. NEADS ID techs are worried that the White House is slow off the mark in dealing with the threat to Washington. But they still think American Airlines Flight 11 is in the air.

ID Tech: Hi, this is Huntress calling, umm, I was told to give you a buzz for our, our Mission Crew Commander. Any information? I guess three aircraft out of Boston are missing and apparently two of them have hit the World Trade Center and one is en route to Washington, did you get that information?

ID Tech: Yeah.

ID Tech: American one one is not the aircraft that crashed, it is still airborne, did you get that information?

ID Tech: That's what we just found out.

ID Tech: We don't know where it is though, it's headed toward Washington, was the last known information.

Senior ID Tech: Washington better get on the loop.

ID Tech: Right, and I don't know but somebody's gotta get the President goin'. This is not good.

Senior ID Tech: They'd better start looking for this guy.

ID Tech: Ah, yeah, we just hung up. I'm not goin' to say too much right now, but, ah, I wanted to give you a heads up. Ah, do you have any information though where American one one is, or anything?

Senior ID Tech: See this guy, they, Boston is the only one givin' us any kinds of decent, freaking input.

ID Tech: Just want to, just want to say one more thing, too, ah, Washington, I don't know if they don't think this is serious, or not, but they are not, unless they hear from like the centers. If you could give them a heads up and let them know that this is–

ID Tech: Washington Center, they're not really, not at
all, OK sir?

Srenior ID Tech: We've got to get a point out on that
American Airlines.

ID Tech: Boston is calling Washington right now.

Senior ID Tcch: They got him?

Unknown: I don't know if he's on him yet, but Langley
is scrambled to intercept (indistinct) and headed for
Washington (indistinct) the fighters over (indistinct).

ID Tech: (Indistinct) I just talked to them.

Senior ID Tech: And I'd have the President airborne,
wherever.

Senior ID Tech: What's up?

ID Tech: Uh, Boston has no clue where they are and he's
goin' let Washington Center know that this is very
serious.

Senior ID Tech: Good.

ID Tech: (Indistinct).

Senior ID Tech: Yeah, fuckin'–

ID Tech: So.

Senior ID Tech: Hey–

Unknown: American Airlines headed toward DC
(indistinct).

ID Tech: I do, I lat long–

Senior ID Tech: Hey, anybody good at math? Take a lat,
last lat long and they were doin' two hundred and
ninety knots.

ID Tech: Did you get the third call sign?

Senior ID Tech: Headed toward Washington.

Sr. ID Tech: The Z point that was the American Airlines
one.

Senior ID Tech: No, our first our first Z point, yeah, that

was the American Airlines, that was our lat long on
him.

**9.32 a.m. Still thinking American Airlines Flight 11 is on
its way to Washington, a NEADS ID tech calls the FAA's
Washington Center to let them know. During the call, the
military is finally told that AA Flight 77 is also missing.**

ID Tech: Open line.

ID Tech: Huntress ID, unsecure line.

Washington Center: Huntress ID, this is Washington
Center, the Operations Manager, ah–

ID Tech: Go ahead sir.

Washington Center: OK, I guess you'd called here a
couple of times, you never talked to me, but if there's
anything you need, or anything I can help you with,
let, let me know what it is right now please.

ID Tech: OK, ah, do you want me to let you know what
we have going on, sir?

Washington Center: I would, yes, well I have a pretty
good idea, but yes.

ID Tech: OK, there are three aircraft missing out of
Boston. We spoke to Boston, and they said they're not
sure of the third aircraft call sign but they do have two,
one of them is United one seven five.

Washington Center: Uh huh.

ID Tech: And one is American one one. They thought
that the American one one was the aircraft that
crashed into the World Trade Center with the
United one seven five. However, American one one
is not the aircraft that crashed. He said the pilot on
American one one was talking to him, having a rough
time telling him what's going on, there was threats

in the cockpit being made. This was the initial, ah, hijack information that we got, American one one, it's a seven sixty seven, from Boston to Los Angeles. Proposed route he was headed towards JFK at the time that they lost contact, but that was not the aircraft headed ah into the World Trade Center, that hit it.

Washington Center: OK.

ID Tech: What Boston's saying, he, the last known, and I'm not sure where we heard it, through the grapevine, people calling, is that American one one was headed toward Washington, and that's the only thing.

Washington Center: Was headed toward where?

ID Tech: Washington.

Washington Center: OK.

ID Tech: So, your AOR, and I just wanted to give you a heads up.

Washington Center: OK, now–

ID Tech: The last …

Washington Center: OK. Go ahead.

ID Tech: The last lat long that we had, primary target only, was four zero three eight north, zero seven four zero three west on American one one.

Washington Center: OK.

ID Tech: But again, remember nothing has been confirmed as far as which aircraft have hit the World Trade Center but the other one we have is information headed towards Washington.

Washington Center: OK, now let me tell you this; I, we've been lookin', we also lost American 77.

ID Tech: American 77.

Senior ID Tech: OK, American 77 lost.

ID Tech: Where was he proposed to head, sir?

Washington Center: Excuse me.

ID Tech: Where was he proposed to head?

Senior ID Tech: American 77.

Washington Center: OK, he was going to LA also.

Senior ID Tech: He was goin' to LA.

ID Tech: He was goin' to LA.

Washington Center: Now, uh–

ID Tech: From where, sir?

Washington Center: Ah, I think he was from Boston, also.

Senior ID Tech: Boston to LA.

Washington Center: Now let me tell you this story here. Ah, Indy, Indianapolis Center was workin' this guy–

ID Tech: What guy?

Washington Center: American 77.

ID Tech: OK.

Washington Center: At flight level three five zero, however they lost radar with him, they lost contact with him, they lost everything and they don't have any idea where he is or what happened. So what we've done at the round – surrounding centers here is to tell everyone to look out for limited codes, primary targets or whatever the case may be.

ID Tech: OK.

Washington Center: And that was the last time, that was about fifteen minutes ago, since I talked to the Indianapolis Center, ah, Operations Manager.

ID Tech: Do you have a type aircraft sir?

Washington Center: That was a seven sixty seven I believe.

Senior ID Tech: Seven sixty seven.

ID Tech: OK, and, ah, right, so I don't call Indianapolis unless I have to–

Washington Center: Somebody else is talking. I'm sorry. I can't hear you in background.

ID Tech: Umm, all I need is the lat long, last known position of the seven sixty seven.

Washington Center: Well, I don't know, that was Bos– that was Indy Center. But they said somewhere, it was, last time I talked to 'em they said that it was east of York, and I don't even know what state that is.

ID Tech: OK, sir, well I'm goin' to go ahead and just give them a call.

Washington Center: OK.

9.35 a.m. Worries mount that a hijacked plane is heading for the White House … but first they need the right phone number.

Rountree [NEADS]: Huntress ID, Sgt (indistinct) how can I help you?

Scoggins [Boston Center]: Our latest report the aircraft VFR [Visual Flight Rules] six miles southeast of the White House.

Rountree: Six miles southeast of the White House?

Scoggins: Yep. East. He's moving away.

Rountree: Southeast of the White House?

Scoggins: Aircraft is moving away.

Rountree: He's moving away from the White House?

Scoggins: Yeah.

Rountree: OK, but, what, he was a DVFR [Defense Visual Flight Rules]?

Scoggins: We believe just, we just know it's a VFR aircraft, we're not sure who he is, ah, if you want to hold on a second. We got–

Rountree: OK, copy.

Scoggins: We have people down there lookin'.

Rountree: OK, copy.

Scoggins: Where was that position?

Scoggins: Six, six southwest, six southwest of the White House deviating away.

Rountree: Deviating away, you don't have a type aircraft, you don't know who he is?

Scoggins: Nothing, nothing.

ID Tech: It's a DVFR?

Scoggins: We're in Boston, so I have no clue. Hopefully someone in Washington would have a better, information for you.

Rountree: OK.

Scoggins: Is this a good number to keep calling?

Rountree: Yeah. This is a great number to keep calling.

Scoggins: OK, all right.

Rountree: Washington, OK. So it's six miles. You guys have him primary target only?

Scoggins: We just have a telcon. We don't have any target at all up here, we're just on a telcon. We just heard that and wanted to make sure you got that information.

Rountree: OK, can you do me a favor and go ahead and fill, uh, Bo– umm Washington in on this?

Scoggins: I'll try and give 'em a call. I don't have a number for them.

Rountree: OK, I'll give you a good number, then. Washington's number is, nine

Scoggins: What is it?

Rountree: OK, the number DSN is xxx-xx.

Scoggins: And what was New York's?

Rountree: New York number that we've got for them is

ah, x-xxx.

Scoggins: Oh, so you don't have a DSN?

Rountree: No, I don't have a DSN for New York, we have a shout line.

Scoggins: OK, I have that already.

Rountree: OK.

Scoggins: They do have a DSN, I just don't (indistinct).

Rountree: (Indistinct) on the DVFR, sir, that was six miles?

Scoggins: No, no information at all. You would be better talking with Washington.

Rountree: I'm sorry, sir, is it a deviating aircraft or is it a DVFR?

Scoggins: OK, that's what you have?

Rountree: No, no sir, on the one that was six miles southeast of the White House?

Scoggins: Yeah, southwest.

Rountree: Southwest?

Scoggins: Yeah, southwest.

Rountree: OK, southwest of the White House. Was he a DVFR? Or you don't have any codes on it, but was he an actual deviating aircraft?

Scoggins: We believe, he, I guess, yes, they believe now he was a deviating aircraft.

Rountree: OK, copy.

Scoggins: You'd get more out of Washington than you would from me.

Rountree: OK, copy.

Scoggins: I'm just passing information.

9.36 a.m. Too late, the military jets are heading for Washington … and they still haven't got the authority to intercept.

Unknown: That came from Boston?

Sergeant William Huckabone [NEADS]: We're goin' to turn and burn and crank it up, OK, here we go, this is what we're gonna do here.

Nasypany: Sir, we've got an aircraft (indistinct) east of the White House right now.

Huckabone: The monster mash.

Nasypany: OK.

Unknown: What happened?

Nasypany: Run 'em.

Radio transmission: Team two one, do you us want relay?

Nasypany: Authorizing AFIO [authorisation to intercept], right now? You want to authorize it?

Background: I can't get through.

Radio transmission: Yeah, we're hearing him loud and clear.

Unknown: What're we doin'?

Background: Goin' direct DC [Washington] with our guys.

Nasypany: AFIO?

9.36 a.m. A military cargo pilot tells controllers he has spotted the stray airliner near the capital … and it's coming down fast.

Reagan National Tower Controller: Gofer zero six, traffic is eleven o'clock and five miles north bound, fast moving, type and altitude unknown.

Gofer 06 [Call sign for military cargo plane]: Gofer 06.

We have the traffic in sight, twelve o'clock.

Reagan National Tower Controller: Ah, you have the traffic, do you know what kind it is? Can you see?

Gofer 06: Looks live a seven fifty seven, sir.

Reagan National Tower Controller: A seven fifty seven, can you estimate his altitude?

Gofer 06: Ah, looks like he's at low altitude right now, sir.

Gofer 06: That, ah, traffic for Gofer zero six is still in a descent now, and, uh, looks like he's rolled out northeast bound.

Reagan National Tower Controller: Alright. Thank You.

Reagan National Tower Controller: Gofer eight six [sic] climb and maintain, ah–

(Background)Unknown: You got a military?

Reagan National Tower Controller: Yeah, stand by. Gofer eight six, turn right and follow the traffic please.

Reagan National Tower Controller: Gofer eight six, turn right heading zero eight zero, we're gonna vector you for the traffic.

Gofer 06: OK, zero eight zero, Gofer zero six (indistinct).

Reagan National Tower Controller: Dulles, I'm keeping Gofer eight six, um, zero six with me for a while.

9.37 a.m. American Airlines Flight 77 crashes into the Pentagon.

9.38 a..m The military cargo pilot reports the passenger jet has hit the Pentagon.

Gofer 06: And, uh, Washington, this is Gofer zero six.

Reagan National Tower Controller: Gofer zero six, go ahead.

Gofer 06: Yes sir, that aircraft is down, he's in our twelve o'clock position, ah, looks like it's just to the northwest of the airfield at this time, sir.

Reagan National Tower Controller: Gofer eight six, thank you. Descend and maintain two thousand.

Gofer 06: OK. We are down to two thousand. And, uh, this is Gofer zero six, it looks like that aircraft crashed into the Pentagon, sir.

Reagan National Tower Controller: Gofer eight six, Gofer zero six, thank you.

Gofer 06: Understand you still want Gofer zero six to descend to two thousand sir.

Reagan National Tower Controller: Gofer zero six, you can maintain three thousand and, ah, turn left heading two seven zero.

Gofer 06: OK. Left turn to two seven zero, Gofer zero six, ah, any chance we can circle around the Pentagon, sir, on our two seven zero turn.

Reagan National Tower Controller: Gofer zero six, approved as requested.

Gofer 06: Gofer zero six.

Reagan National Tower Controller: Gofer, ah, zero six, OK, they're asking if you would go ahead and move away now towards the west, two seventy heading and, ah, two thousand for now.

Gofer 06: Roger, we're climbing to three thousand sir and it looks like that aircraft has impacted the west side of the Pentagon.

Reagan National Tower Controller: Alright. Thank you.

9.38 a.m. The military at NEADS doesn't yet know about the Pentagon strike.

ID Tech [NEADS]: Washington, Huntress, ah, Boston just called us. They said they had information about

some aircraft that was six miles southwest of the
White House that appeared to be deviating.

Washington Center: Boston does?

ID Tech: Boston called and said that I'd have to get the
information from you on it. They don't have a call
sign for the aircraft. They don't have any codes for the
aircraft. They just know that there's one that was six
miles southwest of the White House.

Washington Center: OK, well Boston's airspace doesn't
even come close to that, I don't know how they got
that information, but ah, we don't– hey– OK, we, we
don't know anything about that.

ID Tech: OK, you don't know anything about that.

Washington Center: No, we do not and it's probably
just a rumor, but ah, you might want to call ah, ah,
National or Andrews somebody, somewhere like that
and find out, but we don't anything about that.

**9.39 a.m. NEADS Commander Major Nasypany wants
the fighter jets from Langley Air Force Base over to
Washington in a hurry. But he finds out they aren't even
close – they were sent east over the ocean.**

Nasypany: OK, (indistinct) if need be. I don't care how
many windows you break.

Unknown: Langley had them (indistinct) in three eight
six.

Nasypany: Why'd they go up there?

Unknown: Because Giant Killer sent them out there.

Nasypany: God damn it. OK. Pat, push 'em back.

UNITED AIRLINES FLIGHT 93
**9.28 a.m. Something is clearly wrong in the cockpit of
United Airlines Flight 93.**

Cleveland Center Controller: United 93, that traffic for you is one o'clock, twelve miles eastbound, three seven zero.

UA93: Negative contact, we're looking, United ninety three.

UA93: Hey (indistinct yelling).

Cleveland Center Controller: Somebody call Cleveland?

AA1060: Roger American, ah, 1066, with you. We're at three seven oh, we're, ah, slowing, ah, due to the delays if possible going eastbound.

Cleveland Center Controller: That's American 1066?

UA93: (Indistinct yelling) mayday (indistinct yelling).

Cleveland Center Controller: You got United 93?

Cleveland Center Controller 2: United 93, south of Chardon, descended.

Cleveland Center Controller: What's that?

Cleveland Center Controller 2: I just sayin' it looks like he descended there.

Cleveland Center Controller: I don't think so. United 93, verify three five zero.

Cleveland Center Controller 2. United 93, Cleveland.

Cleveland Center: Go ahead (indistinct).

Cleveland Center Controller 2: Do you have United 93 south of Chardon?

Cleveland Center: We hear some funny noises we're trying to get him. Do you have him?

Cleveland Center Controller 2: No.

Cleveland Center: Thank You. United 93, Cleveland.

Cleveland Center Controller: United 1523 did you hear your company, ah, did you hear, ah, some interference on the frequency, ah, couple a minutes ago, screaming?

United1523: Yes, I did seven ninety seven and, ah, we couldn't tell what it was either.

Cleveland Center Controller: OK. United 93, Cleveland, if you hear the center, ident.

AA1060: American 1060. Ditto on the other transmissions.

Cleveland Center Controller: American 1060, you heard that also?

AA1060: Yes sir, twice.

Cleveland Center Controller: Roger, we heard that also, thanks, just wanted to confirm it wasn't some interference.

9.32 a.m. Hijacker Ziad Jarrah tries to frighten Flight 93 passengers into compliance by telling them there is a bomb on board.

Ziad Jarrah: (Indistinct) Please sit down and remain sitting. We have a bomb on board, so (indistinct) …

Cleveland Center: Ah, calling Cleveland Center, you are unreadable, say again slowly.

Unknown: Yeah, that transmission you said was unreadable, it sounded like someone said they had a bomb on board.

Cleveland Center: That's what we thought, we, ah, we didn't get it clear. Is that United 93 calling?

Cleveland Center: ExecJet 956 that aircraft we believe was transmitting is twelve o'clock one five miles turn left heading two two five, I'll get you away from him.

ExecJet 956: two two five, ExecJet 956.

Cleveland Center: One six mike foxtrot fly heading one two zero, I'll get you away from that.

Fox: Flying one twenty I'm heading, Mike Fox.

Cleveland Center: 561 Alfa Charlie fly heading zero nine zero.

561AC: Zero nine zero, one alfa charlie.

Cleveland Center: Roger, American ten sixty fly heading eight niner zero.

Cleveland Center: Roger.

ExecJet 956: Center, ExecJet 956, what's that traffic for us again?

Cleveland Center: Say again.

ExecJet 956: That traffic we're turning for, is that about a two to three o'clock?

Cleveland Center: It is one to two o'clock, yeah, two to three o'clock as you turn.

ExecJet 956: Alright, we've got him on TCAS, I think we got him.

Cleveland Center: He's climbing, so I want to keep everyone away from him.

ExecJet 956: OK, I think we've got him in sight.

Cleveland Center: Delta 1989, ah, Cleveland.

D1989: Yes sir.

Cleveland Center: Delta 1989, ah, turn right to a heading of, ah, three two zero.

D1989: Alright, Delta 1989, heading three two zero.

Cleveland Center: OK, Delta 1989, we're gonna go the other way, fly a heading of, ah, two six zero.

D1989: Alright, two six zero, Delta 1989.

Cleveland Center: Delta 1989.

9.39 a.m. Jarrah again says a bomb is on board Flight 93 and claims he is flying back to the airport.

Ziad Jarrah: This is the Captain. I would like you all to remain seated. We have a bomb on board and are going back to the airport and have our demands, so please remain quiet.

Cleveland Center: OK, that's United 93 calling? United 93 understand you have a bomb on board, go ahead.

ExecJet 956: Command Center, ExecJet 956, that was the transmission.

Cleveland Center: ExecJet 956, did you understand that transmission?

ExecJet 956: Affirmative, he said there was a bomb on board.

Cleveland Center: That's what you got out of it also?

ExecJet 956: Affirmative.

Cleveland Center: Roger, United 93, go ahead.

9.41 a.m. A private jet keeps a visual on United Airlines Flight 93.

Cleveland Center: United 93 do you hear Cleveland Center? OK, American ten six and Executive 956, we just lost the target on that aircraft.

ExecJet 956: OK. 956. We had a visual on him. Just stand by.

Cleveland Center: Do you have a visual on him now?

ExecJet 956: Ah, we did, but we lost him in the turn. We just make a quick–

Cleveland Center: I had a thirty seven aircraft right behind you on a vector also, that maybe who you saw. Do you have a visual on him now, ah, Executive 956? If you could make a turn back to two twenty heading, let me know if you could see him.

ExecJet 956: Yeah, he's still there, we got him for 956.

Cleveland Center: He's still there, ah, northwest of you about 25 miles?

ExecJet 956: Affirmative for 956.

9.31 a.m. Taking stock.

Herndon Center: OK, stand by please.

Herndon Center: OK, looks like I have everyone on here
   except Boston Center. This is the air traffic command
   center the TMO on duty in the west area. I need to
   have all traffic management units do an inventory,
   basically an inventory of all airborne traffic, ensure
   that you do not have any unusual situations or any
   aircraft that are not accounted for. If you have any
   unusual situations or unaccounted for aircraft identify
   them and contact us here at the Command Center.

Cleveland Center: United 93 may have a bomb on board.

Herndon Center: OK, United 93. Who's speaking?

Cleveland Center: Cleveland Center.

Herndon Center: OK, Cleveland, what's his origination
   and destination?

Cleveland Center: Out of Newark going to San
   Francisco. His position is, twenty, fifteen east, actually
   he's further than that. He's east of Dryer. His exact
   position is 30 miles east of Dryer.

Herndon Center: OK. You have a transponder on this
   aircraft or did he go primary?

Cleveland Center: At this time he's, ah, code one five two
   seven, and we still have a transponder.

Herndon Center: OK, and can you give me any
   additional information as to why you believe there
   may be a bomb?

Cleveland Center: Ah, because he's screaming that on the
   frequency.

Herndon Center: OK, very good. Anyone else? Alright,
   I'm disconnecting now.

9.34 a.m. Air traffic controllers tell FAA headquarters that Flight 93 may have a bomb on board.

Herndon Center: We just had another report, United 93, who was in Cleveland Center's airspace, somewhere around Dyer [sic] Intersection, just reported that they heard screaming on the frequency and the people have a bomb on board. The aircraft departed Newark en route to San Francisco was the report.

FAA HQ: Know what type?

Herndon Center: No, I don't have that information.

FAA HQ: OK. We're still tracking it now, right?

Herndon Center: Correct. We're still tracking, at this time.

FAA HQ: OK. Thanks bud.

Herndon Center: Alright.

9.36 a.m. Is anyone trying to get fighter jets over to Flight 93?

Cleveland Center: Our question here is, our aircraft that we have has climbed, turned, and is not talking to us. Ah, do we want to scramble? We have a couple of local military here?

Herndon Center: OK, that's a decision that has to be made at a different level. Cleveland Center: Is someone talkin' about it at least?

Herndon Center: What's the call sign again?

Cleveland Center: It's United 93. He's right over Cleveland.

Herndon Center: Over Cleveland now? OK, we'll call you right back.

9.41 a.m. More talking.

Herndon Center: United 93, we spoke about him before–

FAA HQ: Yes.

Herndon Center: He is reversing course over Akron.
They just lost his transponder. He's heading
eastbound.

FAA HQ: What kind of airplane, do we know yet?

Herndon Center: Ah, just a second, seven fifty seven.

FAA HQ: Thanks buddy.

Herndon Center: The aircraft is descending.

FAA HQ: OK. He is descending.

Herndon Center: Correct.

FAA HQ: Go ahead.

Herndon Center: Is 29 miles out of, errr, 29 minutes out
of Washington DC, 29 minutes out of Washington
DC, and tracking towards it, this is the one who
reversed course in Ohio.

FAA HQ: Yes. Go ahead.

Herndon Center: That's all I have.

FAA HQ: OK, the, ah, United 93 is 29 minutes out of
where?

Herndon Center: Uh, he's heading toward the
Washington area. He has, he was at flight level three
five zero turned around at Akron, Ohio, and is
tracking toward the Washington area at this time.

**9.49 a.m. Ten minutes has passed and still no decision
has been made to scramble fighter jets. And everybody
just left the room.**

FAA HQ: All right, they're pulling Jeff away to go talk
about United 93.

Herndon Center: Ah, do we wanna think about, ah,
scrambling aircraft?

FAA HQ: Ah, (sighs) oh God, I don't know.

Herndon Center: Uh, that's a decision someone is gonna

have to make probably in the next 10 minutes.

FAA HQ: Uh, you know everybody just left the room.

9.58 a.m. Getting closer to Washington.

Herndon Center: United 93 is two zero miles northwest of Johnstown.

FAA HQ: Two zero miles northwest on primary?

Herndon Center: Ah, well that's a report from another aircraft.

10 a.m. Another pilot sees Flight 93 rocking its wings (the hijackers were later thought to have been trying to send passengers rushing the cockpit off balance).

Herndon Center: United 93.

FAA HQ: Yes.

Herndon Center: Was waiving his wings as he went past the V, the VFR aircraft, they don't quite know what that means. Rockin' his ring– wings.

FAA HQ: K.

10.03 a.m. United Airlines Flight 93 crashes into a field in Shanksville, Pennsylvania.

10.07 a.m. Black smoke seen in Shanksville, Pennsylvania.

Herndon Center: OK, there's now on that United 93.

FAA HQ: Yes.

Herndon Center: There is a report of black smoke in the last position I gave you, 15 miles south of Johnstown.

FAA HQ: Uh, from the airplane or from the ground?

Herndon Center: Uh, they're speculating it's from the aircraft, ah, who, it hit the ground. That's what they're, that's what they're speculating. It's speculation only.

FAA HQ: OK.

(Background) FAA HQ Unknown: We're getting a preliminary report that United 93 hit the ground about 15 miles south of Johnstown, or thereabouts.

10.07 a.m. Still behind with the news at NEADS, the military are trying to get the fighters to Flight 93.

ID Tech [NEADS]: Huntress ID, nonsecure line.

Cleveland Center: I believe I was the one talking about that Delta 1989.

ID Tech: Go ahead.

Cleveland Center: OK, well, uh, disregard that, ah, did you–

ID Tech: What we found out was that he was not a confirmed hijack, however–

Cleveland Center: OK. I, I don't want to even worry about that right now. We've got a United 93 out here, are you aware of that, that has a, that has a bomb on board.

(Background) Senior ID Tech: We've got three more hijacked airborne.

ID Tech: A bomb on board? And is this confirmed? Do you have a mode 3, sir?

Cleveland Center: No we lost his transponder. Um, what we want to know is did you scramble airplanes on that Delta 1989?

(Background) Senior ID Tech: We have a bomb on board, Boston–

ID Tech: We did, out of Selfridge and Toledo, sir.

Cleveland Center: Did you, did you? Are they in the air?

ID Tech: Yes they are.

Cleveland Center: Is there any way we can get them to where this United is?

A CIA chart of all nineteen 11 September hijackers, showing the four different flights. AA Flight 11 and UA Flight 175, respectively, attacked the North and South Towers of the WTC in New York; AA Flight 77 was crashed into the Pentagon building in Washington DC; and UA Flight 93 was crashed into a field in Somerset County, Pennsylvania.

Above: The Twin Towers of New York's World Trade Center on fire after two hijacked airliners had been crashed in to them, 11 September 2001. (*© Spencer Platt/Getty Images*)

Right: Smoke engulfs the North Tower as its twin collapses in a vast cloud of dust at 9.59 a.m., 56 minutes after being struck by the Boeing 767-200 of United Airlines Flight 175.

(*© Lee Snider/Photo Images/Corbis via Getty Images*)

Left: Civilians take cover as a dust cloud from the collapse of the World Trade Center envelops lower Manhattan.

(*© Mario Tama/Getty Images*)

Left: The wreckage of the World Trade Center's Building Number 7 after the 9/11 attacks completely destroyed the Twin Towers. The structure was 370 feet from the North Tower and was not hit by either of the hijacked aircraft.

(© Jacques Langevin/Sygma via Getty Images)

Right: An unidentified New York City firefighter walks away from what would come to be known as Ground Zero after the collapse of the Twin Towers. *(© Anthony Correia/Getty Images)*

Left: Security-camara footage shows the moment when American Airlines Flight 77 was crashed into the west side of the Pentagon, Washington DC, at 9.37 a.m. on 9/11.

(© CNN via Getty Images)

Left: The aftermath of the terrorist attack on the Pentagon using a hijacked Boeing 757 airliner; 200 people died in the attack.

(© *Mai/Getty Images*)

Right: Emergency workers search the site where the Boeing 757 of United Airlines Flight 93 crashed near Shanksville, Pennsylvania. Courageous action by crew and passengers thwarted the terrorists' plan to attack either the White House or the Capitol. (© *Gary Tramontina/Sygma via Getty Images*)

Left: Khalid al-Mihdhar. One of the al Qaeda hijackers who flew a plane into the Pentagon in Washington DC, the Saudi national was known by the CIA to be in the United States eighteen months before 9/11 – but the agency kept their intelligence from the FBI and the domestic security services.

Right: Nawaf al-Hazmi. Another hijacker involved in the Pentagon attack, he entered the USA with Mihdhar in January 2000 after being followed from Kuala Lumpur by the CIA. He told friends in America he would be famous one day.

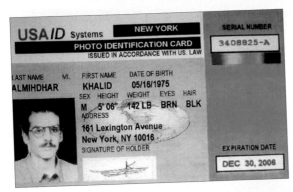

Left: Khalid al-Mihdhar's US ID card. The al Qaeda sleeper agent used his own name while living openly in America before the attacks – as did all the 9/11 hijackers.

Right: Mohammed Atta (left) with UA Flight 93 pilot Ziad Jarrah filmed during the planning stage. Atta, the 9/11 ringleader, was identified by the US military operation Project Able Danger more than a year before the attacks.

Left: Anwar al-Awlaki. The US-born imam was spiritual adviser to two of the hijackers and a regular customer of Washington's vice girls. He was eventually killed in Yemen by an American military drone on the orders of President Obama.

(© *Tracy Woodward/The Washington Post via Getty Images*)

Above left: The arm-wrestler terrorist from East London. Omar Sheikh went from an East London private school to becoming one of the world's most feared terrorists. He was believed to be a paymaster for 9/11 and was part of the gang that kidnapped *Wall Street Journal* reporter Daniel Pearl, who was beheaded by his captors. (© *Getty Images*)

Above centre: The twentieth hijacker. Zacarias Moussaoui raised suspicions after saying he wasn't interested in take-offs or landings at his flight lessons in the USA. But the French citizen's links to the 9/11 plot weren't discovered until it was too late, despite warnings about the number of young Muslims from the Middle East signed up for US flight schools. (© *Sherburne County Sheriff's Office/Getty Images*)

Above right: 9/11 mastermind Khalid Sheikh Mohammed. This US government photograph shows KSM after his arrest in 2003. He has still not been brought to trial. (© *NY Daily News Archive via Getty Images*)

Below: Crisis summit. President George W. Bush meets with his friend Prince Bandar bin Sultan, Saudi Arabia's Ambassador to the USA, on 13 September on the Truman Balcony at the White House, along with Dick Cheney, Condoleezza Rice and Bandar's aide, Rihab Massoud. They were sending a message – that the special bond between the two nations was unbroken despite the fact that fifteen of the nineteen hijackers were Saudis.

Above left: The CIA chief. Former CIA Director George Tenet was adamant that the agency did everything in its power to prevent the 9/11 attacks.

Above right: The Cassandra of counterterrorism. The warnings of Richard Clarke, America's National Crisis Manager and head of counterterrorism at the time of 9/11, kept being ignored. He was not informed about the CIA operation involving Mihdhar and Hazmi, and now believes that the agency made a failed attempt to 'turn' the terrorists. (*© Scott J. Ferrell/Congressional Quarterly/Getty Images*)

Below left: Former FBI Special Agent Mark Rossini. Rossini is still tormented by the CIA order that prevented him from telling his FBI bosses that two al Qaeda terrorists were in America eighteen months before 9/11.

Below right: The commissioner. 9/11 Commission Director Philip Zelikow was given the job of connecting the dots around the attacks and putting an end to the speculation. But the 9/11 Commission Report only left more questions. (*© Chip Somodevilla/Getty Images*)

Above: The campaigner brother. Matt Campbell has been fighting for twenty years to learn the truth about how his brother, Geoff, died in the North Tower of the World Trade Center. In 2020 he launched a new campaign to have his brother's inquest reopened. In this photo, Matt is pictured centre, with Geoff, right, and their other brother, Rob, left.

Below left: The Jersey Girl. Kristen Breitweiser's husband Ronald died in the South Tower and she became one of the famous 'Jersey Girls' who forced President Bush into forming the 9/11 Commission to investigate the atrocity. She is seen here speaking at a press conference in Washington DC in September 2004. (© *Matthew Cavanaugh/Getty Images*)

Below right: 9/11 survivor Tim Frolich. He made it down from the upper reaches of the South Tower only to suffer a debilitating leg injury as he fled the collapsing building. Now he is one of the 9/11 victims leading the campaign to force the authorities to come clean about what really happened.

10.09 a.m. Two airliners have hit the Twin Towers, one crashed into the Pentagon and the other ended up in a Pennsylvania field and the military are still trying to get their fighters to the right place. Even if they had got there, they still didn't have permission to intercept.

Major Nasypany [NEADS]: One five two seven, mode 3, do we have a track number? 1527, mode 3 we got a track number?

Nasypany: OK, we got a mode 3 on this, ah, United 93.

Nasypany: How close are you?

(Background) Unknown: (Indistinct).

(Background) Senior ID Tech: (Indistinct) three nine five one north.

Nasypany: Three nine five one north.

(Background) Senior ID Tech: Zero seven eight four six west.

Nasypany: Zero seven eight four six west.

(Background) Senior ID Tech: This is the guy with the bomb on board.

Nasypany: Got it.

(Background) Unknown: I just got off the phone with the Colonel and he has one E3 on, that's on its way out here (indistinct).

Nasypany: Toledo was–look for him. Hey, I need a track number.

Nasypany: OK. Hey, Brian, OK, 2 Syracuse birds will be airborne in less than 20 minutes, any weapons?

(Background) Unknown: (Indistinct) near Pittsburg, mode 3, one five two seven.

Nasypany: We don't know. Just press with that.

(Background) Unknown: We have any committed on the one aircraft with a bomb on it?

Nasypany: We're gettin to it. We don't know where it is, we're gettin' track on it.

Unknown: Pass that to weapons.

Nasypany: Yeah. OK. Got it.

(Background) Unknown: United nine three, mode 3, one five two seven.

Nasypany: Negative, negative clearance to shoot.

Nasypany: Jamie?

(Background) Unknown: One five two seven Brian.

Nasypany: God dammit. Foxy?

Fox: I'm not really worried about code words.

Nasypany: Fuck the code words. That's perishable information. Negative clearance to fire. ID type, tail. Hey, let your guys know also.

10.11 a.m. Still trying to get the fighter jets off the ground.

Nasypany: Sir, how're you doing?

Syracuse Commanding Officer: I'm doin', well, as good as can be expected. Ah, I've got guys that will be launching in about 15 minutes.

Nasypany: Appreciate it. Are they loaded?

Syracuse CO: We've got hot guns, that's all I've got.

Nasypany: Hot guns, well that that's good enough for me, for the time being. Only words I've got, I've got another aircraft with a possible bomb on board. It's in, ah, Pennsylvania, York? approximate area.

Syracuse CO: Yeah, that's south.

Nasypany: Yeah, south of us, and there's also the possibility of another one that's possibly at Cleveland area.

Syracuse CO: OK. You have vectors on those?

Nasypany: Not yet. Looks like one, the one, over Cleveland turned around looks like he's headin' back. The guy down at York, Pennsylvania, he's heading north, northwest.

Syracuse CO: OK. We might be able to get those two.

Nasypany: Yeah, and the call sign for the guy in York is United 93, mode 3 of fifteen twenty seven.

Syracuse CO: OK, doesn't help us. We can't interrogate.

Nasypany: OK. I got, and I got this other guy out west, he's American.

(Background) Unknown: Who's that guy? Track just faded over Cleveland.

Nasypany: Excuse me. OK, I've got one that just faded over Cleveland, Delta eight niner, mode 3. Uh, I know that's not going to help you, but if you're talking to FAA they might be able to help you, thirteen oh four.

Syracuse CO: OK. When we get our guys airborne they are going to contact you on two six zero point nine, I've got two jets right now, do you need more than two?

Nasypany: Can you bring up two more?

Background Voice: Get four, sir.

Syracuse CO: Yep, yeah.

Nasypany: OK, thank you sir, and if you want to talk to Colonel, ah, Marr he is up at six four oh three, sir.

Syracuse CO: Thank you.

10.14 a.m. Washington air traffic controllers finally let NEADS military chiefs know that Flight 93 has crashed.

ID Tech [NEADS]: I also want to give you a heads up Washington.

Washington Center: Go ahead.

ID Tech: United nine three, have you got information on that yet?

Washington Center: Yeah, he's down.

ID Tech: He's down?

Washington Center: Yes.

ID Tech: When did he land?

Washington Center: He did not land.

ID Tech: He is down, down?

Washington Center: Somewhere northeast of Camp David.

ID Tech: Northeast of Camp David.

Washington Center: That's the last report, they don't know exactly where.

10.32 a.m. Belatedly, Mission Crew Commander Nasypany gets permission from Vice President Dick Cheney to shoot down civilian airliners.

Floor Leadership: You need to read this. Region Commander has declared that we can shoot down tracks if they are not responding to our, uh, directions.

MCC Position: OK. I'll pass that to weapons.

Floor Leadership: OK.

MCC Position: The Region Commander has declared that we can shoot down aircraft that do not respond to our direction. Copy that?

Weapons: Copy that sir.

MCC Position: So, if you're trying to divert somebody and he won't divert–

Major Fox: D-O is saying no.

MCC Position: No? It came over the chat. Foxy, you got a conflict on that, you got a conflict on that direction?

Fox: Right now, no, but–

MCC Position: OK.

Floor Leadership: Hey–

MCC Position: OK.

Floor Leadership: You read that from the Vice President, right? The Vice President has cleared–

MCC Position: Vice President has cleared us to intercept tracks–

Floor Leadership: Of interest–

MCC Position: And shoot them down if they do not respond, per CONR CC [The First Air Force, responsible for the USAF air defense mission].

11.03 a.m. The military jets are now in the air and ready for action. They do not know the threat has already passed and are told to be prepared to engage.

Controller: I told them our mission is to protect major centers and we're goin' to take you and drag you down to Pittsburgh, and do this, because I got a tanker comin' now. But, ah, I just want to give them an ROE because it's gonna' be auto-ops once he's down there. So I want to make sure I got clear concise words to him before he leaves. Granted they only got four turrets of guns.

(Background) Unknown: If they don't, ah, if they do not, don't respond to divert to hand signals and divert procedures and are headed toward a major area then you are cleared to engage.

Controller: Wilco.

Controller: Cobra and Apex, this is Huntress.

Cobra One: Huntress.

Huntress [NEADS]: OK, there is still a bit of traffic airborne, they're not all completely down, I imagine it's all low south of you, if you'll hold two loops before the tanker gets, ah, Oh, shit, I need a check list.

Cobra One: Cobra One copies.

Controller: OK, I have ah ROE instructions, are you ready to copy?

Cobra One. Stand by, Huntress.

Cobra One: This is, ah, Cobra One, go ahead.

Controller: OK the direction ah protectin' the major centers, when you're overhead the major center, be it Pittsburgh in this case, you're, you have intercept authority on any traffic in the area. And if, if the traffic does not respond to, ah, hand signals, divert procedures, anything like that, and they continue to press in a threatening manner towards the major center, you're cleared to engage.

Cobra One: Cobra copies.

Unknown: This is a new type of war, that's what it is.

Earlier, at 9.11 a.m., two US military surveillance techs try to make sense of it all.

Surveillance Tech 1: Is today like a national terrorist day or something that we missed out on?

Surveillance Tech 2: Actually, ah, this is a day (indistinct) for a long time.

Surveillance Tech 1: September 11th, 2001.

Chapter Twelve

The Brother

Lanzarote, Spain, 2.30 p.m., 11 September 2001

Matt Campbell was standing on a beach in Lanzarote when his world fell in.

He was relaxing in the sun with wife, Mel, their two girls, Esme, then two, and Phoebe, who was just six months, and his mother, Maureen, taking a break from his fast-paced life as an IT company boss in the City of London. It was an exciting time. His brother Geoff, younger by a year, worked for Reuters news agency in New York and was helping Matt explore expanding his business into the Big Apple. But first, Matt was taking his family on a sunshine break before going all steam ahead with the new venture.

At lunchtime on 11 September, 2001, their second Tuesday in Costa Teguise, a sandy resort on the east coast of the island, Mel took Phoebe for a walk, trying, like mothers everywhere, to get her baby daughter to settle down for a nap in her buggy. She was shocked to see locals and tourists huddled around TV sets in bars and restaurants watching footage playing over and over of a plane crashing into what looked like the World Trade Center.

Running back to where the rest of the family were sunning themselves on the beach, she told Matt and his mother what she had seen. 'Something seems to have happened in New York,' she said. And they worried, like the rest of the world, about the lives that may be lost and who was responsible for such a terrible thing. By the time they had gone over to see the TV for themselves, the second of the Twin Towers had collapsed. The commentary, however, was in Spanish, and the reception poor, so it was hard at first to tell exactly what had happened and even whether it was an accident or an act of terrorism.

The good thing, Matt reassured Maureen and Mel, was that Geoff's office was in Times Square in Midtown Manhattan, a safe distance away from the horror that was unfolding further south. There was no reason to worry unduly.

It was only when Matt called his partner, Henry, in London that the first seeds of fear began to grow in his mind. Matt didn't know it at the time, but Henry had just looked at an email from Geoff timed at 8.03 a.m. in New York,saying he was running late for a conference that was due to start at 8.30 a.m. at the Windows on the World restaurant on the 106th floor of the North Tower of the World Trade Center. Geoff was planning to network at the conference, put on by the London-based Risk Waters Group to discuss the latest financial technology. For now, Henry just told Matt he was trying to locate his brother.

Matt had left his mobile phone back in the hotel room, so he used a pay phone to try, unsuccessfully, to call first Geoff and then his Bostonian fiancée Caroline Burbank. He finally reached his other brother, Rob, who told him he had managed to talk to Caroline. He also broke the news to Matt that Geoff had, indeed, been at the Risk Waters conference in the North Tower, which he had just watched crashing to the ground on a beachside café TV.

'I just dropped the phone,' said Matt. 'That was the moment we realised that the worst had happened. We knew he had been in the building and had obviously gone to the conference and it was on the 106th floor. It's not like he was on the 20th floor and there was a good chance to get out. It wasn't 100 per cent at that point, but nobody could get hold of him. It didn't look good.'

The family would later discover that none of the eighty-one people who attended the conference from England, Canada, Japan and cities all over America survived.

But there was still hope that morning that maybe Geoff was running so late he didn't make the event in time; that maybe he was among the injured or had simply lost his phone in the chaos. As he called his father, who was taking a group of hikers on a walk in Wales, and made arrangements to fly to New York, Matt clung on to the hope that he could get a call any time saying that his brother was still alive. The call never came.

The Campbells flew back to the UK on Thursday and Reuters got Matt, Rob and their parents on one of the first flights over to New York on the Saturday. Most of the other families of the sixty-seven British victims of 9/11 would follow a day or two later.

Matt was given a glimmer of hope by an article in a British newspaper that said survivors were in hospitals unconscious or unable to speak, but it soon became clear, after visiting a hospital where the injured were being cared for, that very few of those left alive were unidentified. They joined the thousands of relatives left hoping against hope that their loved ones had been saved by some sort of miracle. Geoff was officially a missing person, but with each hour and each day that passed, his family had little choice but to accept that he was gone. 'I remember just sitting down on the kerb outside this hospital and just thinking that he was dead. I had to accept it,' said Matt. 'They were still digging, and it was too early to give up, but probably on the Sunday we knew.'

A police officer took a photograph of Matt with Caroline and Maureen at Ground Zero on the Wednesday. Caroline hasn't been back; it was simply too painful.

The trauma of being caught in fate's sliding doors was the overriding emotion then; the fading hopes and the realisation that the last time they each spoke to Geoff would be the last time they would ever get to hear his voice. The 'if only' thoughts that screamed through every quiet moment.

Matt met some friends in a noisy Manhattan pub full of firefighter families. 'I wasn't in a good space, but I liked beer and I wanted to talk to people about my brother, and I remember it being really busy and suddenly the whole place went quiet when Bush came on the television,' recalled Matt. 'I hadn't really been exposed to that big patriotic American thing and I just wasn't impressed. I found it really hard to listen to whatever nonsense he was saying.'

Matt had not yet thought too much about the events of 9/11; like most of us, he'd taken it largely at face value. The reality of what had happened to his family was still too raw, but perhaps this was when he first started questioning the leaders who were delivering the official narrative.

On the Friday, 21 September, nearly a week after they arrived in New York, the family met Prime Minister Tony Blair and former President Bill Clinton following a moving memorial service at St Thomas's Church in Manhattan for the British victims of the attacks. Blair gave a reading at the service, but Matt felt the prime minister lacked compassion in a meeting with the families afterwards. 'Blair was stiff, cold and useless,' he said. 'Mum burst into tears in front of him and Caroline gave an interview later saying he was a weak leader. We were not impressed.'

In stark contrast, Clinton, tall and demonstrative with his distinctive mop of silver-grey hair, wrapped Matt's brother Rob in a massive bear hug.

There was a memorial service back home on 30 September at Our Lady of Perpetual Succour, the Catholic church in Northampton where Matt and Mel were wed, that was packed to the rafters with family and friends and a 'Campbell-style piss-up wake' afterwards at the King Billy pub, where stories about Geoff, who packed a lifetime of success, travels and good memories into his thirty-one years, were toasted with champagne. Then Caroline, Matt and the rest of Geoff's loving family braced themselves for what would be the hardest part of all; trying to get on with their lives without him.

The problem for Matt was that he was becoming increasingly disturbed by the disparities in the official version of his brother's death. And the more time that passed after 9/11, the more questions he had. He understood that, in the confusing aftermath of the biggest attack on mainland America in its history, he wasn't going to get all the answers right away. But he never expected the British government to be so shamefully peremptory in their investigation into the deaths of sixty-seven citizens or the Americans to be so deceptive and secretive in telling their version of what happened.

It was around the beginning of November 2001 that Matt started feeling that he could no longer ignore the disquiet he felt over the way his brother's murder was being handled. His co-director, Henry, sent him an article by the pioneering former *Daily Mirror* Chief Foreign Correspondent John Pilger that touched a very raw nerve. It was published at the end of October, soon after the launch of the allied attack on the

Taliban in Afghanistan, and was titled: 'This War Is a Farce'. It started with:

'The war against terrorism is a fraud. After three weeks' bombing, not a single terrorist implicated in the attacks on America has been caught or killed in Afghanistan.

'Instead, one of the poorest, most stricken nations has been terrorised by the most powerful – to the point where American pilots have run out of dubious "military" targets and are now destroying mud houses, a hospital, Red Cross warehouses, lorries carrying refugees. Unlike the relentless pictures from New York, we are seeing almost nothing of this. Tony Blair has yet to tell us what the violent death of children – seven in one family – has to do with Osama bin Laden.'

Matt was struck by the issues raised in the article – and by how few of them had been raised in the mainstream media. 'None of those directly involved in the September 11 atrocity was Afghani,' continued Pilger. 'Most were Saudis, who apparently did their planning and training in Germany and the United States.

'The camps which the Taliban allowed bin Laden to use were emptied weeks ago. Moreover, the Taliban itself is a creation of the Americans and the British. In the 1980s, the tribal army that produced them was funded by the CIA and trained by the SAS to fight the Russians ...' Pilger didn't agree with the war in Afghanistan and was vituperative about Bush's War on Terror and the support offered by British Prime Minister Tony Blair. 'There is no war on terrorism. If there was, the Royal Marines and the SAS would be storming the beaches of Florida, where more CIA-funded terrorists, ex-Latin American dictators and torturers, are given refuge than anywhere on earth.

'There is, however, a continuing war of the powerful against the powerless, with new excuses, new hidden agendas, new lies. Before another child dies violently, or quietly from starvation, before new fanatics are created in both the east and the west, it is time for the people of Britain to make their voices heard and to stop this fraudulent war – and to demand the kind of bold, imaginative non-violent initiatives that require real political courage.

'The other day, the parents of Greg Rodriguez, a young man who died in the World Trade Center, said this: "We read enough of the news to sense that our government is heading in the direction of violent revenge, with the prospect of sons, daughters, parents, friends in distant lands dying, suffering, and nursing further grievances against us. It is not the way to go … not in our son's name."'

Matt began thinking more deeply about all the circumstances surrounding the attacks: how fifteen of the nineteen hijackers had Saudi Arabian passports; how America appeared to be building up for war before 9/11 even happened; and how many clues there appeared to have been in the lead-up to the attacks that were either ignored or disregarded.

That first Christmas was tough. Geoff had lived in Copenhagen and Istanbul before moving to America in 1999, so it wasn't the first holiday they had been apart. But this was different. There would be no coming back with stories from his travels. Geoff had been taken from them; it was hard not to feel bitter.

Up until this point, it was like Geoff had vanished into thin air. There was nothing left – even now, the families of more than 1,000 'vaporised' victims have not received any remains – and he was still, officially at least, a missing person.

But in June 2002, news came from New York that Geoff's shoulder blade had been formally identified. As a boy on holiday in Scotland, he had broken his collar bone and when she was told it had been found, a day before her birthday, Geoff's mother, Maureen, took it as a positive omen. In times of great loss, such are the things we hold on to.

Vacuum-packed in aluminium foil, the remain was flown over with a British police officer and handed to Geoff's family and Matt kept it at his house for two years until three more bone fragments – from his thigh, shoulder and part of his spine – were identified and sent on to England, where the family were finally able to hold a burial service at St John the Baptist's Church in Clayton, West Sussex. They laid thirty-one white roses on top of Geoff's casket for every year of his life. They were finally able to say goodbye.

But still, the feeling kept gnawing at Matt that things were not right. 'I felt that there was an element that the Americans had somehow let it happen, but I didn't know how to articulate that,' said Matt. 'I just started reading everything I could lay my hands on. It is insane looking back at my Amazon purchases. Almost anything with 9/11 in the title I was buying, even things like graphic novels, poetry and art.'

A bright light came with the birth of Mel and Matt's third daughter, Evi, in 2008, but Geoff's death had triggered a depression that his brother was having difficulty shaking off. While other members of the family tried to find some sort of closure, Matt was becoming increasingly consumed by the questions that continued to grow about 9/11.

War had been waged on countries the US claimed to be behind the attacks – although it quickly became clear that the Bush and Blair case against Iraq was irrevocably flawed – and yet not one individual involved in the mass murders in New York, Washington DC and Pennsylvania had been charged with a crime. It made no sense to Matt. 'I found myself going down the rabbit hole of conspiracies,' he admitted. 'I'm normally a quite happy, head in the clouds sort of person. The idea of me being depressed would seem ridiculous, but I guess that's probably true for a lot of people. I had lost a lot of weight and was into raw food and running and keeping healthy, but I was also drinking a fair bit and I probably spent a lot of time moaning about state-sponsored terrorism and things like that.'

By now, Matt had wound up his IT company in the City and moved with his family to Thailand in 2006, following in the footsteps of his brother, Rob. The family had also received some more remains. This time there were fragments of Geoff's scalp, hair, teeth and skin, offering some solace because the hair wasn't singed, meaning it was unlikely he had been caught in the infernos that erupted after the plane struck. That November in 2008, just before Evi's September birth, they had a second burial for Geoff.

In October 2011, the Campbells returned to England for good and Matt tried his best to get on with his life. He decided not to go to the January 2013 London inquest into the 9/11 deaths of ten UK victims, including his brother, fearing it would only frustrate him further. But he did get the audio from the inquest and a transcript of the proceedings. 'It was quite astonishing,' he said. 'You had the biggest-ever terrorist attack in America, involving a large number of British people and Europeans, and it was all done and dusted in about one hour and forty-five minutes.

'My brother was dealt with in about three minutes,' said Matt. 'You got the impression that the people who prepared the report for the coroner were just cutting and pasting the things the Americans said and that was it. They wrote down the wrong year of death for my brother and they got the flights going into the buildings confused, omitting the names of the

AA Flight 11 hijackers, fundamental things like that. It was very distressing to me to see how little was really done to find out what happened to my brother and the other victims.'

The ten deaths investigated by the coroner were the only ones of the sixty-seven who died to leave any remains, meaning the other families didn't even get this much.

Despite his scepticism over the official 9/11 narrative and the urging of his wife Mel to take action, rather than rage alone over the way his family and others had been misled, Matt had never gone public with his concerns. That was about to change.

The catalyst proved to be a court case in Horsham, about a twenty-minute drive from home in West Sussex, involving a 9/11 activist who was determined to make a very public stand in order to air his controversial views that the attacks were part of an establishment plot stretching across the Atlantic to involve not only the governments of Blair and Bush, but state-run corporations like the BBC.

About a hundred supporters – including Matt – turned up to Horsham Magistrates Court in February 2013 to see Tony Rooke, who was representing himself, argue that the reason he had not paid his TV licence was because he didn't want to give money to an organisation that, he said, was 'funding the practice of terrorism'.

His argument centred on a strange story from the BBC on the morning of 11 September that has long been promoted by some of the more extreme conspiracy theorists. Amid the chaos and confusion of events unfolding in New York, the BBC reported that 7 World Trade Center – the third building that collapsed in the wake of the planes hitting the Twin Towers – fell to the ground a full twenty minutes before it actually happened.

'I am withholding all funds from the BBC, the government

and subsidiaries under Section 15 of the Terrorism Act,' Rooke told a BBC inspector after refusing to pay his licence.

Rooke told the court: 'I believe the BBC, who are directly funded by the licence fee, are furthering the purposes of terrorism and I have incontrovertible evidence to this effect. I do not use this word lightly, given where I am.'

On the collapse of World Trade Center Building 7, he continued: 'The BBC reported it twenty minutes before it fell. They knew about it beforehand. Last time I was here I asked you (the judge): 'Were you aware of World Trade Center 7'?

'You said you had heard of it. Ten years later you should have more than heard of it. It's the BBC's job to inform the public. Especially of miracles of science and when laws of physics become suspended [one key aspect to his argument was the 2.25 seconds of freefall acceleration that scientists say could not have been caused by fire].

'They have made programmes making fools of and ridiculing those of us who believe in the laws of gravity. American reports have shown that the fall was nothing but a controlled demolition. I am not looking at who demolished it – that is impossible – but the BBC actively tried to hide this from the public.'

While the BBC put it down to an honest mistake made in the process of reporting a rapidly evolving live story, Rooke contended that the British broadcaster had prior knowledge of the building's collapse and that the cause was not the fires caused by the planes but controlled demolitions planted by shadowy state assassins. We will examine some of these perplexing conundrums, looking into how and why the three buildings fell into themselves so dramatically in more detail later but, needless to say, the Horsham magistrates weren't crazy about Rooke using the court to push his theories.

He won a moral victory in avoiding a big fine but was found guilty of watching his TV without a licence, given a six-month conditional discharge and told to pay £200 costs. District Judge Stephen Nicholls told Rooke: 'This is not a public inquiry into 9/11. This is an offence under Section 363 of the Communications Act.'

Matt was inspired enough to try the same thing two years later, but Hastings Magistrates Court refused to allow him to argue his case that the BBC was covering up the truth about 9/11 and he was advised to plead guilty by his lawyer and pay a £75 fine with £320 costs.

Undeterred, Matt sought a different path to force the authorities to take a more transparent look at 9/11 by seeking to re-open his brother's inquest.

Going public opened Matt up to the crazier fringe of the 9/11 Truther movement. Some suggested he was making the whole thing up, that there were no planes and the attacks were mocked-up using Hollywood green screens to create the iconic images of the Twin Towers being hit. Others accused him of being a government agent spreading 'lies' about his brother's death.

But in joining forces with the families of other UK victims and with activists seeking answers to the questions he had been asking, he at least felt like he wasn't alone any longer. He flew over to New York to meet with the forensic scientists still working painstakingly to identify the more than 7,000 body parts from 9/11 that had not been paired with a victim, and he went to Guantanamo Bay to see at first hand one of the pre-trial hearings involving alleged 9/11 mastermind Khalid Sheikh Mohammad and his al-Qaeda co-defendants Walid Muhammad Salih bin Mubarak bin Attash, Ramzi bin a-Shibh, Ali Abdul Aziz Ali and Mustafa Ahmed Adam al-Hawsawi.

There was a setback in his hopes for a new inquest with the death in October 2015 of Labour MP Michael Meacher, an outspoken critic of America's 9/11 response, who was helping him meet the legal requirements to petition the attorney general for the inquest to be re-opened. Matt needed to show that there was new evidence, that the investigation had not been sufficient or that there had been some kind of fraud.

He was certain the UK end of the 9/11 investigation hadn't gone nearly far enough and relied almost entirely on the findings of the American authorities, but he did learn there were nearly 363 boxes of documents related to the probe, codenamed Operation Exchange, in police storage. The report for the coroner had been prepared by DS Nigel Levitt (of Counter Terrorism Command/SO15), but Matt was unable to obtain a copy as it has been classified 'Exempt from Disclosure'. The public hasn't been allowed to see any of it.

'I don't expect to get all the answers,' said Matt, who is now working as a reflexologist in West Sussex. 'I don't have any faith in the American authorities to do the right thing and the legal process there is so expensive. I don't have any trust in the CIA or the FBI either, as they have been compromised.

'It's not beyond the realms of fantasy that explosives were planted in the buildings. Explosives were used in the 1993 World Trade Center bombings. You only have to read what thousands of architects and the engineers are saying about the government putting it down to structural failure. The Americans won't even provide, via a Freedom of Information request, the authenticated flight manifest for the plane that crashed into the North Tower and killed my brother. Why are they keeping so much from us? That's what I want to know.'

With the twentieth anniversary of his brother's death looming, Matt and his family decided to have another attempt at striking off Geoff's initial inquest and forcing the re-opening of another, more conclusive, hearing.

On 11 September 2020, Matt submitted an application under the 1988 UK Coroners Act to then Attorney General Suella Braverman, seeking her permission to apply to the High Court for an order granting a fresh inquest. He argued that the coroner's original findings – that the impact of the aircraft into the tower caused the building's total destruction – is contradicted by evidence suggesting the collapse may have been caused 'by the use of explosives and incendiaries'.

This time, Matt was represented by a top London barrister, Nick Stanage, an adviser to the United Nations on fair trial and human rights, who also sat as an Assistant Coroner and as a Legally Qualified Chair of Police Misconduct Hearings. His hope was that, if the Americans were going to continue to obfuscate the truth about 9/11, maybe he could force the British government to shake them up a little on behalf of their citizens who died that day. It didn't seem too much to ask.

'What I am still hoping is that the British authorities will have to explore the fact that there is so little to back up the official narrative,' he said. 'I just want them to do some work. And if it goes nowhere, it goes nowhere.

'I just want the same as everyone else – to be told the truth.'

Chapter Thirteen

The Firefighter

**New York City, 9.30 a.m.,
11 September 2001**

Pete Davidson was just eight years old when his father, Scott, climbed onto the Hook and Ladder 118 fire truck with his five buddies at Middagh Street firehouse in Brooklyn Heights and headed across the bridge towards the towering inferno that dominated the New York skyline.

The events of that terrible morning would shape the comedian's life in myriad ways, just as it would for the families of the other 342 firefighters who died as heroes trying to save the lives of others. There was pride, but of course there was also sorrow, a deep sense of loss in knowing that so many sons and fathers, daughters and wives, brothers and sisters, would never be coming home.

The call to 74 Middagh Street, the little, red-brick home of Engine Co. 205 and Hook and Ladder Co. 118, came moments after the second plane hit the World Trade Center. Without hesitating, Scott, thirty-three years old, joined fellow crew members Vernon Cherry, forty-nine, Leon Smith, forty-eight, Joey Agnello, thirty-five, Robert Regan, forty-five, and Pete Vega, thirty-six, on the fire truck, and they were on their way.

An iconic photo of the bright red truck speeding across the Brooklyn Bridge with the burning towers as a grim backdrop would be featured on the front page of the *New York Daily News* a few weeks later. By then, it was known that this was their last run.

Once across the bridge, Ladder 118 arrived at the Marriott World Trade Center Hotel and the six firefighters headed up the stairs into the doomed building. Any fear they may have felt was cast aside in the knowledge that so many lives were in jeopardy. As the debris-covered evacuees ran for their lives from the devastated buildings, the firefighters dashed deeper in.

They were last seen on the 15th floor in the North Tower, on the way up. Survivors remember seeing the six, the number 118 emblazoned on their helmets, running up the stairs into thick, black smoke just moments before the towers collapsed, crushing the hotel at 3 World Trade Center. More than 900 guests and scores of Marriott employees escaped, many with the help of the men of Ladder 118.

In a twist of fate, a falling body – one of the more than 200 people who jumped rather than face the inferno – fell on a fireman outside the Marriott and members of Engine Company 205, also based at Middagh Street, were taking him to an ambulance when the hotel was obliterated and their lives were saved.

Scott was a devoted dad to Peter and Casey, who was just four when he died, and known as a fiercely competitive sportsman with an equally fierce sense of humour. He had been a fireman since January 1994, a job he called the 'greatest in America'.

Saturday Night Live star Pete has acknowledged his own struggles with mental health, telling *Variety*: 'I've been in and out of mental health facilities since I was nine. I tried to drown myself in the pool when I was in the fourth or fifth grade. I was trying to get my head stuck in the ladder in the deep end, so I would not be able to get up. But I'm too much of a pussy, and my head is too small.'

But he also believes that the tragedy, happening when he was so young, helped set him on the path to fame. 'If my dad didn't die, I wouldn't be a comic,' he said. 'I'd be a construction worker in Staten Island or a basketball coach. I learned what death was. And you're not really supposed to learn about that until high school, when one of your friends falls asleep in the garage, or whatever … to learn how anything can just be taken away from you early gave me this sense of "Fuck it. Whatever, dude".

'I'm able to do stand-up and fuck around because hopefully the worst thing that has ever happened to me happened.'

At school, he pulled all his hair out until he was bald and told the *New York Times* in an interview that he became a 'lab rat' for doctors studying the effects of 9/11 on the children of the victims. 'It was overwhelming,' he told the *Times*. 'It was sad how sad he was growing up,' added his mother, Amy.

In memory of his dad, the comedian had the firefighter's badge number – 8418 – tattooed on his left forearm, a tribute also paid by his former girlfriend, pop star Arianna Grande, who got the numbers inked on the top of her foot.

Over the years, he has remembered his father on social media, once writing on Twitter: 'All jokes aside. There's not a day that goes by where I dont think of u. Ur my hero. Cant wait to see u again someday.'

Although his mother, Amy, is signed up to a lawsuit seeking answers about 9/11, Pete has little time for conspiracy theories or, as an Instagram post makes clear, for conspiracy theorists. After a trailer was released for *9/11*, a 2017 movie starring

Charlie Sheen and Whoopi Goldberg, he wrote: 'Spoiler alert: I know how it ends … I would respect this movie more if it had Vin Diesel driving a Lambo out of Tower 2 at the last second. F-ck this movie. NOT ONLY THAT BUT YOUR STAR OF THE MOVIE CHARLIE SHEEN IS A 9/11 CONSPIRACY THEORIST. YOU F-CK.'

He was right about one thing: Sheen was heavily involved at one time in the 9/11 Truther movement, speaking at a Los Angeles convention in 2006 with far-right radio host and conspiracy theorist Alex Jones and discussing his controversial views on network TV with late-night US chat-show host Jimmy Kimmel.

His theory, which would hit close to home for Pete Davidson and other family members who lost loved ones on 9/11, was that the collapse of the World Trade Center towers was the result of a controlled demolition rather than the heat from fires sparked by the planes and their tanks full of fuel.

'I know I got lot of heat for the opinions I had that weren't just my own,' Sheen told the *Hollywood Reporter* in 2017. 'I was not just coming up with stuff about 9/11. I was parroting those a lot smarter and a lot more experienced than myself, who had very similar questions. If I offended anyone, I apologise; and if I inspired anyone, then so be it.'

Unrepentant, he added: 'There are still a couple of things just rooted in simple physics that beg some measure of inquiry. I was in contact with a lot of family members and they were in concert with a lot of my questions.'

Sheen isn't the only celebrity to raise the issue in public. 'It is impossible for a building to fall the way it fell without explosives being involved,' actress and TV personality Rosie O'Donnell insisted in March 2007. 'For the first time in history, steel was melted by fire. It is physically impossible,' she said.

While few are going to be convinced by a daytime TV host and an actor with a reputation for outrageous behaviour, more than 3,300 architects and engineers have signed a petition calling for a new investigation into the collapses of the North and South Towers, as well as 7 World Trade Center. They claim to have gathered 'impeccable evidence' pointing to the theory of controlled demolition using explosives and incendiaries planted in advance and triggered all at once on the morning of 11 September.

The group, Architects and Engineers for 9/11 Truth, veers into muddier waters when it suggests that elements in the US government were part of a murderous cabal that planned the attacks to stoke outrage against Islamic terrorists and generate support for wars to boost America's footprint in one of the most geopolitically important regions in the world.

As we shall see later in this book, the US does have some form for concocting bogus plots to mislead foreign governments, but it is still difficult to see even the most voracious hawk in the Bush administration planning the deaths of nearly 3,000 innocent people, many of them Americans. The science, however, does offer an intriguing conundrum when you remove the burden of appointing blame, as does the first-hand evidence from emergency responders – especially from the fire services – who were convinced at the time that the towers were being blown up.

The memories of more than a hundred surviving firefighters, collected as oral histories by Thomas Von Essen, New York's Fire Commissioner on 11 September, point to the possibility of explosions being the critical factor in the collapses. They don't prove anything, but they certainly make interesting – and dramatic – reading. They are the recollections of those who were actually there, the ones that made it through. Here is a selection from the FDNY archives.

Richard Banaciski (South Tower): 'We were there, I don't know, maybe ten, fifteen minutes and then I just remember there was just an explosion. It seemed like on television they blow up these buildings. It seemed like it was going all the way around like a belt, all these explosions ... Not thinking that this building is coming down. We just thought there was going to be a big explosion, stuff was going to come down.'

Brian Becker (South Tower – as experienced from inside the North Tower): 'I'd say we were in the 30th or 31st, 32nd floor, or something like that, and a few of the guys were lying wiped out on the floor, you know, taking a break with their masks off and lying in the hallway, when there was a very loud roaring sound and a very loud explosion, and the – it felt like there was an explosion above us ...'

Richard Boeri (South Tower): 'We had our backs to the tower and under that pedestrian bridge, walking south, myself, Eddie Kennedy and the officer, when you heard the crackling. You looked up and you saw the one floor explode on itself and the top start to slide.'

Gregg Brady (North Tower): 'We were standing underneath and Captain Stone was speaking again. We heard – I heard three loud explosions. I look up and the North Tower is coming down now, 1 World Trade Center ... At that time, when I heard the three loud explosions, I started running west on Vesey Street towards the water.'

Timothy Burke (South Tower): 'Then the building popped, lower than the fire, which I learned was, I guess, the aviation fuel fell into the pit, and whatever floor it fell on, heated up really bad and that's why it popped at that floor. That's the rumour I heard. But it seemed like I was going, "Oh, my god, there is a secondary device", because the way the building popped, I thought it was an explosion.'

Edward Cachia, (South Tower): 'As my officer and I were looking at the South Tower, it just gave. It actually gave at a lower floor, not the floor where the plane hit, because we originally had thought there was like internal detonation explosives because it went in succession, boom, boom, boom, boom, and then the tower came down.'

Fernando Camacho (South Tower): 'As we came in through the revolving doors, the lights went out. A second or two later everything started to shake. You could hear explosions. We didn't know what it was. We thought it was just a small collapse. As I looked straight ahead of me, I saw total darkness. Everything was coming our way like a wave.'

Frank Campagna (North Tower): 'That's when it went. I looked back. You see three explosions and then the whole thing coming down. I turned my head, and everybody was scattering.'

Craig Carlsen (South Tower): 'I guess about three minutes later you just heard explosions coming from building two, the South Tower. It seemed like it took forever, but there were about ten explosions. At the time I didn't realise what it was. We realised later, after talking and finding out that it was the floors collapsing to where the plane had hit. We then realised the building started to come down.'

Dean Coutsouros (North Tower): 'I happened to be looking up at it, and from the fire floor down, it was just like a really loud crackling noise; it sounded like a million firecrackers, and just a wave, right from the fire floor down, just a wave that started to come down.'

Frank Cruthers (South Tower): 'And while I was still in that immediate area, the South Tower, 2 World Trade Center, there was what appeared to be at first an explosion. It appeared at the very top, simultaneously from all four sides, materials shot out horizontally. And then there seemed to be a momentary delay before you could see the beginning of the collapse.'

Paul Curran (South Tower – while low in the North Tower): 'With that, all a sudden the tower went completely – a horrendous noise, a very, very tremendous explosion, and a very heavy wind came through the tower. The wind almost knocked you down.'

Karin Deshore (South Tower): 'I had no clue what was going on. I never turned around because a sound came from somewhere that I never heard before. Some people compared it with an airplane. It was the worst sound of rolling sound, not a thunder. I can't explain it, what it was. All I know is – and a force started to come hit me in my back. I can't explain it. You had to be there. All I know is I had to run because I thought there was an explosion. I was unaware what was happening. I thought it was just a major explosion. I didn't know the building was collapsing ... I just felt like the darkness, the loneliness and being alone was the worst thing I ever experienced in my life and not being able to breathe. There was no air. Whatever this explosion was simply sucked all the oxygen out of the air. You couldn't breathe and the feeling of suffocation ...' (Then in the North Tower): 'Somewhere around the middle of the World Trade Center, there was this orange and red flash coming out. Initially it was just one flash. Then this flash just kept popping all the way around the building and that building had started to explode. The popping sound, and with each popping sound it was initially an orange and then red flash came out of the building, and then it would just go all around the building on both sides as far as I could see. These popping sounds and the explosions were getting bigger, going both up and down and then all around the building. I went inside and told everybody that the other building or there was an explosion occurring up there and I said I think we have another major explosion … So here these explosions are getting bigger and louder and bigger and louder, and I told everybody if this building totally explodes, still unaware that the other building had collapsed, I'm going in the water. I'm still standing there, trying to figure out what my next move should be, when the same sergeant says, "Fucking shit, it's coming at us", and that's a quote. Again, I didn't see what was happening behind me, but knowing of all the explosions I thought here was another explosion coming and this sound again and this wave of this force again.'

George DeSimone (North Tower): 'After that, I still thought it was an explosion. I thought it was some kind of thermal explosion where I'm either going to get burnt – and I had kind of ideas that it was going to be something like Hiroshima where all this heat was coming at me and we were going to get burnt – or if the heat didn't burn me, I thought that all the parts coming out of this building, the windows, metal, all the things like that, that I might be severed in half. I don't think we understood the magnitude of what was going on. I was fearful that there were bombs in the building. That was my first thought, being the military kind of guy that I am.'

Brian Dixon (South Tower): 'I was watching the fire, watching the people jump and hearing a noise and looking up and seeing – it actually looked – the lowest floor of fire in the South Tower actually looked like someone had planted explosives around it because the whole bottom I could see – I could see two sides of it and the other side – it just looked like that floor blew out. I looked up and you could actually see everything blew out on the one floor. I thought, geez, this looks like an explosion up there, it blew out. Then I guess in some sense of time we looked at it and realized, no, actually it just collapsed. That's what blew out the windows, not that there was an explosion there, but that windows blew out. As I just got in under the entrance there, I got just a little ways back and it was just like – you hear the noise, a boom, and then a blast of air.'

Michael Donovan (South Tower): 'I got up, I got into the parking garages, was knocked down by the percussion. I thought there had been an explosion or a bomb that they had blown up there.'

Robert Dorritie (South Tower): 'I guess we got about three-quarters of the way across when we were deciding which way to go into the South Tower. That's when I looked up, and the tower started coming down, which at the time I said I thought it was a secondary device. I had warned the guys about secondary devices on the way down.'

James Drury (South Tower): 'We were in the process of getting some rigs moved when I turned, as I heard a tremendous roar, explosion, and saw that the first of the two towers was starting to come down.' (North Tower): 'We started to hear the second roar. That was the North Tower now coming down. I should say that people in the street and myself included thought that the roar was so loud that the explosive – bombs were going off inside the building. Obviously, we were later proved wrong. Seeing that first tower come down was unbelievable. The sound it made. As I said, I thought the terrorists planted explosives somewhere in the building. That's how loud it was, crackling explosive, a wall.'

Christopher Fenyo (South Tower): 'About a couple minutes after George came back to me is when the South Tower, from our perspective, exploded from about midway up the building. We all turned and ran. At that point, a debate began to rage because the perception was that the building looked like it had been taken out with charges. We had really no concept of the damage on the east side of 2 World Trade Center at that point, and, at that point, many people had felt that possibly explosives had taken out 2 World Trade, and officers were gathering companies together and the officers were debating whether or not to go immediately back in or to see what was going to happen with 1 World Trade at that point. The debate ended pretty quickly because 1 World Trade came down.

Thomas Fitzpatrick (South Tower): 'All we saw was a puff of smoke coming from about two-thirds of the way up. Some people thought it was an explosion. I don't think I remember that. I remember seeing, it looked like sparkling around one specific layer of the building. I assume now that that was either windows starting to collapse like tinsel or something. Then the building started to come down. My initial reaction was that this was exactly the way it looks when they show you those implosions on TV. I would have to say for three or four seconds anyway, maybe longer. I was just watching.'

Gary Gates (South Tower): 'I looked up, and the building exploded, the building that we were very close to, which was one tower. The whole top came off like a volcano. So, the explosion, what I realised later, had to be the start of the collapse. It was the way the building appeared to blow out from both sides. I'm looking at the face of it, and all we see is the two sides of the building just blowing out and coming apart like this, as I said, like the top of a volcano.'

Jerry Gombo (South Tower): 'It felt sort of like an earthquake. The sky darkened and you heard this thunderous roar. It was like a volcano, if you will, not that I ever experienced a volcano, but I guess that's the way I could describe it, and this cloud just coming down. The ground was shaking and this roar …' (North Tower): 'No sooner did we get, I would say, several yards down Vesey Street, heading east to west when the second tower came down, and once again this huge mushroom cloud …'

Gerard Gorman (After both towers have collapsed): 'At that point I did not know the first building collapsed. Still didn't know. We thought it was a missile attack or something like that. We thought we were under attack. They didn't have any idea that this building could collapse. So, on the overhang, I remember seeing a frigging bomb squad cop and I asked him, "What the hell blew up?"'

Steve Grabher (South Tower): 'I looked over my shoulder and you could see the whole top of the South Tower leaning towards us. It looked like it was coming over. You could see the windows pop out just like in the picture, looked like a movie. I saw one floor of windows pop out, like poof, poof. I saw one and a half floors pop out. It looked almost like an explosion.'

Stephen Gregory (South Tower): 'At that point in time I called Manhattan. I was answered. I asked them if they were aware of an explosion at the World Trade Center. I told them basically what I thought had happened. I thought that when I looked in the direction of the Trade Center before it came down, before No. 2 came down, that I saw low-level flashes. In my conversation with Lieutenant Evangelista, never mentioning this to him, he questioned me and asked me if I saw low-level flashes in front of the building, and I agreed with him because I thought – at that time I didn't know what it was. I mean, it could have been as a result of the building collapsing, things exploding, but I saw a flash, flash, flash, and then it looked like the building came down. [It was] the lower level of the building. You know like when they demolish a building, how when they blow up a building, when it falls down? That's what I thought I saw. And I didn't broach the topic to him, but he asked me. He said, "I don't know if I'm crazy, but I just wanted to ask you because you were standing right next to me." He said, "Did you see anything by the building?" And I said, "What do you mean by see anything?" He said, "Did you see any flashes?" I said, "Yes, well, I thought it was just me." He said, "No, I saw them, too." I don't know if that means anything. I mean, I equate it to the building coming down and pushing things down; it could have been electrical explosions, it could have been whatever. But it's just strange that two people sort of say the same thing and neither one of us talked to each other about it. I mean, I don't know this guy from a hole in the wall. I was just standing next to him … I know about the explosion on the upper floors. This was like eye level. I didn't have to go like this. Because I was looking this way. I'm not going to say it was on the first floor or the second floor, but somewhere in that area I saw, to me, what appeared to be flashes.'

Gregg Hansson (North Tower): 'Then a large explosion took place. In my estimation, that was the tower coming down, but at that time I did not know what that was. I thought some type of bomb had gone off.'

Timothy Hoppey (South Tower): 'That's when we heard the rumble. I looked up, and it was just a black cloud directly overhead. At that point, I was thinking it was a secondary explosion. It looked to me like it was much lower than where the planes had gone in. I thought the top half of the building was falling off, and I was thinking of it falling outward, not really imploding upon itself like it did.'

Paul Hyland (North Tower): 'I just saw the top half of the North Tower sink and sort of just sat down on itself, sat down, and then just started shattering and just blowing out like a Christmas tree.'

Timothy Julian (South Tower): 'That's when I heard the building collapse. First, I thought it was an explosion. I thought maybe there was bomb on the plane, but delayed type of thing, you know, secondary device. You know, and I just heard like an explosion and, ah, then ah cracking type of noise, and then it sounded like a freight train, rumbling and picking up speed, and I remember I looked up, and I saw it coming …'

George Kozlowski (North Tower): 'As we were walking, we heard – we thought it was another plane coming. It was like a big shhhhh. A thousand times louder than that. It sounded like a missile coming and we just started booking. We took off like bats out of hell. We made it around the corner and that's when the shit hit the fan right then and there. We heard that loud and then ba-boom. I just – it was like an earthquake or whatever. A giant, giant explosion. Then this big gust came, and I just went flying, maybe thirty, forty feet. Tumbling. I got up, got on my hands and knees because all of the white shit was all over me. I just kept crawling. My ears were like deaf, you know, when you hear a giant firecracker or something.'

Kirk Long (South Tower, experienced from inside the North Tower): 'When the building shook, I was right next to an elevator shaft with Andy, crawling down the hallway. I was waiting for a flame to come up from the basement because I believed something in the basement blew up. Nothing like that happened, so I was waiting for a flame to come down from a plane. Nothing like that happened. Still, at that time, I never knew that the South Tower had gone down.'

Paul Mallery (South Tower): 'I said it sounds just like this, this is exactly what it sounds like, here's another one, thinking it was a third plane. Meanwhile the sound to me was four distinct events. They all sounded the same. The two plane crashes and the two collapses, except the collapses lasted longer. I don't know if this is nuclear attack. I don't know what this is any more.'

John Malley (South Tower): 'As we walked through those revolving doors, that's when we felt the rumble. I felt the rumbling, and then I felt the force coming at me. I was like, what the hell is that? In my mind it was a bomb going off. The pressure got so great, I stepped back behind the columns separating the revolving doors. Then the force just blew past me. It blew past me, it seemed, for a long time. In my mind, I was saying, what the hell is this and when is it going to stop? Then it finally stopped, that pressure which I thought was a concussion of an explosion. It turns out it was the down pressure wind of the floors collapsing on top of each other.'

Julio Marrero (South Tower): 'I heard a loud bang. We looked up, and we just saw the building starting to collapse. I looked over and started to scream at my partner, which he was inside the vehicle … I was screaming from the top of my lungs, and I must have been about ten feet away from her and she couldn't even hear me, because the building was so loud, the explosion, that she couldn't even hear me.' (North Tower): 'That's when I just broke down and cried at Bellevue Hospital, because it was just so overwhelming. I just knew that what happened was horrific. It was a bombing.'

James McKinley (South Tower): 'Then all of a sudden I heard this huge explosion. I didn't know what it was 'cause nobody was telling me anything … I was this close to it, and I didn't know what was going on. After that, I heard this huge explosion; I thought it was a boiler exploding or something. Next thing you know, this huge cloud of smoke is coming at us, so we're running.'

Joseph Meola (South Tower): 'As we are looking up at the building, what I saw was, it looked like the building was blowing out on all four sides. We actually heard the pops. Didn't realize it was the falling – you know, you heard the pops of the building. You thought it was just blowing out.'

Craig Monahan (South Tower): 'When it sounded like the explosion stopped, the steel hitting, when it all seemed to stop, this just like a fire storm of wind and material, a sandstorm kind of, just came and wailed by, really flew past us quick.'

Keith Murphy (South Tower, as experienced from the ground floor of the North Tower): 'I had heard right before the lights went out, I had heard a distant boom, boom, boom, sounded like three explosions. I don't know what it was. At the time, I would have said they sounded like bombs, but it was boom, boom, boom, and then the lights all go out. I hear someone say, "Oh, shit", that was just for the lights out. I would say about three, four seconds, all of a sudden this tremendous roar. It sounded like being in a tunnel with the train coming at you. It sounded like nothing I had ever heard in my life, but it didn't sound good. All of a sudden, I could feel the floor started to shake and sway. We were being thrown like literally off our feet, side to side, getting banged around and then a tremendous wind started to happen. It probably lasted maybe fifeen seconds, ten to fifteen seconds. It seemed like a hurricane force wind. It would blow you off your feet ...'

Michael Ober (South Tower): 'Then we heard a rumble, some twisting metal; we looked up in the air, and to be totally honest, at first, I don't know exactly ... but it looked to me just like an explosion. It didn't look like the building was coming down, it looked like just one floor had blown completely outside of it ... After hearing this and looking up and seeing the building, what I thought was an explosion, everyone was running ...'

Janice Olszewski (South Tower): 'I didn't think it was safe. I didn't know what was going on. I thought more could be happening down there. I didn't know if it was an explosion. I didn't know it was collapse at that point. I thought it was an explosion or secondary device, a bomb, the jet-plane exploding, whatever.'

Thomas Piambino (South Tower): 'The South Tower had fallen, but at that time I didn't know what it was. All I heard was a tremendous explosion. The tower I was in shook really bad.' (North Tower): '... and then the North Tower started to fall, and my perception was that, when I looked back at the tower as it was starting to come down, – I was booking – was that there was, I thought it exploded, and I didn't realise it had collapsed. It looked to me like an explosion ... I wound up taking refuge behind an ESU truck, I believe it was, a Police

Department ESU [Emergency Service Unit] truck, I think, and I just rode it out until first there was the explosion or the concussion, and then there was very, very strong wind, and then there was the black …'

John Picarello (South Tower): 'In about a second or two, you just heard like a ba-ba-ba-boom, and everything just came down and everything was pitch black.'

Angel Rivera (South Tower, experienced from inside the Marriott Hotel): 'When we hit the 19th floor, something horrendous happened. It was like a bomb went off. We thought we were dead. The whole building shook. The brick coming out of – the door to the hallway into the hotel blew off like somebody had thrown it all over the place. It shook all over the place. We were thrown on the floor … The building was still shaking and we're still hearing explosions going on everywhere, so we decided, let's get out of here.' (North Tower, again, from inside the Marriott): 'Mike Mullan walked one flight up, and then the most horrendous thing happened. That's when hell came down. It was like a huge, enormous explosion. I still can hear it. Everything shook. Everything went black. The wind rushed, very slowly [sound], all the dust, all the – and everything went dark. We were rolling all over the floor, banging against the walls. When the second tower came down, we had no idea what was going on. We thought another plane, another bomb, another as a second device.'

Daniel Rivera (South Tower): 'Then that's when I kept on walking close to the South Tower and that's when that building collapsed. It was a frigging noise. At first, I thought it was – do you ever see professional demolition where they set the charges on certain floors and then you hear, "pop, pop, pop,

pop, pop"? That's exactly what – because I thought it was that. When I heard that frigging noise, that's when I saw the building coming down.'

Terence Rivera (South Tower): 'As I run towards it, I know that I'm not going to escape the – escape it, so I dive under – I don't know even know which rig it was. I dive under a rig. At the same time, it felt like an explosion. I got bounced around underneath the rig.'

Kenneth Rogers (South Tower): 'We were standing there with about five companies and we were just waiting for our assignment, and then there was an explosion in the South Tower, which according to this map, this exposure just blew out in flames. A lot of guys left at that point. I kept watching. Floor after floor after floor. One floor under another, after another, and when it hit about the fifth floor, I figured it was a bomb, because it looked like a synchronised deliberate kind of thing.'

Anthony Salerno (North Tower): 'Putting out all those fires, in that interim, the second building had come down. I remember hearing a lot of explosions, the street turning completely grey, grey clouds of smoke all over the place. Everybody had stopped what they were doing and ran back up the block.'

Howie Scott (South Tower): 'We just made our turn to go in towards the lobby of tower two. For whatever reason, I just happened to look up and saw the whole thing coming down, pancaking down, and the explosion, blowing out about halfway up.'

Richard Smiouskas (South Tower): 'All of a sudden there was this groaning sound like a roar, grrrr. The ground started to shake … It looked like an earthquake. The ground was shaking. I fell to the floor. My camera bag opened up. The cameras went skidding across the floor. The windows started exploding in. I didn't know exactly what was going on outside. I'm thinking maybe the building snapped in half. I'm thinking maybe a bomb blew up. I'm thinking it could have been a nuclear.'

Frank Sweeney (South Tower): 'I bent over to pick up the hose, and I hear what sounded like firecrackers and a low rumble. I look up, and the South Tower – I could see the top part of the siding overlapping the bottom side of the siding … I ran …'

Jay Swithers (South Tower): 'I took a quick glance at the building and while I didn't see it falling, I saw a large section of it blasting out, which led me to believe it was just an explosion. I thought it was a secondary device, but I knew that we had to go.'

David Timothy (North Tower): 'The next thing I knew, you started hearing more explosions. I guess this is when the second tower started coming down.'

Thomas Turilli (South Tower): 'The door closed [in an elevator], they went up, and it just seemed a couple seconds and all of a sudden you just heard like it almost actually that day sounded like bombs going off, like boom, boom, boom, like seven or eight, and then just a huge wind …'

Thomas Vallebuona (South Tower): 'I heard "boom", an exploding sound, a real loud bang. I looked up, and I could see the Trade Center starting to come down, the South Tower, which I guess I was about a block away from. (North Tower):

'And "ba-boom" again, the same sound, the same noise, the same shuddering, shrilling noise of the metal falling as it cascades down.'

James Walsh (North Tower): 'The building didn't fall the way you would think tall buildings would fall. Pretty much, it looked like it imploded on itself.'

If the eyewitness accounts reflect the shock and confusion of the firefighters as they tried to understand what was happening around them, it was hardly surprising; nothing like it had ever happened before. A steel-framed skyscraper had never suffered a complete collapse because of a fire or a number of fires.

The question was obvious – was fire the real reason for such a calamitous collapse?

According to the official narrative, the answer was yes. It's definitely the easy option, avoiding any uncomfortable issues raised by the alternatives.

First on the scene were experts from the Federal Emergency Management Agency (FEMA) and the American Society of Civil Engineers (ASCE), who were tasked to explain what happened and make recommendations to ensure nothing like it could ever happen again.

The FEMA report, published in May 2002, blamed the fires sparked by the fuel-filled planes for causing sufficient structural damage to ultimately bring down the towers, but even its authors admitted a closer look may be needed because of their lack of access and authority, and the apparent hindrance by the FBI and the National Transportation Safety Board, the body responsible for investigating air crashes.

As a result, in October 2002, President Bush agreed to a congressional plan to give wider powers for a second, more exhaustive inquiry by the Maryland-based National Institute of Standards and Technology (NIST), which at least had some experience of investigating past building failures.

Their findings concluded that although a fire should not have been able to bring down a 110-storey building – that's what happened. The reason, they said, was that it wasn't a conventional fire but involved massive impact from the planes, which damaged the structure of the building and its fireproofing insulation. The NIST report said the floors, their fireproofing voided by the extreme temperatures, sagged and caused the girders to fall in and the exterior walls to buckle. With the core columns severed by the impact of the planes, the result was that the outside walls eventually caved in on themselves and fell like a house of cards.

Then we have the mysterious collapse of World Trade Center Building 7, which wasn't hit by any planes, but was supposedly set ablaze by flames from the neighbouring towers. NIST cited the firefighters' inability to stop fires from burning on six floors for the failure of the fireproofing. The steel columns, trusses and girders eventually bowed in the extreme heat and the forty-seven-storey building was brought down seven hours after the Twin Towers.

This is the building collapse that the BBC reported before it actually happened and that has been at the heart of conspiracy theories that 9/11 went much deeper than a renegade band of terrorists doing the bidding of a terrorist kingpin with a grudge against the West.

If you really believe that the power elite in Washington had a hand in America's worst-ever domestic terror attack, then this is the one for you.

Chapter Fourteen

The War on Gravity

Building 7, World Trade Center, 5.21 p.m.,
11 September 2001

The road to Damascus for Richard Gage was closer to California's iconic Pacific Coast Highway, a full 6,000 miles from the ruins of the World Trade Center. Up until 29 March 2006, his work as an architect would have been more concerned with designing buildings to resist earthquakes in the Golden State than terrorist attacks in the Big Apple.

A dyed-in-the-wool Ronald Reagan Republican, he hadn't thought to question the official 9/11 narrative and supported the War on Terror 'to get those bastards that did this to us'.

Driving home from a construction meeting that spring afternoon, Gage switched the radio station to a talk show featuring 9/11 researcher David Ray Griffin, a retired American theology professor, who was discussing the firefighter testimonies (see pages 188–203), offering first-hand accounts of explosions going off in the World Trade Center in the hours after the planes hit the North and South Towers. He was, quite simply, blown away by the interview, so much so that he had to pull over and try to digest what he heard. Griffin had struck a deep nerve in the mild-mannered architect, who suddenly started questioning everything he thought he knew about 11 September.

Right there, sitting stunned by the side of the road, Gage resolved to use his expertise to discover the truth about how and why some of the world's highest buildings would fall as fast as a bowling ball. The government's explanation, he quickly decided, defied nature, science and common sense.

He went to see Griffin speak a couple of days later in Oakland and started making his own inquiries, eventually making a presentation to the fifteen other architects in his firm. They thought he was 'nuts' when he first spoke of the evidence that bombs had been planted in the towers. But by the end of the presentation, all fifteen agreed with his conclusions.

Gage has spent the intervening years speaking around the world, seeking wider audiences for his views and those of the organisation he founded, Architects and Engineers for 9/11 Truth, about what they are convinced is the truth about the three World Trade Center towers. He is unapologetic about the evidence, despite being dismissed by some as a conspiracy theorist. He says he has no alternative, knowing that controlled demolition – that is, bombs – was the actual cause of the destruction of the towers.

But it is Building 7, the third tower to collapse on 9/11, that consumes him above all else. It is, he insists, the smoking gun to the 'crime of the century'.

It's hard to believe that the total collapse of a reddish granite-fronted, forty-seven-storey building next to the World Trade Center housing, among others, the US Secret Service, the CIA, the Department of Defense, the Securities and Exchange Commission and New York City's emergency command centre, could end up a footnote in history.

Most people would tell you that the Twin Towers and the

Pentagon in Washington DC were destroyed on 11 September 2001. Many would forget that 7 World Trade Center also dropped like a rock in seven seconds, symmetrically into its own footprint, that same day in one of the biggest riddles of 9/11, whether or not you believe in any conspiracy theories. Its destruction didn't even get a mention in the 9/11 Commission's official report.

How could a 610-foot-tall (190-metre-tall) building, with 1,868,000 square feet of office space – one of the biggest in the city – collapse into itself in seven seconds of freefall? The Twin Towers fell, first the South and then the North, soon after being hit by the hijacked planes, American Airlines Flight 11 and United Airlines Flight 175.

World Trade Center Building 7 collapsed later that day at 5.21 p.m., without being hit by a plane, only debris fired out as the North Tower cascaded to the ground 370 feet away.

The debris started small fires on several floors that were allowed to burn throughout the day and firefighters, hindered by poor water pressure and stretched to breaking point across the plaza in the Twin Tower rescues, were powerless to stop them. According to the NIST investigation, it was the fires and not the structural damage caused by the impact of the debris on the south side of the building that caused the eventual collapse. Floor beams expanded to push a main girder off its seat on the 13th floor, causing the nine floors below to crash to the 5th floor, which caused columns to buckle.

Other than an alleged but unproven bulge in the southwest corner between the 10th and 13th floors, none of this could be seen from outside the building. There didn't appear to be too much to worry about once the people were evacuated safely. There was so much to worry about elsewhere. Fire chiefs were told that the building had structural damage and was at risk of collapse. The NIST findings made WTC 7 the only steel skyscraper to have ever collapsed as the result of fire alone.

The unprecedented, precipitous collapse of all three skyscrapers triggered alternative theories right from the start. The most controversial – and enduring – is the insistence that the explosions heard by hundreds of people, including the emergency service workers at the scene, were caused by pre-planted explosives which, in the case of the North and South Towers, were detonated an hour or so after the point the hijacked planes struck.

Specifically, Richard Gage and his followers claim that evidence of the incendiary nano-thermite was found in the World Trade Center dust; sophisticated, ignitable material that, as he puts it, is 'made in the most advanced defence-contracting laboratories, not in a cave in Afghanistan'.

Although it was the second to be hit, the South Tower fell first, 56 minutes after impact. It was 102 minutes before the North Tower collapsed. The pride of America – an architectural marvel that was once the tallest in the world (the North Tower was 1,368 feet (417 metres) tall and the South Tower was just behind at 1,362 feet (415.1 metres)) – was no more.

When the Twin Towers were completed to great fanfare in 1973, the engineers boasted they could withstand the impact of a Boeing 707. Not even in their worst nightmares could they ever have conceived that two Boing 767s with tanks full of fuel and travelling at 590 miles per hour (UA Flight 175) and 475 miles per hour (AA Flight 11) would crash into them twenty-eight years later. The official version claims jet fuel poured down the lift shafts, sending fires that were raging on the upper floors swiftly down the building.

But Gage and Architects and Engineers for 9/11 Truth point to comments made by John Skilling, the World Trade Center's chief structural engineer, who told the *Seattle Times* in 1993 that even the extremely unlikely possibility of a jet colliding with the building had been taken into account in its design.

'We looked at every possible thing we could think of that could happen to the buildings, even to the extent of an airplane hitting the side,' Skilling told the *Seattle Times*. 'However, back in those days people didn't think about terrorists very much.

'Our analysis indicated the biggest problem would be the fact that all the fuel [from the plane] would dump into the building. There would be a horrendous fire. A lot of people would be killed [but] the building structure would still be there.'

He said at the time that he did not believe a single 200-pound car bomb would bring the towers down because the columns were closely spaced, so that if some were destroyed, the others could still support the load.

'However,' he said in the interview following the first World Trade Center bombing in 1993, 'I'm not saying that properly applied explosives – shaped explosives – of that magnitude could not do a tremendous amount of damage. I would imagine that, if you took the top expert in that type of work and gave him the assignment of bringing these buildings down with explosives, I would bet that he could do it.'

NIST blamed the fireproofing failure amid the blazes, which it says were burning at 1,800°F (982°C) – and it is the temperature that is key to the argument over the structural failure.

Those espousing the controlled demolition theory point to what they insist is overwhelming evidence. Melting steel requires heat exceeding 2,800°F (1,538°C) and up to 4,000°F (2,200°C) – more than four times the temperatures at which jet fuel burns, which, according to its manufacturer, ME Petroleum, is only 600°F (316°C).

The only possible explanation for the extreme temperatures is thermite and nano-thermite, says Gage, who points to the discovery of particles of the incendiaries found in the World Trade Center dust, as documented in the FEMA report and other official studies. According to Architects and Engineers for 9/11 Truth, thermite is a mixture of one metal, usually aluminium (Al), with the oxide of another metal, usually iron oxide (Fe_2O_3), in a granular or powder form. When ignited, the energetic Al–Fe thermite reacts and produces molten iron and aluminum oxide, with the molten iron reaching temperatures well in excess of 4,000°F (2,200°C). Nano-thermite, it adds, is an ultra-fine-grained variant of thermite that can be formulated to be explosive by adding gas-releasing substances.

The government's experts claim, however, that the steel in the buildings needn't have melted altogether; just weakened, for which a lower temperature would be sufficient. Besides, they argued, the fires were also fuelled by office furniture, computers, piles of paper and curtains that would have sent the temperatures soaring even higher, perhaps high enough to warp steel girders.

Whether the cracks and pops and blasts and puffs of smoke that were seen and heard by eyewitnesses in both towers were caused by the unique combination of circumstances as the building burned is arguable.

World Trade Center Building 7 feels harder to explain, maybe because pictures of its downfall look so similar to controlled demolitions on TV. Truthers point to a comment from Larry Silverstein, the owner of the building, who said it should be 'pulled' because of the raging fires.

'I remember getting a call from the fire commander telling me they were not sure they were going to be able to contain the fire,' he told PBS in the documentary *America Rebuilds: A Year at Ground Zero*. 'I said, "You know we've had such terrible loss of life, the smartest thing to do is pull it," and they made that decision to pull and then we watched the building collapse.' He later clarified that he meant the fire crews should be pulled from the building in case it collapsed.

Gage argues that both FEMA and NIST declared that no firefighting operations were undertaken in WTC 7 on 11 September.

NIST lead investigator Shyam Sunder, unveiling the institute's 'final word' on WTC 7 at a press conference in Gaithersburg, Maryland, told journalists: 'Our take-home message today is that the reason for the collapse of World Trade Center 7 is no longer a mystery. WTC 7 collapsed because of fires fuelled by office furnishings. It did not collapse from explosives or from diesel fuel fires.'

Claiming the collapse was the result of an 'extraordinary event', he added, 'For the first time, we have shown that fire can induce a progressive collapse.' The report claimed that explosive blasts 'would have resulted in a sound level of 130 dB [decibels] to 140 dB at a distance of at least half a mile', but none that loud were either reported or caught on tape.

Undeterred, Gage and his Architects and Engineers for 9/11 Truth, in particular, refused to accept the NIST findings, and they funded a four-year computer modelling study by researchers at the University of Alaska Fairbanks (UAF) in the hope that it would clarify the truth.

Revealing the results of the draft report in 2019, UAF civil engineering professor Leroy Hulsey, the study's principal investigator, claimed: 'Our study found that the fires in WTC 7 could not have caused the collapse that was recorded on video. We simulated every plausible scenario, and we found that the series of failures that NIST claimed triggered a progressive collapse of the entire structure could not have occurred. The only thing that could have brought this structure down in the manner observed on 9/11 is the near-simultaneous failure of every column in the building below floor 17.'

The study essentially claims there were several fundamental engineering flaws in the NIST report. Some of these were concerning the heat generated by the fire and the stiffness of the building, as well as key structural elements omitted by NIST.

'Fires could not have caused weakening of displacement of structural members capable of initiating any of the hypothetical local failures alleged to have triggered the total collapse of the building,' the study says. 'Nor could any local failures, even if they had occurred, have triggered a sequence of failures that would have resulted in the observed total collapse.'

The 125-page UAF report argued that the free-fall collapse was the result of a sudden event, rather than a progressive collapse triggered by a failure of one column in the building causing subsequent sequential failure.

'In a typical building collapse (given a localised structural steel failure), WTC 7 would be expected to experience a combination of axial rotation and bending of members, resulting in a disjointed, asymmetrical collapse at less than free-fall acceleration,' it adds.

As a result of the findings, the group, backed by eighty-eight architects and structural engineers and ten 9/11 family members, demanded in 2020 that NIST reversed its 'outlandish' decision that fires alone caused the destruction of Building 7.

They argue that it defies nature to believe that fires caused Building 7 to collapse into its own footprint, free-falling more than a hundred feet at the rate of gravity for two-and-a-half seconds of its seven-second destruction.

To Richard Gage, the results of the study were yet another vindication of his Damascus moment back in 2006. 'You have a major university study proving that the official narrative is false, that this building could not have come down by fire alone, that in order to bring that building down, the study concludes that you'd have to have all eighty columns being removed within a second of each other. How the hell does fire do that?' he asked.

Regarding the Twin Towers, before you get to the question of why anyone would want to hide explosives in those towers while also planning to use hijacked planes as guided missiles, you have to wonder how the perpetrators were able to plant them at strategic spots in the buildings.

Gage speculates that construction workers renovating the lifts had the perfect opportunity. 'What we know is that [in] the nine months prior to 9/11, there was the largest elevator modernisation going on in the world,' said Gage, who claimed that outside operatives could have gained access while the work was being carried out 'because the elevators ran immediately next to those columns'.

He is not alone in suggesting that the lift renovations may have offered a possible cover for would-be bombers, but there is no evidence that the elevator company or any of its employees had any involvement in suspicious activity. There is little that the government experts can do in order to convince their detractors, and the same is true in reverse. All that remains of the 43,000 windows in the Twin Towers is a tiny shard of glass the size of a box of matches.

The 104-storey Freedom Tower, with an enormous 408-foot steel spire antenna, now rises out of the ashes of the Twin Towers and a new 52-floor WTC 7 replaced the demolished original in 2006. You can pick your side in the ongoing debate over how the towers fell, but you will only get a clear sense of what really happened by listening to Richard Gage and people like him – serious, informed people with a real expertise in these complex issues – and carefully examining the evidence they continue to present that controlled demolitions, and not fires, brought down the World Trade Center buildings.

The conundrum for many is that if you agree with Gage and Architects and Engineers for 9/11 Truth, then you must open your mind to some even more disturbing questions. Who would do such a thing? And why?

Gage posed this question to me, as he would to anyone reading this book. 'Do you have the courage to do it, though?' He insists there is an immense groundswell of support from the public, not just in America but around the world. 'There are millions who agree with the obvious truth, backed by evidence, that we're talking about today in the 9/11 Truth movement,' he said. 'There are fewer among elected representatives and almost no one in the mainstream media willing to talk about this.'

He insists 9/11 was a 'false flag' operation, with one party, presumably a faction of the US government, trying to pin the blame on another, Osama bin Laden, for its own devious ends. 'It's a passion and mission for me personally, and for those of us within the 9/11 Truth movement, who are working day and night, trying to expose this to the American people and wake them up,' he says. 'We're very hopeful. More and more people are becoming aware of the 'false flag' attack of COVID-19, with this engineered virus and the fear-mongering and control of the people through the propaganda. It's helping to wake people up.

'All people have to do is to follow the evidence.'

Chapter Fifteen

The Survivor

South Tower, World Trade Center, 9.03 a.m.,
11 September 2001

Tim Frolich loved the sweeping views from the window by his desk on the 80th floor of the South Tower of the World Trade Center, especially with the cobalt blue sky on a late summer morning like this one. But when he saw the flames and smoke billowing from the North Tower, just 200 feet across the New York skyline, he knew something was terribly wrong. The Fuji Bank accountant had no way of knowing that America was under attack. He certainly never dreamed that before the morning was out, both the Twin Towers would be reduced to rubble. All he knew in that moment was that he had to act fast and get his fellow bank employees down to safety.

As a volunteer fire warden for his floor, Tim wanted to do all he could to get his colleagues away from the threat of danger as fast as possible. That meant going up Stairway A to the 81st and 82nd floors to advise other members of the Japanese-owned bank's staff that they should head down.

One of the costliest mistakes made in the immediate aftermath of the disaster was the instruction from emergency services to stay in place and wait for help, rather than to evacuate the burning buildings. Countless lives would be lost in both towers as a result. Some managed to get all the way down to the bottom of the South Tower, only to be told to go back up again to their offices and wait to be told what to do. Many of those victims perished needlessly.

The Port Authority, which ran the buildings, had told Tim and his fellow fire warden, via walkie-talkie, to ensure people stayed at their desks, insisting it was a 'controlled situation' in the North Tower and that there was nothing to worry about for people across the way in the South Tower. They disagreed and quickly decided to get their staff down as quickly as possible. Some of Fuji Bank's senior managers, worried about going against the official advice, decided to stay put.

Having helped the rest of the bank staff towards the stairs, Tim joined the slow-moving queue, progressing in barely suppressed panic downward, pausing briefly back on the 80th floor to see if there were any more instructions, or, at least, some advice that made more sense to them. At just before 9 a.m., an announcement over the South Tower's public address system declared the building 'secure' and told workers to return to their offices. Tim preferred to keep moving down.

Exhausted, the accountant moved out of the stairwell to take a break on the 60th floor. That was when United Airlines Flight 175 hit the South Tower, knocking him off his feet and sending the roof tumbling down around him, dust and debris everywhere. He was just able to see his friend across the floor and crawled back to the stairs where he could catch a breath and get back to his feet.

The plane struck the South Tower at 9.03 a.m. between floors 77 and 85 – exactly where Tim would have been if he had decided to follow orders and remain at his desk. Nearly 2,000 people were at or above the points of impact in the two towers. Only eighteen of those survived.

Tim and his fellow fire wardens successfully evacuated 120 members of the Fuji Bank staff from their offices on the 79th through to the 82nd floors of the South Tower. The twenty-three who remained or returned to their desks died in the attack.

Descending again, Tim came upon a woman who worked at Morgan Stanley, who suffered from asthma and was having a severe panic attack. He stood with her as the waves of evacuees flooded past them to safety. Slowly, they edged down through the floors, knowing that every step took them a little closer to survival.

Finally, exiting through the lobby, Tim emerged blinking into the sunlight, his eyes burning from the smoke. As a medic rinsed his eyes and he began to realise the immensity of his escape, there was a monstrous rumble from behind him.

'Run for your life!,' the medic shouted, and Tim forgot his tired legs and lurched as fast as he could away from the Twin Towers along Fulton Street, chased by a giant black cloud. Unable to see anything in the sudden darkness and engulfed by a hurricane of deafening sound and objects falling all around him, his life was once again hanging by a thread.

Then a hand came out and shoved Tim into the Millennium Hotel and both he and the New York City firefighter who pulled him off the street tumbled down a flight of stairs. As soon as he fell, Tim felt his left foot and ankle snap like twigs.

The fireman went for help and returned thirty minutes later with another firefighter and a Port Authority police officer, Captain Kathy Mazza, who together lifted him up the stairs and set him down to wait for an ambulance.

Although he has had a series of surgeries to repair the

serious nerve damage in his left foot and ankle and still suffers from the injury to this day, Tim got to go home to his family, against all the odds. Some of his close friends and fellow employees were not so lucky, including his 'personal hero' Captain Kathy Mazza, who continued to help with the North Tower effort and was killed when it collapsed a short while later that morning.

Fast forward nineteen years and Tim is at the White House. The pain in his right foot is a daily reminder of what was lost on 9/11, but this is a day of hope. Much has been said about 9/11 by first George W. Bush and then Barack Obama, but Donald Trump is the first US president to agree to meet the victims' families and the survivors on the anniversary.

In the intervening years, questions from the families had been met with a wall of silence and a stubborn lack of transparency, which in turn left them disappointed, shocked and outraged. Tim, like the others a strong patriot, couldn't understand why the leaders of his own country, the people who pledged to defend and to support him, were so determined to hide the truth about the attacks that changed his life so dramatically.

Finally, this was an opportunity to redress those wrongs. President Trump had intimated that he was on their side. Invitations to the White House to twenty 9/11 family members suggested he was true to his word.

Arriving in Washington DC on 10 September 2019, there was a real sense among the families that their long wait was nearly over. Whatever their personal feelings about Trump, he wasn't playing the same games as his predecessors, and there was certainly no love lost between him and the intelligence community he had consistently derided since coming to power in 2016. If there was something to hide, perhaps he was the man to haul down the screens.

Such was the optimism as Tim and the families filtered into the South Lawn to join a minute's silence, overseen by President Trump and First Lady Melania before he crossed to the Pentagon, where 184 people were killed eighteen years earlier.

'We are united with you in grief,' Trump said at the ceremony in a message to the families. 'We offer you all that we have: our unwavering loyalty, our undying devotion, our eternal pledge that your loved ones will never, ever be forgotten.'

The families had already decided that, if they got a chance to speak to the president on his return to the White House later that morning, they would ask him the same thing. They wanted to know the name of a Saudi Arabian state official who had been identified in FBI inquiries as being directly involved in helping the San Diego al-Qaeda hijackers Nawaf al-Hazmi and Khalid al-Mihdhar.

They wanted to know the full extent of Saudi Arabia's involvement in 9/11. They wanted the president to open up the CIA and FBI files to show what America really knew about the attacks. They wanted an end to the secrecy from their own government. But for now, this one name would be a start. It would show that Trump really was on their side and not just another pawn to the powers of money and influence.

They got their opportunities after being ushered inside and posing with the Trumps for a publicity photo. One after another in the Blue Room, they were announced and given a few minutes to chat with the president.

Reaching out for a handshake, Tim said: 'We are here to remember all of those we lost, but we also need your help.'

'Don't worry,' Trump interrupted him. 'It's done.'

'I was caught offguard,' said Tim. 'I was ecstatic and when we went into the Red Room next door, I spoke to some of the other families and I told them, "He is going to do it". Some of the others spoke to him about making the name public and he told them the same thing, that he'd get it done.'

The buoyant families even dared to dream that Trump would, indeed, go over the heads of all the intelligence chiefs who had covered their tracks and provide all the answers to their questions.

Others family members told how Trump became animated at learning that former FBI directors Robert Mueller and James Comey had been among the officials blocking the release of key documents.

'Hey Melania. Listen to these guys – the same scum that is fighting me is now fighting the 9/11 families,' said Trump. 'Don't worry, I'm going to help you guys.'

It turned out, of course, that it wasn't 'done' at all. The next day, the families were told that the name of the Saudi official would be given to their lawyers but could not be passed on or made public in any way. Worse, the FBI and CIA reports on 9/11 would never be released. Attorney General William Barr said they were 'state secrets'. Not only that, the reason for them being declared state secrets was also a state secret.

Barr and the Acting Director of National Intelligence Richard Grenell argued that disclosure of the Saudi official's name could cause 'significant harm to national security'.

In other words, Trump had doubled down on the actions of the previous two presidents and reinforced the wall of silence, preventing them from learning what America's own intelligence services had discovered about 9/11 and any foreign involvement. A fishy situation had become a whole lot smellier.

'We felt like we'd been stabbed in the back,' said Tim.

Interestingly, in an apparent nod to claims that the US worked with Saudi intelligence in the run-up to 9/11, Jill Sanborn, the FBI's assistant director of counterterrorism, argued that making internal FBI files public would deter foreign governments from working with the agency in the future.

To put the legal conflict in some sort of context, there may have only been twenty representatives at the White House, but the majority of the victims' families and survivors of the attacks are signatories to two lawsuits targeting Saudi Arabia's alleged links to 9/11. It was only possible to bring those lawsuits after sustained pressure enabled the passing of the controversial Justice Against Sponsors of Terrorism Act (JASTA), a 2016 bill allowing US citizens to sue foreign governments, even if they have not been designated as state sponsors of terrorism.

US Congress took nearly seven years to ponder the bill and had to overcome an attempted veto by then President Obama – a bid to halt the law seen as a betrayal by many 9/11 families. The 9/11 families had written to Obama five times asking for a meeting to help him understand their feelings about JASTA, as it has become known, and why it was so important to them. He ignored every request and would later delay the release of twenty-eight pages of classified court documents that contained key information about Saudi Arabia, despite admitting he had never actually read them.

Obama issued his veto on 23 September 2016, claiming JASTA would leave the US open to reciprocal legislative attacks. A two-thirds majority in both the House of Representatives and the Senate was enough to overcome the veto and provide the launchpad for the Saudi lawsuit.

'The victims of 9/11 have fought for fifteen long years to make sure that those responsible for the senseless murder of thousands of innocent men, women and children, and injuries to thousands others, are held accountable,' Terry Strada, national chair of the 9/11 Families and Survivors United for Justice Against Terrorism, said at the time. 'JASTA becoming law is a tremendous victory toward that effort. We rejoice in this triumph and look forward to our day in court and a time when we may finally get more answers regarding who was truly behind the attacks.'

The families also had to overcome an attempt by Saudi Arabia to quash the bill. The Saudis were reportedly spending $1.3 million a month on lobbying and public relations to spread misinformation about the law, including paying for trips to the capital for US veterans to oppose the bill. Voting JASTA into law meant that two lawsuits could be filed against the Saudis.

Motley Rice, headquartered in Mount Pleasant, near Charleston, South Carolina, first filed litigation in 2002 for 500 family members and survivors, aimed at holding responsible the individuals, banks, corporations and charities historically implicated in sponsoring al-Qaeda's terrorist activities. Now they represent more than 7,000 9/11 clients and added Saudi Arabia as a defendant on 17 March 2017, soon after JASTA was signed into law.

New York firm Kreindler & Kreindler also represents victims' families and survivors in a lawsuit, also filed in March 2017 against Saudi Arabia, and they added a further 10,000 plaintiffs to the litigation three months later.

The lawsuits, the biggest in US history both in the number of plaintiffs and the potential for billions of dollars levied by the courts against Saudi Arabia if they succeed, are being fought tooth and nail by the Saudis, who are adamant they played no official part in either the planning or the execution of the attacks. As a consequence, the cases are moving at a snail's pace through the Manhattan courts.

But Jim Kreindler is convinced that his legal mission to uncover the truth will eventually win out. With his father, he won a record $2.7 billion payout from Libya for the families of the victims of the Pan Am 103 Lockerbie disaster, still the only case involving a country paying compensation for a terrorist attack.

Speaking to students at Dartmouth College in January 2002, he predicted they would be 'revolted and horrified' at what prominent members of the US government – including past presidents – have done to cover up the truth about 9/11. He claimed the attacks happened with the 'active intent and cooperation of eleven known Saudi government officials, alleging they were 'accomplices without whom there never would have been a 9/11 attack'.

Kreindler is adamant the Saudis have long worked hand in glove with al-Qaeda – and bin Laden himself – to protect the House of Saud from the kind of Wahhabi fundamentalist revolution that deposed the Shah of Iran.

Ironically, it wasn't a lawsuit or a subpoena that finally revealed the name of the so-called 'third man', the mysterious Saudi state official who had supposedly aided the San Diego hijackers and who Trump had promised to unveil. It was a bureaucratic mistake.

Michael Isikoff, chief investigative correspondent for Yahoo! News, revealed that the FBI had inadvertently included the name in a court declaration filed in federal court in April 2020. Once the error was exposed, the declaration was withdrawn, but it was too late to prevent the name of Mussaed Ahmed al-Jarrah, a former mid-level official at the Saudi Embassy in Washington DC, from entering the public domain.

The error was hailed by lawyers for the 9/11 families as an apparent confirmation that the FBI knew of a link between the Saudi government and the hijackers. They claim that Jarrah passed on instructions to the Saudi consulate in Los Angeles to ensure Mihdhar and Hazmi got the assistance they needed when they landed on the West Coast, although the FBI was never able to gather enough evidence to build a case against him.

Was the failure to redact Jarrah's name in one instance in the declaration really a mistake? That's the question being asked by people with knowledge of how the intelligence services work in America.

Or was it a warning shot across the bows of Saudi Arabia to ensure the kingdom holds its nerve and doesn't bow to pressure to finally reveal all it knows about 9/11?

It is certainly true that no chances were being taken in the days after the attacks when it became apparent that Saudi Arabia was likely to come under scrutiny over possible involvement.

More than 300 Saudi nationals were allowed to fly out of the US immediately after 9/11, some while planes across the US were still officially grounded. Many of those who left in such a hurry were members of the bin Laden family, and all of them left with the assistance of the White House and the blessing of the FBI.

Chapter Sixteen

The Pentagon

**Dulles Airport, Washington DC, 7.35 a.m.,
11 September 2001**

We pick up Nawaf al-Hazmi and Khalid al-Mihdhar dropping off their old Toyota car at the Dulles Airport car park outside Washington DC early on 11 September, having failed on at least part of their mission; neither had learned to fly. With them in the cramped car was Hani Hanjour, who had stuck to the task and was a barely proficient pilot, along with Hazmi's brother, Salem, and a fifth hijacker, Majed Moqed. All five were from Saudi Arabia.

Salem al-Hazmi had arrived from the United Arab Emirates a couple of months earlier on 29 June and Moqed had flown in on 2 May from Dubai. They all lived together in a flat in Paterson, New Jersey, before checking into a Marriott in Herndon, Virginia, a short distance from Dulles, for their final night together on 10 September.

Crucially, at this late stage of the game, Mihdhar and Hazmi had somehow slipped the authorities who had followed them so closely to America and then from the West Coast across to the East. They were now on the official Terrorist Screening Database watchlist. All pretense of 'turning' them now shorn, their names were finally added on 24 August 2001 after the FBI were officially alerted to their presence in the US.

But there was still time to stop them. Only Hanjour, who had spent more time in America and spoke better English, walked through security at Dulles at 7.35 a.m. without being stopped for a secondary search.

At around 7.29 a.m., the Hazmi brothers, dressed in smart, button-down shirts, were flagged up because of their poor English and suspicious behaviour. Those concerns were heightened because the brothers didn't show adequate identification, although a part of Nawaf's driving licence would later be found amid the rubble in the Pentagon's north car park. Nawaf also set off two metal detectors, according to an airport surveillance video.

They were shown to a security counter where Salem's bag was checked for explosives and they were then allowed through. The only consequence was that their luggage was held up until they had both boarded the flight.

Mihdhar and Moqed also set off metal detectors as they passed through security a few minutes earlier at 7.18 a.m. Moqed set off another alarm and was manually checked by a screener.

Still, no agents checked the contents of their bags. If they had, they would have found the box-cutters they would use later that morning to take control of AA Flight 77 to Los Angeles and divert it towards Washington with Hanjour at the controls.

It is true that knives with blades shorter than four inches that were not deemed 'menacing' were allowed in hand luggage at the time, a fact it is easy to forget now that a bottle of Evian water is seen as a potentially deadly weapon. But even if the knives had been confiscated, the lives of the other fifty-three passengers on the flight, as well as the six crew and the 125

Pentagon staffers, who died when the plane crashed two hours later, might have been spared.

The plane took off at 8.20 a.m. with all five terrorists on board – the pilot and his 'muscle'. In a similar configuration to the other hijacked flights, Hanjour was up front in seat 1B, the Hazmi brothers were in first-class seats 5E and 5F and Moqed and Mihdhar back in economy in seats 12A and 12B.

Less than thirty-five minutes later, they had overwhelmed the crew and Hanjour was flying towards the Pentagon. The Boeing 757 crashed into the western side of the building in Arlington County, Virginia, at 9.37 a.m. at full throttle – about 530 miles per hour.

The plane took out several streetlamps before hurtling 310 feet into the first floor of the recently renovated Pentagon. The resulting entry holes left in the building led conspiracy theorists to question whether a plane could have even caused the damage.

In his books, *9/11: The Big Lie* and *Pentagate*, French author Thierry Meyssan went so far as to claim that Flight 77 never existed, and a remote-controlled missile drone was fired at the Pentagon as part of a military coup orchestrated by a right-wing faction in the US government. 'What became of the passengers of American Airlines Flight 77?' he asked. 'Are they dead?'

Despite pushback from the Pentagon, which called the claims 'a slap in the face and real offence to the American people, particularly to the memory of victims of the attacks', *9/11: The Big Lie* was a bestseller in France when it was published in 2002 and has been translated into twenty-eight languages.

In these pages, we are not going to add insult to injury by suggesting the hijackings were somehow faked. The suffering of too many people was all too real.

At first glance, it does seem strange that a plane with a 125-

foot wingspan and 155 feet long should leave a hole 75 feet wide in Ring E, the Pentagon's exterior wall, and 12 feet wide further in the building in Ring C.

However, closer examination showed one wing hit the ground and the other was sheared off by the reinforced load-bearing columns on the outside wall. 'If you expected the entire wing to cut into the building, it didn't happen,' Mete Sözen, a professor of structural engineering at Purdue University and a member of the team that investigated the crash, told *Popular Mechanics*.

The official report said the Ring C damage was caused by the landing gear and not the fuselage.

Blast expert Allyn E. Kilsheimer, the first structural engineer to the scene, dismissed conspiracy claims that there was no debris from the plane, saying: 'It was absolutely a plane, and I'll tell you why. I saw the marks of the plane wing on the face of the building. I picked up parts of the plane with the airline markings on them. I held in my hand the tail section of the plane, and I found the black box.

'I held parts of uniforms from crew members in my hands, including body parts. OK?'

The involvement of Mihdhar and Hazmi in the atrocity was, however, a huge cause for concern. As we have heard, CIA Director George Tenet was gobsmacked to see their names on the flight manifest; it meant all his worst fears had been realised.

When Robert Mueller was sworn in as the sixth director of the FBI on 4 September 2001, he had no clue he was about to inherit the biggest intelligence disaster in US history. Essentially a decent man with a courageous past, winning a Bronze Star for heroism in the Vietnam War for rescuing a wounded colleague under enemy fire in an ambush that claimed half of his platoon, Mueller's biggest post-9/11 role was to cover up the mess that allowed the hijackers to remain free and save his beleaguered agency. It meant rewriting history to steer prying eyes away from the truth.

In his statement to the Joint Intelligence Committee Inquiry on Capitol Hill, Mueller sought to deflect any kind of suggestion that there may have been an undercover operation shadowing some of the perpetrators.

'While here, the hijackers effectively operated without suspicion, triggering nothing that alerted law enforcement and doing nothing that exposed them to domestic coverage. As far as we know, they contacted no known terrorist sympathizers in the United States,' he said.

'They committed no crimes with the exception of minor traffic violations. They dressed and acted like Americans, shopping and eating at places like Wal-Mart and Pizza Hut. They came into different cities, moved around a lot and did not hold jobs. When three got speeding tickets in the days leading up to September 11, they remained calm and aroused no suspicion. One of the suicide hijackers, Nawaf al-Hazmi, even reported an attempted street robbery on May 1, 2001, to Fairfax, Virginia Police – he later declined to press charges.

'None of the nineteen suicide hijackers are known to have had computers, laptops or storage media of any kind, although they are known to have used publicly accessible Internet connections at various locations. They used 133 different pre-paid calling cards to call from various pay phones, cell phones and land lines.

'The nineteen suicide hijackers used US checking accounts accessed with debit cards to conduct the majority of financial activity during the course of this conspiracy. Meetings and communications between the hijackers were done without detection, apparent surveillance flights were taken, and nothing illegal was detected through airport security screening. In short, the terrorists had managed very effectively to exploit loopholes and vulnerabilities in our systems. To this day we have found no one in the United States except the actual hijackers who knew of the plot and we have found nothing they did while in the United States that triggered a specific response about them.'

From what you have read in the preceding chapters, even if you are reserving judgement on how much blame the intelligence services should shoulder, much of what Mueller told Congress was misleading.

The hijackers had contacted known terrorist sympathisers in the US, there were certainly people in the country who knew about the plot and their behaviour had triggered a response when Hazmi and Mihdhar were put on a terrorism watchlist, however belatedly.

'Clearly, these nineteen terrorists were not supermen using extraordinarily sophisticated techniques,' Mueller concluded in his statement to lawmakers. 'They came armed with simple box-cutters. But they also came armed with sophisticated knowledge about how to plan these attacks abroad without discovery, how to finance their activities from overseas without alarm, how to communicate both here and abroad without detection and how to exploit the vulnerabilities inherent in our free society.

'There were no slip-ups. Discipline never broke down. They gave no hint to those around them what they were about. They came lawfully. They lived lawfully. They trained lawfully. They boarded the aircraft lawfully. They simply relied upon everything from the vastness of the Internet to the openness of our society to do what they wanted to do without detection.

'And just like the CIA, we do not think the threat has subsided. Those who masterminded and financed these attacks are still capable of doing so. Capturing a number of important operatives has been a huge victory, but there are others, still loosely connected and still a potent threat. Nor should we forget that thousands of 'foot soldiers' – those who trained in the camps – remain disbursed. And there are those who, without direction or control, are compelled for ideological reasons to pursue jihad and kill Americans.'

He did include an extremely veiled nod to the breakdown in communications involving the 'wall' that prevented CIA and FBI intelligence operatives from sharing information with their colleagues, saying: 'These realities to me mean we need a different FBI, one that does not just think in terms of cases and prosecutions. We need new structures, new training, new levels of cooperation, new technologies, more analytical capacity and a different mindset. All of these things are being put in place. Nothing can be paramount to preventing the next attack. When we looked back, there were clearly things we should have done better or differently. But there are also many things we have done quite well and things we should do more of.'

The CIA had basically left Mueller and the FBI carrying the can for the botch-ups that led to 9/11. The CIA could hide behind their shady veil of secrets, imagined and otherwise. The FBI not only had to investigate the attacks on New York and Washington, they also had to explain the events that allowed them to happen, even if they had largely been left in the dark.

Mueller also faced the unenviable task of saving the FBI as an organisation. By doing so, he had no choice but to hide ˋ the truth.

The old adage goes that the best form of defence is attack, and George Tenet strongly resisted any criticism of the CIA in the wake of 9/11 and made the agency central to the Bush administration's War on Terror strategy going forwards. It was certainly in President Bush's interests to give the agency a pass; a scandal over the intelligence failure would have involved demands for scapegoats and his presidency, still in its infancy, would have been in peril.

So, Tenet was bullish, not only in pushing back at his critics, but also in formulating America's response. He was held at fault for failing to set up an effective management strategy to tackle al-Qaeda before the 9/11 attacks, a charge he took issue with, and managed to ride the worldwide condemnation of CIA torture tactics involving waterboarding and other methods barred by the Geneva Convention at black sites, where terror suspects were held without trial. But America's failure to prove Iraq had any weapons of mass destruction finally proved to be his undoing.

Watergate journalist Bob Woodward wrote in his book *Bush at War* that Tenet told Bush that his intelligence supporting the claim was a 'slam dunk'. When the issue looked like imperiling Bush's re-election campaign in 2004, Tenet was forced to fall on his sword.

He left office after seven years, saying his head was still held 'very, very high'. He had faced one of the most testing times of any CIA chief and, in one regard at least, he had been successful against all the odds. He had kept the biggest secret of all – America's failure to prevent 9/11.

Perhaps the true feeling in Washington was summed up by Senator Richard Shelby, a former Senate Intelligence Committee chairman, who said: 'There were more failures of intelligence on his watch as director of the CIA than any other [director of Central Intelligence] in our history.'

Chapter Seventeen

The Fighters

**On Board Flight 93, 9.35 a.m.,
11 September 2001**

Thirty minutes of recordings from the cockpit of the doomed United Airlines Flight 93 were redacted from the original official transcript. It may be because officials wanted to save relatives from the pain of reliving their loved ones' last moments, but the absence did the families a disservice because it goes some way to disproving claims from conspiracy theorists that one of the great stories of heroism from 11 September was a work of fiction.

As we have already seen, Vice President Dick Cheney's order to shoot down any hijacked passenger jets following the attacks on the Twin Towers and the Pentagon came too late to do any good. Any moral navel-gazing about the decision was academic.

Yet speculation persists that a US drone missile was fired at Flight 93 to bring it down in a field in Shanksville, Pennsylvania, or that it was shot by a mysterious white plane or an F-16 flown by a pilot who was, in fact, thousands of miles away in Montana at the time.

Now you can head down the rabbit hole and refuse to

believe anything anyone says about 9/11. The lack of body parts and debris at the crash scene as a result of the shattering obliteration that occurred on the impact of the crash have led some people to conclude it never even happened.

The white plane was probably a Dassault Falcon 20 business jet that was in the vicinity of the hijacked plane and was actually asked by the FAA to drop from 3,000 feet to 1,500 feet to check if they could see any signs of a crash – reporting a cloud of black smoke. There was also a C-130 military cargo plane within twenty-five miles of the passenger jet when it crashed.

If you believe the 'shot-down' theory, you may be willing to go even further and give credence to the 'Bumble Planes' conspiracy that suggests the three earlier hijacked flights were landed in secret and decoys took off to confuse flight controllers while the bemused passengers were all ferried to DC to be herded on board Flight 93 and destroyed over Pennsylvania. It would be easy to ridicule if it wasn't that so many families are still grieving. The conspiracy theorists hiding behind their social-media handles, their radio shows and their desks in academia seem to care little for such feelings.

There were countless acts of heroism, large and small, on 9/11, but Flight 93 is a story worthy of its Hollywood treatment. The passengers on board were the only ones from the four flights to have some inkling about what was happening to them. They learned from panicked calls to loved ones on the ground that hijacked planes had already been weaponised in New York and Washington DC, and it didn't take much to imagine the fate their own captors had in store. Investigators said later that the hijackers of Flight 93 had targeted either the White House or the Capitol building.

From calls from ten passengers and two crew members,

we can build a picture of the last minutes on board the plane. According to the accounts, passengers Todd Beamer, Tom Burnett, Mark Bingham and Jeremy Glick and others came up with a plan to storm the cockpit and overwhelm the hijackers.

'They're talking about crashing this plane into the ground. We have to do something. I'm putting a plan together,' Burnett said in a call to Deena, his wife.

Beamer, talking to an airphone operator, can be overheard talking to another passenger who asks him, 'Are you ready?'

'Let's roll,' says Beamer, before the lines go dead.

Cynics still claim, with some justification, that there is no proof what happened after that. The accepted version was that the terrorists, fearing that they were about to be overpowered, crashed the plane in a field. Relatives of those on board believe the passengers successfully stormed the cockpit and may have even killed one of the hijackers before hitting the ground.

The redacted section from the cockpit recording was played for the first time in a packed courtroom in Alexandria, Virginia, during the trial of Zacarias Moussaoui. The recording was also broadcast live to 9/11 families in courtrooms in six other US cities.

The cockpit recording was the only one recovered from the four planes. It begins at 9.32 a.m., four minutes after the hijacking, when Ziad Samir Jarrah, the Lebanese terrorist who had taken over the controls, tells passengers that there is a bomb on board. He actually presses the wrong button, alerting air traffic control in Cleveland to the hijacking.

Two minutes later there is the sound of a scuffle.

'Please, please, don't hurt me,' a man says.

'Down, no more,' says one of the hijackers.

'Oh, God, I don't want to die,' says the same man.

The passengers are told repeatedly to sit down.

Another minute later, at 9.45 a.m., one of the female flight attendants can be heard pleading, 'I don't want to die.'

'No, no, down, down,' says a hijacker.

'I don't want to die. I don't want to die,' she continues, before loud cries are heard.

'Everything is fine. I finished,' a hijacker says, speaking in Arabic.

At 9.39 a.m., with the plane flying at 17,000 feet, Jarrah switches course from San Francisco, the plane's intended destination, to Washington DC, and tells passengers to sit down, warning them there is a bomb on board.

Once again, he thinks he is speaking on the plane's loud-speaker but is, in fact, speaking directly with air traffic control. He doesn't respond to appeals from controllers and turns off the transponder, making it more difficult for the plane to be tracked.

'This green knob?' says one of the hijackers in Arabic. 'Yes, that's the one,' replies Jarrah.

The passengers were forced to the back of the plane where some of them managed to get in touch with the authorities and family members and quickly learned what had happened to the other flights.

Shortly afterwards, Todd Beamer famously told his fellow passengers, 'Let's roll', as a signal to start fighting back.

The recording puts the passenger assault on the cockpit at 9.57 a.m.

'Is there something? A fight?' a hijacker can be heard asking in Arabic.

'Yeah,' comes the reply.

'Oh, Allah. Oh, Allah. Oh, the most gracious,' says an Arabic voice close to the mic in the cockpit.

Muted voices can then be heard saying, 'In the cockpit. In the cockpit.'

'They want to get in here,' says a voice in Arabic. 'Hold, hold from the inside. Hold from the inside. Hold.'

At 9.59, there are sounds of breaking glass and shouting.

'Is that it? Shall we finish it off?' says an Arabic voice.

'No. Not yet. When they all come, we finish it off,' answers another hijacker, again in Arabic.

There appears to have then been another charge on the cockpit. 'In the cockpit! If we don't, we'll die,' says a male passenger.

'Roll it,' says another passenger, believed to be a reference to a drinks cart that may have been used as a ram.

'Cut off the oxygen,' shouts a hijacker, repeating the order another two times.

'Pull it down,' says an Arabic voice. 'Pull it down.' This is presumably the moment the hijackers decided to crash the plane short of their target, an acknowledgement that the passenger revolt was on the brink of succeeding.

'Allah is the greatest. Allah is the greatest!,' an Arabic voice shouts over and over – the last words heard on the tape before it goes silent at 10.03 a.m. when Flight 93 slammed at full speed into a disused coal field in Shanksville, Pennsylvania.

Chapter Eighteen

The Brokers

40 Wall Street, New York City, 9.55 a.m., 11 September 2001

In the hours after the 9/11 attacks, it was only natural for Wall Street to worry about the shockwaves that would inevitably be sent through the US economy. The 2008 recession was some years off and greed was still the order of the day. Donald Trump, fifteen years away from his unlikely rise to the White House, appeared to be more interested in the idea that the demise of the Twin Towers meant one of his buildings, 40 Wall Street, would be the tallest in downtown Manhattan.

Asked about the damage caused by the collapses in an interview with local TV station WWOR, the property billionaire replied: 'I mean, 40 Wall Street actually was the second tallest building in downtown Manhattan, and it was actually, before the World Trade Center, the tallest, and then when they built the World Trade Center it became known as the second tallest, and now it's the tallest.'

The claim was not actually true; the nearby 70 Pine Street skyscraper was twenty-five feet taller than Trump's building, but the episode, as insignificant as it was, illustrated the bullish attitude that prevailed at the time – the bigger and showier, the better.

The immediate fear was that the attacks on the very heart of America's financial machine would send confidence, and thus stocks, tumbling. What few gave much thought to initially was that traders would benefit from what happened. It was not so much that money could not be made in such circumstances; disasters, after all, had traditionally been seen by some more ruthless manipulators of the money markets as an opportunity to profit from the misery of others.

But this was different and altogether more disturbing – a pattern of insider trading that suggested that traders knew the 9/11 attacks were going to happen. In the days before 11 September, an 'extraordinary' number of 'put options' – investments which grow in value as the stock price goes down – were taken out on two airlines, American Airlines and United Airlines. They were, of course, the airlines whose planes were hijacked and crashed by the terrorists. Essentially, they were betting that the airlines' stock prices would fall.

The 'puts' involved at least 450,000 American Airlines shares and red flags were raised because they far outnumbered the 'call' options, which are taken out in the hope the stock would rise. CBS News, reporting just days after the attacks, said the 'puts' and 'calls' are usually reasonably even matched, but in this case an unprecedented 80 per cent of the orders were 'puts', an imbalance that had never been seen before.

When the stock of AMR Corporation, American's parent company, plummeted by 39 per cent after 9/11, the gamble paid off with a profit of more than $5 million for the people taking out the 'puts'.

UAL Corporation, United Airlines' parent company, reported a similar imbalance that paid out huge profits after the company's stock fell by 42 per cent. One single $2.5 million 'put option' trade on United Airlines reportedly went unclaimed following the attacks.

Estimates of the profits made ranged from several million dollars to as much as a billion.

According to the Associated Press, on 6 and 7 September, when there was no significant news or stock price movement involving United Airlines, the Chicago exchange handled 4,744 put options for United stock compared with just 396 call options. On 10 September, an uneventful day for American Airlines, the volume was 748 calls and 4,516 puts, based on a check of option-trading records. Tellingly, other airlines did not report the same kind of trends.

'I saw put-call numbers higher than I've ever seen in ten years of following the markets, particularly the options markets,' John Kinnucan, a principal of Broadband Research, an independent telecommunications research firm, told the *San Francisco Chronicle*. 'When one sees this type of activity, the first thing one does is ask oneself, "What is the explanation? What are people worried about?"'

The Securities Exchange Commission and the Chicago Board Options Exchange launched investigations after brokerage firms reported their suspicions. Other countries, including Germany, the UK and Japan, noticed irregular trading involving the US carriers. The obvious concern was that Osama bin Laden may have sought to profit from the tragedy and conspiracy theorists jumped on the trades as proof that the US government was behind the atrocity.

In 2004, the SEC said it found no evidence that any traders had advance knowledge of the attacks after investigating 9.5 million securities transactions that took place in the days before 9/11.

The 9/11 Commission also dismissed the insider-trading claims, saying there were 'innocuous' explanations for the suspicious trades. The commission report said 95 per cent of the United 'puts' were bought on 6 September by a single US-based investor as part of an investment strategy. The investor had 'no conceivable ties to al-Qaeda'. In fact, he or she also bought $115,000 American Airlines shares on 10 September, suggesting there was no knowledge of the terrible events that would befall the following day.

What the 9/11 Commission Report did not mention was that the US-based investor was the American arm of a major bank, whose former chairman became the CIA's executive director in March 2001. It provided fuel for the conspiracy theorists but required a major leap of faith to offer up a Wall Street coup as a reason for causing the deaths of nearly 3,000 people.

The trade in American Airlines 'puts' on 10 September was attributed to a California investment advice newsletter that recommended the trades to its clients.

In truth, the money markets were behaving erratically even before 9/11 with share prices in steady decline over the previous three months because of fears over unemployment in the US, and both airlines were reporting declines in earnings.

Richard Gage, of the Architects and Engineers for 9/11 Truth, believes the 'money trail' provides a crucial clue to unravelling the 9/11 plot. He points to speculation that a fortune in gold was stolen from vaults beneath the towers and that property owners made billions in insurance payouts from the buildings decimated in the attacks.

Wars are, indeed, started for less, but, again, I refuse to believe greed alone is sufficient motive for the sacrifice of nearly 3,000 people. In times of grave national emergency, propping up the economy is one of the top priorities of any government, but after 9/11 there were even more pressing issues. The president and his administration had to decide how to hit back and who to target. With Osama bin Laden and the Taliban already in the frame, and Afghanistan (and Iraq) in the firing line to face America's wrath, George Bush had another matter to handle; he needed to shut down any suggestion that 9/11 could have been prevented on his watch.

Chapter Nineteen

The Cover-Up

The White House, Washington DC, 3.15 p.m.,
13 September 2001

George Bush and his friend, Prince Bandar bin Sultan Al Saud, were smoking cigars at the White House, but the situation they faced could not have been more serious. The US presidency was in the balance and Saudi Arabia faced being blamed for the attacks that shocked the world two days earlier.

With the two men on the Truman Balcony were Dick Cheney, Condoleezza Rice and Bandar's aide, Rihab Massoud. A public message was being sent. Yes, Osama bin Laden was a Saudi, as were fifteen of the nineteen hijackers, but the relationship between the United States and the Desert Kingdom was unbroken.

Privately, the message was just as urgent, maybe even more so.

By now, Bush had been made aware of the scale of the intelligence foul-up and the implications if it got out at such a volatile moment in the country's history. There's no evidence that Bush knew beforehand about the CIA's failed operation to turn Mihdhar, and it seems unlikely that his inner circle was appraised because Richard Clarke, his counterterrorism czar, knew nothing about it. It's possible that even George Tenet, the CIA director, wasn't told until just before 11 September or immediately after the attacks.

The way it was explained to me by a senior source is that if Mihdhar's presence in the US had been raised at the president's daily briefings, the subsequent line of questioning from Bush and his staff – and definitely from Clarke – would inevitably have led to the fact that the CIA had broken the law and knowingly cut out the FBI to run a domestic operation. It wasn't a cul-de-sac that the Alec Station analysts, running the off-the-books recruitment attempt, would have wanted to find themselves trapped in.

Once the planes hit and almost every FBI agent in the nation was investigating what happened, all bets were off, and the only way that the damage could be controlled was by telling the president. Bush and Tenet had a stark choice. They could tell the truth and risk, at the very least, US intelligence operatives being arrested and charged for running an illicit operation, and the dissolution of the CIA, or, at worst, Bush being blamed for the failure on his watch and impeached. Or they could lie and hope nobody ever found out what went wrong.

Bandar also found himself between a rock and a hard place. The backlash against Saudis in America was almost immediate and there were hundreds of members of the House of Saud and other powerful families – including the bin Ladens – who feared for their safety and were clamouring to be allowed to return to the Middle East as soon as possible. Bandar had been a friend of the first President Bush, George H.R., and, as Saudi Arabia's ambassador to the US from 1983 to 2005, was more responsible than anyone else for the close relationship between Washington and Riyadh. Those ties would be blown apart should it become known that the Saudis had collaborated with the CIA to target a 9/11 hijacker on American soil. There would also be a political fall-out at home as, while strict Wahhabis in Saudi Arabia may have condemned Osama bin Laden, they did not condemn his message. To many in the kingdom, he wasn't an international terrorist, he was a holy warrior. As much as his methods may have repulsed many Saudis, there was support for his cause. Bandar had been in constant touch with Tenet since the morning of the attacks and he knew everything they knew.

It would be better, Bush and Bandar agreed, to protect their secret – and their special relationship. The decision to hide the truth would have implications for decades to come and draw in subsequent presidents Barack Obama and Donald Trump. It would lead to fingers being pointed unfairly at the Saudis as partners in crime with al-Qaeda and successive US administrations would be accused of betrayal by the 9/11 families, who were denied the simple facts that they, more than anybody, deserved.

Back then, the hope must have been that once the storm was weathered, the two countries could move on together, bound by the same secret.

There was talk, of course, of Bush's plans to retaliate against the Taliban, bin Laden's protectors in Afghanistan, and maybe even of his unfounded suspicions that Iraq's Saddam Hussein played a part. But never was there a suggestion that the Saudis were in any way responsible. According to Watergate journalist Bob Woodward, Bush told Bandar at the Truman's Balcony meeting, 'If we get somebody and we can't get them to cooperate, we'll hand them over to you.'

It was both a confirmation that America's Saudi intelligence partners were as important as ever and a nod to the rendition policy – skipping around the protections afforded by the

US Constitution by handing over terror suspects to third-party nations to torture – that remains a stain on the Bush presidency.

It was also in line with an understanding between the intelligence agencies of the undercover allies that the Americans would hand over any Saudis they deemed were becoming too radical, rather than arrest them to avoid any 'embarrassment'. The policy helps explain why the CIA was so determined not to arrest Mihdhar and Hazmi and other Saudis that came in their sights before 9/11.

Before they parted ways at the White House on the 13th however, there was one other matter Bandar needed his old friend to attend to. He was under enormous pressure to get members of the royal family and other wealthy Saudis back home, but all flights over America were grounded and security was intense. The only way they could leave was with the president's personal intervention.

In the ensuing days, according to Judicial Watch, a conservative watchdog group that filed Freedom of Information requests for passenger lists of flights that took off after 11 September, as many as 300 Saudis left the US with 'the apparent approval of the Bush administration'.

On 13 September, the same day that Bandar and Bush were together at the White House, a small charter plane reportedly flew three Saudis, all college students from wealthy Saudi families, from Tampa, Florida, to Lexington, Kentucky, where they met a Boeing 727 waiting to take them and other Saudis, who had been buying racehorses, back to Saudi Arabia.

Craig Unger, author of *House of Bush, House of Saud*, wrote in *Vanity Fair* that Saudi royals and members of the extended bin Laden family and their associates were driven or flown under FBI supervision to a meeting point in Dallas and then to

Washington DC to be ready to leave the country when airports re-opened on 14 September.

While the FBI may have known the identities of the 142 Saudis who left on six charter planes and the further 160 who left on fifty-five commercial flights, they certainly did not investigate them all. Their names were matched with terrorism watchlists and some were interviewed, but that was about it. The cover-up, in conjunction with the US administration, was already in full swing.

Recently unclassified FBI files offer a glimpse into the scale of the operation to evacuate the panicked Saudis. They tell how a group of about seventy-five members of the Saudi royal family, including five princes and two princesses and their entourage, arrived in Las Vegas on 9 September 2001 from Los Angeles because they were worried about further earthquakes following a tremor in the LA area the previous day.

Arriving in charter planes and rented limos, they check into twenty-three rooms in Caesar's Palace and another twenty-three rooms in the Four Seasons Hotel, presumably happy to wait out the aftershocks in Sin City.

Once the enormity of the 9/11 attacks became clear, half the party checked out of Caesar's and joined the rest of the party in the Four Seasons and, worried about their security, employed a Beverly Hills private bodyguard and security company to protect them from any perceived threats.

For the next few days, says the FBI, the party desperately tried to charter a plane to take them out of the country but were unsuccessful until 19 September, when they finally managed to snag a chartered Republic of Gabon-flagged Douglas DC-8-73 to fly them to Switzerland.

The organisers were asked for a manifest plus passport details of the fifty-one members of the Saudi royal family and their staff who were travelling and the names were checked against the FBI terrorist watchlist. All appeared to be clean.

The next day, another eighteen Saudi royals and their entourage left Las Vegas in a chartered Boeing 727 bound for Stanstead, England. Again, the FBI cross-checked passports for terror suspects.

It wasn't until 24 September that the FBI got subpoenas for Caesar's Palace and the Four Seasons to hand over their records from the Saudi stays. On that same day, thirty-four members of another Saudi royal party, who had been lodging at the Bellagio Hotel, left Vegas in a chartered American Trans Air L-1011, heading for Paris and then London.

There were similar scenes in Kentucky, where Prince Ahmed bin Salman Abdulaziz Al Saud was attending the Keeneland horse auctions. His son was among the group brought across from Florida and the party flew out on a chartered 727 that was heading first to London and then on to Saudi Arabia on 16 September. The FBI reports insist that the Florida group was driven to Lexington and did not fly in contravention to the four-day Federal Aviation Authority ban on commercial flights.

'They filed a flight plan and were told if they took off, they would be shot down,' says the FBI report. 'Bottom line, the jet never left, at least not on 9/12 and not with the college students.'

One of the most interesting journeys involved Ryan International Flight 441, which became known as the 'Bin Laden Family Flight', which left St Louis, Missouri on 18 September at 11 a.m. with no passengers on board and made four stops before leaving the country two days later.

Thirteen of the group were bin Ladens. One passenger embarked at LA on the same day, another three plus a body-guard came aboard in Orlando, Florida, the next day, followed by another five passengers at a pick-up in Washington DC on the 19th and a further fourteen Saudis with two body-guards from Boston, from where the flight departed on 20 September, arriving in Paris that evening. Among the passengers picked up in Orlando were Osama bin Laden's brother Khalil, his wife, Isabel, and son, Sultan. Afraid for his family's safety, he asked for – and got – an FBI escort to Orlando airport to catch the flight.

The FBI in Los Angeles also drove bin Laden's half-sister, Najiah, to the airport to catch the same flight. In all, twenty of the passengers were interviewed, included Khalil, who was interviewed three times, once on the ride to the airport. They were all cleared to depart, and the plane was searched at every stop.

While there is no suggestion anyone joining the Saudi exodus from the US had anything to do with al-Qaeda – or, indeed the Mabahith/CIA operation – the 9/11 investigation was still in its infancy and the speed and the assistance the fleeing parties received would surprise most investigators. One FBI report even adds that one of the Saudi princes thanked the FBI for its cooperation.

If nothing else, the entire episode illustrates just how far the American authorities would go to protect the Saudis from any awkward questions or embarrassing situations. And, how closely the House of Bush and the House of Saud were still working together.

Updated: 9/19/2001 9:57:00 AM

	Board	Dest.	NAME	D/O/B	PASSPORT #	NATIONALITY
X	LAX	BOS	Jason Blum (LAPD)		▇▇▇▇▇▇	United States
1.	LAX	OEJN	Najia Binladen		▇▇▇	Saudi Arabia
2.	MCO	OEJN	Khalil Binladen		▇▇▇	Saudi Arabia
3.	MCO	OEJN	Sultan Binladen		▇▇▇	Saudi Arabia
4.	MCO	OEJN	Maria M.F. Bayma	7/21/54	▇▇▇	Saudi Arabia
5.	MCO	OEJN	Isabel Bayma		▇▇▇	Brazil
6.	MCO	OEJN	Khalil Sultan Binladen		▇▇▇	United States
7.	IAD	GVA	Shafig Binladen		▇▇▇	Saudi Arabia
8.	IAD	LBG	Akberali Moawalla		▇▇▇	British
9.	IAD	OEJN	Omar Awad Binladen	4/10/70	▇▇▇	Saudi Arabia
10.	IAD	OEJN	Kholoud Osama Kurdi	9/9/79	▇▇▇	Saudi Arabia
11.	IAD	OEJN	Badr Ahmed Binladin	6/25/80	▇▇▇	Saudi Arabia United States
12.	BOS	OEJN	Nawaf Bark Binladen	4/28/71	▇▇▇	Saudi Arabia
13.	BOS	OEJN	Reem Hamza Asar	5/15/78	▇▇▇	Saudi Arabia
14.	BOS	OEJN	Omar Saleh Almadoudi	1/16/77	▇▇▇	Saudi Arabia
15.	BOS	OEJN	Faisal Saleh Almadoudi	4/27/75	▇▇▇	Saudi Arabia
16.	BOS	OEJN	Mohammed Saleh Binladen	9/22/82	▇▇▇	Saudi Arabia
17.	BOS	OEJN	Salman Salem Binladin	9/18/77	▇▇▇	Saudi Arabia
18.	BOS	OEJN	Tamara Khalil Binladen	1/16/81	▇▇▇	Saudi Arabia
19.	BOS	OEJN	Sana's Mohammed Binladen	12/8/61		Saudi Arabia
20.	BOS	OEJN	Mohmmed Awed Aljohi	4/20/72	▇▇▇	Saudi Arabia
21.	BOS	OEJN	Hasan Awed Aljohi	5/24/76	▇▇▇	Saudi Arabia
22.	BOS	OEJN	Suyati BT Sumiran Sadar	6/25/70	▇▇▇	Indonesia
23.	BOS	OEJN	Faisal Khalid Binladen	10/22/80	▇▇▇	Saudi Arabia
24.	BOS	OEJN	Salem Ali Salem Alyafeai	6/21/83	▇▇▇	Yemen
25.	BOS	OEJN	Almtasim Mazen Alsawwaf	8/12/83		Saudi Arabia
26.	BOS	LBG	J.P. Buonono	7/29/55	▇▇▇▇▇▇	United States
27.	BOS	LBG	Joseph Allen Wyka	7/21/68	▇▇▇▇▇▇	United States
28.	BOS	LBG	Ricardo V. Pascetta	12/02/50	▇▇▇▇▇▇	United States

In the days after 9/11, many Saudi families sought to leave the USA, fearing a backlash. This is a copy of the flight manifest for the so-called 'Bin Laden family flight' that carried thirteen members of the al Qaeda leader's extended family out of the country.

Chapter Twenty

The Counterterrorism Czar

Situation Room, White House, Washington DC,
9.45 a.m., 11 September 2001

Richard Clarke was heading a meeting from the Situation Room when Flight 77 hit the Pentagon. He had already ordered the evacuation of the White House following the strikes on the Twin Towers and, in his capacity as national crisis manager and head of counterterrorism, Clarke was desperately trying to summon some military firepower to take back the skies over New York and the capital.

His warnings to George Bush and his new administration that a major domestic attack was overdue had been largely ignored. Now his worst fears were becoming frighteningly real in front of their eyes.

Dick Cheney was in the White House bomb shelter, George Bush was still at the Sarasota school and about to be ferried to a faraway air base, but Clarke was above ground, holding the country's response to the attacks together. It was a meeting that effectively went on for days as air traffic over America was halted and the hunt for the perpetrators began.

All the time, Clarke burned with the knowledge that what had just transpired was exactly what he had been warning everyone about. He was, as the *Guardian* put it, the 'Cassandra of the war on terror'. His prophesies of doom had been ignored.

He was one of the few holdovers from Bill Clinton's administration, prized for his forthright views and ability to make things happen as the national coordinator for counterterror. Almost as soon as Bush moved into the White House in January 2001, Clarke asked for a Cabinet-level meeting to discuss the al-Qaeda danger but complained the new president was more interested in the threats from Moscow and Iraq, to the extent that Bush later ordered him to try to dig up connections between 9/11 and Saddam Hussein, even when it was clear to him that there weren't any.

Clarke had been uncomfortable both with the Republican president's response to his warnings pre-9/11 and with his response to the attacks. The extent of those misgivings became clearer after he quit the administration in 2003 and was asked to appear before the 9/11 Commission the following year.

'Your government failed you, those entrusted with protecting you failed you, and I failed you,' he told the 9/11 families, the first senior administration figure to go public with an apology. 'We tried hard, but that doesn't matter, because we failed,' he added.

Clarke followed up with a controversial book, *Against All Enemies*, accusing Bush of being unprepared for 9/11, which led to a sustained smear attack from the White House, which took potshots at his credibility. The lifelong public servant was supposed to get the point that breaking ranks was not going to be an option. There was too much at stake.

'I think there is a box in the White House that, if anyone escapes and tells the truth, they break open for talking points about what to say,' Clarke told Jon Stewart on *The Daily Show* in 2008.

By this time, he knew about the CIA's failure to pass on the memo about Mihdhar and Hazmi to the FBI and, like many others in his world, was trying to make sense of it. He was adamant that, despite being in charge of antiterrorism at the White House under Clinton and in the early days of the Bush presidency before 9/11, he had not been told that the two al-Qaeda terrorists had entered the United States in January 2000.

If he didn't know, then he assumed that nobody higher up the chain – including Bush, Cheney and Rice – knew about it either. The buck, he assumed, stopped at CIA Director George Tenet, an old friend and colleague who he had worked closely with at the White House.

Clarke didn't stop there. He had been mulling the events of 9/11 over in his mind long enough and had clearly come to the conclusion that it was time to speak out, whatever the consequences. Like FBI agent Mark Rossini, he couldn't just let the matter rest. It was too important to get to the truth.

Sitting down with documentary makers John Duffy and Ray Nowosielski, he admitted that a failed recruitment plot involving the CIA was the only answer that made any sense to him. Wearing a blue suit and wire-framed glasses, he said the CIA shared vast amounts of information with him and his staff in scores of threat committee meetings held while Hazmi and Mihdhar were in the US, but their names never came up once.

'That means one thing to me,' he told the filmmakers. 'There was an intentional and very high-level decision in the CIA not to let the White House know.'

The million-dollar question was why they would play such a high-stakes game. 'I have thought about this a lot, and there is only one conceivable reason that I can come up with. There may be other reasons, but I have only been able to come up with one,' he teased.

'I can understand [the CIA] possibly saying, "We need to develop 'sources' inside al-Qaeda. When we do that, we can't tell anybody about it." And I can understand them perhaps seeing these two guys show up in the United States and saying, "Aha, this is our chance to 'flip' them, this is our chance to get ears inside al-Qaeda." And to do that, we can't tell anybody outside al-Qaeda, until we got them, until they're really giving us information.'

Clarke had come to the same conclusion as Rossini. 'The CIA was trying to "turn" these guys. They failed in that effort. They broke from procedures in that process, and they didn't want to be blamed after the fact.'

He returned to the subject in 2016 after the Obama administration released twenty-eight previously classified pages from the first congressional probe into 9/11, which offered more details of the Saudi involvement in helping Hazmi and Mihdhar in San Diego.

As they continue to do, interested people from 9/11 families through to the emergency services, journalists and conspiracy theorists were still trying to understand the role played by the Saudis and the reason why the CIA kept the al-Qaeda cell's presence in California a secret.

In an article for ABC News, Clarke wrote: 'I believe that the two questions may be linked and that a major element of the 9/11 tragedy may remain unrevealed: a possible failed CIA–Saudi spy mission on US soil that went bad and eventually allowed 9/11 to proceed unimpeded.' He continued:

> My perspective on these issues is shaped by my job in the Clinton and Bush administrations, the national coordinator for counterterrorism, based in the White House's National Security Council. In that role, I was

constantly reading detailed intelligence reports and being briefed by the CIA, the FBI and other agencies concerning possible terrorist plots.

The interagency team I chaired prevented numerous attacks, but not 9/11. Despite the conclusion of the 9/11 Commission that information sharing among the agencies was inadequate, we did actually share reports and analysis on a daily basis. In addition to the formal interagency groups that reviewed reports, the CIA director would frequently call me whenever he saw an important report about al-Qaeda plans.

He never called about the presence of the 9/11 hijackers – even when the CIA knew two of them were in the country and had been tracking them around the world for months.

According to an investigation by the CIA Inspector General, no one in the agency alerted the FBI or White House with that information for over a year, even though fifty to sixty CIA personnel knew it. Quite the opposite: CIA managers issued instructions that the information was not to be shared. Why?

The CIA declined to comment for this report, but the answer may be found in what a small group of Saudi nationals were doing in Southern California in 2000 and 2001.

Two Saudi would-be hijackers, named Khalid al-Mihdhar and Nawaf al-Hazmi, showed up in Los Angeles in 2000. Shortly after they arrived, another Saudi citizen, Omar al-Bayoumi, introduced himself to them, found them housing, provided them with money and took them to Anwar al-Awlaki, an imam who would become a senior al-Qaeda figure, in San Diego.

The official story, found in the 9/11 Commission Report, is that al-Bayoumi was just a good Samaritan who met al-Mihdhar and al-Hazmi by chance at a restaurant after overhearing them speak Arabic with Gulf accents. But the newly released twenty-eight pages shed light on widespread suspicions about al-Bayoumi and raise an important question that has never fully been answered: Who was he, really?

According to the twenty-eight pages, FBI agents involved in the case had received several reports that led them to believe al-Bayoumi was a Saudi intelligence officer, living and working secretly in the US. His cover story was that he worked for an aviation logistics company owned by the Saudi government, but investigators found he never did any work for the company.

Even al-Hazmi suspected al-Bayoumi was a Saudi spy, according to the 9/11 Commission Report.

It is still not known whether al-Bayoumi was totally innocent, whether he was purposefully supporting al-Qaeda operatives on behalf of the Saudi government or whether he was an al-Qaeda sympathiser. The 9/11 Commission Report says there is 'no credible evidence' that he 'knowingly aided extremist groups', and he was found to be an 'unlikely candidate for clandestine involvement with Islamic extremists'.

But there is another theory that the twenty-eight pages and the 9/11 Commission Report do not explore: What if al-Bayoumi was a Saudi spy who was investigating al-Qaeda at the request of the CIA?

I believe that could be the answer and, if he was, could explain why the CIA took measures to prevent the FBI and the White House from knowing that al-Qaeda terrorists had shown up in California.

Al-Mihdhar and al-Hazmi were already known to US and Saudi intelligence as mid-level al-Qaeda operatives. Before they made their way to the US, at the CIA's request, al-Mihdhar's hotel room in Dubai was searched by the United Arab Emirates' intelligence service. At the CIA's request, al-Mihdhar and al-Hazmi were videotaped by the Malaysian intelligence service while attending an al-Qaeda terrorist planning meeting in Kuala Lumpur. At the CIA's request, the Thai intelligence service was asked to track them when they flew to Bangkok after that meeting. The Thais later reported back to the CIA, somewhat slowly, that the two men left on a flight for Los Angeles.

About the time that CIA learned the two men were in Los Angeles, the possible Saudi intelligence officer, al-Bayoumi, found them and befriended them.

The CIA is not authorised to run intelligence operations in the US. Even if it were, most CIA employees would have had a hard time making friends with al-Mihdhar and al-Hazmi.

A fellow Saudi like al-Bayoumi, however, would stand a much better chance, especially if he pretended to be an al-Qaeda sympathiser acquainted with people like the radical imam al-Alwaki. In the parlance of the intelligence world, such approaches to potential sources of information, using false pretenses, are known as false flag operations.

If the CIA asked the Saudi intelligence service to approach al-Mihdhar and al-Hazmi in the US then, it would have come at the same time that the CIA's

Counterterrorism Center (CTC) was trying to develop human sources inside al-Qaeda. It would have been entirely logical for the CTC to try to learn things about al-Qaeda by having someone from a friendly intelligence service run a false flag operation on two known al-Qaeda operatives. Because those two men were in the US, however, the CIA would have needed to coordinate the approach with the FBI.

Had FBI been informed, however, it very likely would have vetoed the idea and moved quickly to arrest the two men. I knew very well the FBI personnel in charge of counterterrorism at the time, and they would not have hesitated to make such an arrest. That is also what I would have requested the FBI to do if the CIA had told me, which it should have and did not.

If the CIA broke the rules about getting FBI approval and, in cooperation with the Saudi intelligence service, ran a false flag operation in the US against al-Qaeda terrorists, that would explain why CIA managers repeatedly made decisions and issued clear instructions not to tell anyone outside the CIA the rather startling and unprecedented news that al-Qaeda operatives were in our country. It is possible that the false flag operation produced no information of value and the CIA lost interest in it.

Finally, eighteen months after the two al-Qaeda men arrived in the US, the CIA, in a very low-key way, passed a report to the FBI about al-Mihdhar and al-Hazmi. It was too late. Their trail had gone cold. They had entered the final phase of preparations for 9/11.

Nothing in the joint congressional investigation, the 9/11 Commission's work or the CIA Inspector General's investigation explains why the CIA hid its knowledge about these two al-Qaeda operatives. Also, nothing in those reports provides any reason to disbelieve the possibility that the CIA, the CTC and the agency's top management hid a false flag operation that went wrong. Anyone involved in such a false flag operation would have good reason to hide it. Had the presence of the two terrorists in the US led to their arrest and interrogation by the FBI, other 9/11 hijackers might also have been caught.

It was fifteen years ago that the 9/11 tragedy occurred, but it is not too late to finish the investigation, to answer the questions that were left open over a decade ago.

Was the reason that a Saudi helped the hijackers in California the same reason that the CIA blocked dissemination of information that those hijackers were in the US? Was that reason that the CIA was trying to use those two terrorists as a potential source of insider information about al-Qaeda?

We all deserve to know.

Chapter Twenty-One

The Widow

South Tower, World Trade Center, 8.50 a.m., 11 September 2011

It wasn't supposed to be like this. Kristen Breitweiser was married to the man of her dreams; they had a beautiful baby daughter named Caroline and a golden retriever called Sam and lived in one of the safest towns in America. She had married husband Ronald in bathing suits and bare feet on a beach five years earlier and their life plan wasn't complicated. They had everything they wanted. They just wanted to grow old happily together.

But Kristen's American Dream was blown apart on the morning of 11 September 2001.

Three days earlier, on the tail-end of a two-week vacation, the family were at the beach in Sandy Hook near their Middleton Township, New Jersey home when Ronald pointed out the World Trade Center, two towering shadows on the horizon, and told Caroline: 'Look, that's where Daddy works.'

On 11 September, Ronald was at his desk on the 94th floor of the South Tower where he worked as a money manager for high-net-worth individuals as a senior vice president with Fiduciary Trust Company International when AA Flight 11 crashed into the North Tower. His first thought was to call his wife. He needed to tell her he was okay.

'The morning of September 11th, he kissed me and our two-year-old daughter and our golden retriever goodbye and went off to work, and he called me from his desk to ask if I had seen what happened and I didn't know what he was talking about,' said Kristen. 'He told me to turn on the television. I did, and I was like, "Oh! my gosh".

'He was saying, "It's crazy. I'm watching people jump out the windows," and he was obviously distressed by that. But he didn't want me to worry and think that it was his building. "It's not, I'm safe. I'm okay. I love you." Then he said, "I gotta go, I'm going to go watch it on the trading floor to try to get more information."

'And we hung up and with the television still on a few minutes later, I saw his building explode right where he was.'

At around 9.40 a.m., thirty-eight minutes after UA 175 hit the South Tower, the phone rang again. Nobody spoke and Kristen didn't know if it was her husband, but she spoke as if it was. 'I told him that I loved him, that he was the love of my life, that we were home waiting for him … I hope if it was him, he could hear me.'

Kristen would never get to speak to Ronald again. They would not get to grow old together. Caroline would have to grow up without her daddy. All they had left were their memories … and his wedding ring, found in the wreckage of Ground Zero a month later. Ronald was thirty-nine when he died.

That day, effectively, was the last of the life Kristen had chosen for herself. She had given up her job as a lawyer to be a stay-at-home mum, who volunteered and gardened and looked after her daughter. She was happy in her family bubble.

But in her grieving, Kristen could not ignore a growing

sense of injustice. With every answer she got about the attacks that killed her husband, she had twenty more questions. She honestly believed her government would do everything it could to help her and other 9/11 families, only to discover it was doing everything it could to prevent them from finding out the truth. She expected transparency and respect, but all she got was lies and deception.

So, the shy, unassuming housewife became the tough, no-nonsense campaigner. Instead of just asking questions, she started demanding answers – and she was not alone.

Three other women from New Jersey also lost their husbands on 9/11 and were also becoming increasingly disillusioned and angry over the way the families had been abandoned by the government.

Like Kristen, Patty Casazza, Lorie Van Auken and Mindy Kleinberg gave up waiting for someone else to give voice to their concerns. Their only chance was to take up the mantle themselves.

The 'Jersey Girls', as they became known, believed that an independent investigation, commissioned by the US government, was the best way to get an accurate portrayal of what happened before, during and after the attacks. Nothing could bring their husbands back, but a proper public accounting of 9/11 would at least help prevent such a catastrophic event from ever happening again. By bringing all the dirt into the open, rather than sweeping it under the carpet, they felt they could gain some kind of closure.

They did not dream back then that, twenty years later, they would still be fighting to get their own government to answer the same questions they were asking in the weeks and months immediately after 9/11. They fully believe that their children, now grown up, will have to continue their fight.

Kristen remembers exactly when she realised she had way more questions than answers.

'I was reading *Newsweek* magazine and there was a photo of President Bush reading to schoolchildren and the caption said, "President Bush, after the second plane hit the second building". And I was left wondering, why is the President of the United States still reading a book while my husband just got blown up by a plane? And it just didn't make sense to me. From then on, I just got involved with some other families of widows, particularly in fighting for an investigation into the attacks, why they happened, why they weren't prevented and what we learned in the course of that,' she added.

'My husband worked on Wall Street and I was a stay-at-home mum. I had no experience whatsoever. I am a very shy, private person and getting thrown out there publicly to the wolves to try to fight for the 9/11 families is extremely uncomfortable for me. I'm not a very public person, like anyone who knows me personally will tell you. They will tell you I hate being out at parties or anywhere like that. But along with the other widows that I work with, we're forced to do it because, genuinely, what we see happening and the information that we know is just so godawful wrong means we are just compelled to do something about it.

'We tell everyone that we meet, "Do not blindly assume that someone else is going to take care of this for you. Don't assume that other people are going to protect your rights. Don't assume that someone else will do it." The only way anything has ever gotten done for us is if we fought for it; you have to get up and fight for your rights and what you believe in because no one else is going to do that for you. Your government is not going to make sure that the 9/11 families are protected. If anything, if you're not out there, you're going to get trampled and your rights are going to get thrown under the bus, which is what we've learned repeatedly for the last nineteen years.

'I would love nothing better for my government to have done its job in protecting people on 9/11. That morning, they told people like my husband to stay at his desk. If they had told people in Tower Two to immediately escape, lives would have been saved. And then, in the aftermath of 9/11, there's been nothing but cover-up, a lack of accountability and a total disregard to the rights that we should have as this nation's largest group of terrorist victims. I would have loved for all that to have been magically taken care of by our elected officials.'

For nearly twenty years, the widows and other family representatives have had a fairly thankless task trying to get to the truth.

'It's not for a lack of asking for nineteen years,' said Kristen. 'The other widows and myself have relentlessly asked everyone and anyone. No one could say, "Oh, we didn't know you wanted to know that information."

'I mean, even to this day, I think it's the ninth pending requests to the FBI to get a case update. One of the reasons the FBI is not giving us access to information that we know exists against the Saudis is because they "quote unquote" have an ongoing investigation in the United States. If the FBI has an ongoing investigation and you're a victim of part of that crime, you are entitled to a case update by the FBI. We've requested it every year, but we have not had a case update since 2012. Now listen, any other victim of any other crime had no problem getting a case update, but for some weird reason, 9/11 families don't get case updates. The FBI, when they investigate things and have information that's valuable to a victim to hold the perpetrators accountable, the FBI and the Justice

Department and the prosecutors, they share that information with the victims. For some reason, with 9/11, we don't get that cooperation. We get stonewalled. I don't know why that is, but it's awfully unfair and strange.

'It's a huge cover-up of the failure and, I have to tell you, when you study it and you learn about the failure, failure, failure upon failure, you see a pattern. It is inconceivable to think that there were that many failures across that many sections of the US government that contributed to the mass murder of 3,000 people. That's an awful lot of failures in an awful lot of sectors.'

Kristen is still close to the other Jersey Girls. 'We were on a conference call this morning with the State Department and with the Senate Foreign Relations Committee and emailing them on the issue. So yes, we are still fully active and engaged, which is beyond pathetic and sad that nineteen years of my life has had to have been focused on these issues.

'I really would like to have a regular life and to move on beyond this and if my government would just treat us the way they treat every other victim, I could do that. But for some reason, when it comes to 9/11, there's cover-up and there's all sorts of other stuff that just, you know, does not help us.

'We are in this until we get truth, transparency, accountability and justice.

'That's what we started in October of 2001 and we haven't gotten it yet, and we are not going away – and, frankly, we have children and they will carry the torch once we're gone. We've raised them in a way and they've seen us as their mums for the last twenty years doing this, it's ingrained in them.

'The truth is not being given to us – it is being covered up and it shouldn't be. The people that deserve to be protected the most are completely being screwed over. It's very hard to get the information out to the American public so that they know what's going on.'

She said she believes the government underestimated the widows' 'sticktuitiveness'. 'When you've lost everything, you've got nothing to lose,' she continued. 'There's nothing left for us to lose. We've already lost everything. We are not lobbyists looking for a professional career in Washington. I'm not looking to make friends; I don't need to worry about where my next job is going to be in DC.

'I think that they definitely thought they'd wear us out and that we'd go away. And we haven't, and we won't until we get answers and accountability and justice and, that's just the way it is.'

Kristen believes the US authorities will go to extreme lengths to steer the spotlight away from criticism over its handling of 9/11. She thought, for example, that I would face officially sanctioned smears for highlighting the families' case in this book and claimed she had faced pressure to back down.

'I was invited to a United Nations meeting for victims of terrorism and there were all these hundreds of people talking and the UN is giving its spiel on how victims of terrorism are entitled to this, that and the other thing, and I'm listening to people from other nations, some of which are looked at in a very negative light, standing up and saying what their countries do for them.

'Finally,' she said, 'I stood up and I just wanted everyone to know that I'm so glad that you all get the help that you need because in the United States, we don't get help. If anything, they go out of their way to harm us. I rattled off a litany of things, and at the end of the meeting, I got tapped on the shoulder and I turned around and it's two people from the Department of Justice. They wanted to talk to me and make sure that I knew that they had heard what I said and, you know, blah, blah, blah, blah, blah. They needed my contact information and all kinds of stuff. They weren't happy that I stood up and said that.

'I was like, really? I got invited to this and after hearing about how these "quote unquote" lesser countries and third-world nations help their terrorism victims more than you people do. I don't know. I think I'm entitled to say that.'

Kristen is unapologetic. She had her life mapped out and it took a tragic turn on that fateful day. Because, like her husband, she prizes family above all else, she will not be derailed from the road less travelled. She can't allow another wife to become a widow and face the same brick wall.

'My husband was an amazing man,' she said. 'He was the best dad. He was an incredible husband. And I watched him blown up on live television. And when I turned to my government to know that my daughter and I would be safe and make sure that no one else would ever have to walk in my shoes, my government walked off and not only didn't help, but they went out of their way to harm me. We have been wholesale abandoned, and then, while I'm abandoned, they have made it storm and given me an earthquake underneath my feet.

'Did they need to do that? It's already been bad enough.'

Chapter Twenty-Two

The (Official) Cover-Up

Washington DC, 22 July 2004

The 9/11 Commission Report was supposed to be the last word on what really happened on 11 September 2001. To the families who lost loved ones, and particularly for Kristen and the Jersey Girls, it finally represented an opportunity to connect the dots.

They hoped that, perhaps, the reason for the lack of transparency from the Bush administration, the confusion over the true circumstances and the paucity of prosecutions was that the chaotic tentacles of the biggest investigation in the nation's history were simply too spread out to keep track of. This would bring it all together and offer some sense of closure.

If anything, the result was the exact opposite.

Underfunded, ill-informed and certainly not independent, the 9/11 Commission was a lion without teeth, designed to paint an official picture of the attacks that reflected the Bush administration's version of what happened. If its political appointees had any hopes of uncovering uncomfortable truths that veered from the official narrative, they were quickly quashed. As a public relations exercise, it had every chance of success; as an investigative body determined to reach the unvarnished truth about 9/11, it was set up to fail.

As members of the 9/11 Family Steering Committee, the Jersey Girls played an important role in pushing for the 9/11 Commission and helped to get Bush's first choice as chairman, Henry Kissinger, thrown out by highlighting his business interests involving Saudi Arabia, including members of the bin Laden family.

They were less effective in their opposition to Professor Philip Zelikow's appointment as executive director, citing his ties to the Bush White House and to National Security Advisor Condoleezza Rice in particular. He stayed, despite their fears he would orchestrate a whitewash.

By the time the commission was ready to start work, Kristen was already convinced the inquiry was set up to fail.

'No one at that time wanted any kind of investigation into 9/11,' she said. 'There was a joint inquiry, which was very limited. They didn't get access to a lot of information. They were still involved. But the 9/11 Commission was supposed to look at everything, not just the intelligence agencies.

'We had worked all along and had been fighting for the commission to get access while at the same time fighting the commissioners themselves to ask the questions that we wanted to get answers to for a more thorough investigation. Behind the scenes, we were battling for the commission to have the ability to do a thorough and true investigation. We were arguing with the commissioners that they weren't doing a good enough job, that they weren't asking the right questions. They weren't going to the proper areas – and we had conference call after conference call after conference call. With every topic they looked at, we were asking, "Why aren't you looking into this? Why aren't you asking this person those questions? Why aren't you providing answers as to why this happened?" They just didn't do it right.

'And I think the way that the investigation was structured, it was very compartmentalised and that was done purposefully, so that not one person or group could see the entire story in one linear way. Everybody was focused on one little topic and they had to stay on that topic because the danger is, when you take that one little topic and you hand it to the other little topic and you add it to the other little topic, it looks pretty bad.

'We were very involved in the selection of the commission, and I had done research on them all. So, we knew that they all were there for a purpose. Each and every one of them was there to protect one particular interest or several interests. They all were conflicted. Zelikow obviously was the staff director and he had a huge conflict of interest. He had no business being on that commission.

'We had hoped that the commission would result in some answers, but it really didn't. I mean, there's unfortunately many, many unanswered questions, many pieces of evidence that don't add up, and it's unfortunate because I think the American public deserves to know the truth. Quite frankly, we went to war in Iraq on a lie. Hundreds of thousands of people were killed, billions of dollars – trillions of dollars – were spent, and in my opinion, we've never been told the truth.

'It's unconscionable. I think what's really bad is that, twenty years out, we're still trying to get documents and evidence. And literally, the United States Department of Justice sits on the side of the Saudis in the courtroom and blocks evidence. My husband was killed and nearly 3,000 others were murdered in broad daylight and the government itself did not prosecute one person.'

The 9/11 Commission Report, when it was published on 22 July 2004, made for an interesting read, a detailed account of what was known about the attacks. But it didn't give the families the answers they had hoped for. It didn't explain the question marks that were growing over Saudi Arabia's involvement in the conspiracy, saying only that there was no evidence that there was anything suspicious. It suggested Bayoumi, the Saudi spy in San Diego, was simply a good Samaritan helping out his fellow Saudis in distress. It told how the CIA kept information about Mihdhar and Hazmi from the FBI; it didn't explain why. It certainly didn't go anywhere near the theory that there had been a doomed CIA attempt to 'turn' Mihdhar.

The dots remained unconnected. At the time, Kristen called the report 'utterly hollow'.

'The report itself is compartmentalised in the same way as the inquiry,' she says now. 'It's not told in a linear fashion, in a story that makes sense. It's told in a very jumbled way and it has you jumping around in different places. The footnotes are at the back of the book and they're written really small.

'And so it's done, in my opinion, purposely to shade the story and confuse people. There's a much easier way to tell the story in a straightforward manner that would raise a lot of questions and the commission was designed to ward that off.

'They did not connect the dots. At the same time, the United States was embarking on the war in Iraq and you were treated as being unpatriotic if you asked questions. It was an environment that was not conducive to questioning intelligence agencies, which to us seemed so stupid because we were wondering, "How are you not investigating these failures?" You're looking to the same intelligence agency to provide you with proof of why you should go to war in another country. And sure enough, we're on record from day one as saying Iraq had nothing to do with 9/11. Nobody listened to us. Nobody.'

The Jersey Girls tried at first to sway with the punches and make the best of what they deemed to be a bad job done by the 9/11 Commission.

'We tried to take some of the recommendations that were benign and support those,' said Kristen. 'But we knew that the commission wasn't a real investigation. We knew that as a staff director, Philip Zelikow was a total plant.'

Kristen said that former New Jersey Governor Tom Kean, who chaired the commission, broke his promise to make all the documents used in the inquiry available to the public.

'We were promised by Tom Kean and Lee Hamilton [the vice chair] that all of the underlying documents that they used would be transparent. We would have access to them. But we don't, to this day. I've spoken to him since he promised us, and he said, "That's an outrage. That's not true at all, they are public."

'I told him, "You told us, and you told the American public that everything that you worked on would be public information and available. And it's not, it's all hidden."'

It would be another thirteen years before Zelikow returned to the claim that a bid to recruit Mihdhar was behind the intelligence shambles before 9/11. He picked a fight with Richard Clarke and Mark Rossini, the FBI agent tortured by his decision to follow the rules and not share the CIA report on Mihdhar and Hazmi with his superiors in the FBI. He didn't know it at the time, but he was also taking on the 9/11 widows and the Jersey Girls again.

Writing a blog on a security services insider website, the Cipher Brief, Zelikow, the professor of history at the University of Virginia, took issue with the claim, asserted in this book, that the CIA intentionally withheld information from the FBI 'that might have prevented the 9/11 attack'.

He insisted there was no evidence to back up the recruitment conspiracy theory, quoting his own 9/11 Commission's inability to find any proof to support it. 'Instead,' he wrote, 'the evidence showed – as we detail in our report – repeated confusion about who was being sought and where. There were several occasions during the work in the first half of 2001 when the dots might have been connected but, due to particular circumstances in each case, unfortunately this did not happen.'

Rossini was quick to respond, saying, 'Speaking only for myself, I arrived at the theory of recruitment as a plausible reason why the draft CIR [Central Intelligence Report] written by my FBI colleague, Special Agent Douglas J. Miller was purposely blocked from being sent to the FBI on or about January 6th, 1999, since no other logical reason could be determined.

'A canard has been floated that the FBI and CIA never shared anything prior to 9/11 and, therefore, that was the reason why SA Miller's CIR was never sent,' he continued. 'As the executive director of the 9/11 Commission, you know that not to be true. You never drilled down as to why of all the hundreds if not thousands of CIRs, IIRs [intelligence information report], LHMs [letter-head memorandum], etc., sent between the two agencies each year, that SA Miller's memo was stopped. There are even instant messages between the person who told me not to speak with the FBI about the contents of SA Miller's memo and deputy unit chief of Alec Station at that time, in which it was decided that SA Miller's CIR was not to be sent to the FBI.'

The forum again offered the opportunity for the widows who felt betrayed at the 2004 findings of the commission to vent at its former executive director.

'My husband was killed in the World Trade Center and, in my experience and opinion, it is Mark Rossini who should be believed,' wrote Kathleen Owens, who lost her husband in the World Trade Center attacks. 'Philip Zelikow loves to say there was "no evidence", but he was instrumental in making sure of that. We are still waiting for thousands of documents to be declassified. The 9/11 Commission Report is not a complete or definitive resource,' she added.

Lorie Van Auken, one of the Jersey Girls, also stood behind Rossini, writing: 'Philip, speaking as a 9/11 widow who fought for the 9/11 Commission, attended all of the commission hearings, regularly submitted questions for the commission, and often met with the staff and commissioners, to be clear, I want to say that I believe Mark Rossini.'

Another Jersey Girl, Mindy Kleinberg, piped in: 'I find it curious that you would feel the need to refute Mark Rossini's supposition. And so emphatically, at that. In footnote 44 of your 9/11 Commission Report you tell the public that an FBI agent detailed to the CIA Bin Laden unit (sounds like agencies working together, but I digress) was told to purposefully withhold information regarding two known terrorists to the FBI. This information, had it been shared, could have possibly thwarted the 9/11 attacks. That's how important that information was. And it was not withheld due to a "wall" between agencies or lack of information sharing but rather purposefully, criminally withheld. And yet the commission report just leaves it at that. No further discussion on why that critical piece of information was withheld, no further investigation of who committed that obstruction and no consequence for the person that committed that crime. Were they left in their position at the CIA? Could the nation be safe with someone like that in that position? Was that not the purpose of the 9/11 Commission to begin with? To make recommendations that would make us safe? So, if what you posit in your article is true, then what was the reason for this withholding of evidence and what have you done about it?'

In a further post, she added: 'The biggest problem is that Zelikow fails to give any hypotheses for the mistakes the CIA officer makes. The fact that Rossini, an agent involved in this incident, and Clarke, a former national security advisor, choose to give us a possible reason is due to the fact that Zelikow does not do that at all. And just whining and complaining that someone is offering an opinion without offering another real reason does nothing to set any record straight.'

In another post, written with Van Auken, Kristen defended Rossini and Clarke and insisted, 'The truth will out.'

They wrote: 'When Zelikow makes comments that "there was simply no evidence" found by the commission to warrant "blah, blah, blah", you must recognise that it was Zelikow's job to ensure that the commission would never find the evidence it needed to make a full assessment and provide a full accounting of the "how" and "why" of 9/11. If an investigator got too close to some malfeasance on behalf of a foreign government? Philip fired them. If an investigator asked a too pointed question about an agency? Philip reassigned them. If too much damning information found its way into the commission's final report? Philip re-wrote it. Funny how, as a self-described historian, Philip fails to comprehend that you don't rewrite history – you report it, straight.'

They added: 'Finally, we want to be crystal clear when we say this: the withholding of the information discussed herein was deliberate and purposeful. Three thousand people were murdered in cold blood as a result. And since the withholding of this information happened AFTER the *Cole* bombing, there is simply no room for excuse – any reasonable person would have foreseen and concluded that death or injury would result by not sharing this information. And that's a problem when a federal grand jury is empanelled for mass murder.'

The last word on the commission goes to Kristen Breitweiser. "In some ways, the 9/11 Commission was our baby," she says now. "So, what do you do when your baby grows up to be a serial killer?"

Chapter Twenty-Three

The Blueprint

**Manila, The Philippines,
6 January 1994**

They join the long line at the 'Stealthy Starbucks' for vanilla lattes and lemon pound cake at the CIA's forest-bound headquarters in Langley, Virginia, rather than head for lunch at old spy watering holes in nearby DC, like the now-closed Chadwicks or Au Pied de Cochon in Georgetown, both restaurants that fell victim to the demise of the James Bond largesse expense account.

Wide-eyed and invariably young, the new breed of CIA analysts, straight out of Dartmouth and Yale, are so well versed in the brave new world of data that many don't see the need to stray too far from their desks. It's all there online, they will tell you, if you know where to look.

To the dying breed of old-school, shoe-leather spooks, who only returned home for a change of clothes and would have to be dragged screaming into the office, the young turks are all that has gone wrong with the modern service. They blame the new breed, or at least the new breed at the turn of the millennium, for missing the clues staring them in the face for years that al-Qaeda was totally committed to, first, bringing down the World Trade Center and, second, using passenger planes to do it.

They know better than to think anyone would carry the can for missing the signs – most of those involved in running the CIA's ill-fated Alec Station Bin Laden unit ended up getting promoted. But the question remains; why didn't the fifty or so CIA staff, working full time on the bin Laden desk in 2001, connect the dots from a failed terrorist plot in 1994 to fly planes into the CIA headquarters at Langley and a handful of other US targets and the slow-burning plans to fly planes into the World Trade Center and the Pentagon on 11 September 2001?

It is clear now that the 1994 Bojinka Plot was the blueprint for 9/11. The same terrorist came up with the idea – Khalid Sheikh Mohammed – and at least part of the plot relied on the same concept of using planes as weapons. Funding was supplied by Osama bin Laden and the death toll was estimated at about 4,000 people, if they pulled it off. The biggest difference was the Bojinka Plot, as it was called by KSM, was foiled by a mixture of luck and detective work.

When they saw the Twin Towers falling on TV in the Philippines, the investigators involved in the 1994 investigation simply could not believe the Americans had allowed it to happen. They thought they had shut down any hopes the jihadists had of an airliner attack and passed on enough information to their US counterparts to ensure it could never happen. It turned out that Bojinka was just a dress rehearsal.

Consider the evidence that was in the hands of the CIA years before 9/11.

The story begins with a complaint to police in Manila on the night of 6 January 1994 that some fireworks had accidentally gone off in a sixth-floor flat at the Doña Josefa apartment building in the city centre, which overlooked the route Pope John Paul II was due to use in a visit to the city a few days later.

Inspector Aida Fariscal decided to take a closer look inside. This is where the luck combined with good police work. Behind the locked door of the burning studio apartment number 603 was a bomb factory and a gold mine of intelligence detailing a massive terror plot that, had it been carried out, would have dwarfed the first bomb attack on the World Trade Center the previous year.

There was clear proof that the Pope was the immediate target. There were maps of his route as well as Bibles, crucifixes and a priest's cassock to be used by a suicide bomber to sneak among the Holy Father's entourage. There were how-to bombmaking kits, gallons of toxic chemicals, a finished bomb and enough timers, switches and equipment to make many more. It was an Aladdin's cave of terrorist hardware.

Perhaps even more importantly, there was software, too. In their haste to leave, the two men who had been living in the flat left behind, on a Toshiba laptop, plans that portrayed the Pope's assassination as just the curtain raiser to a campaign of terror on a scale never seen before.

A file on the computer tagged 'Bojinka' included a list of American and United airline schedules for eleven long-haul flights between the US and Asia, together with the Arabic names of recruits who would plant bombs on board before getting off after the first leg of the journeys. The explosives were synchronised to go off on all eleven flights at the same time over the Pacific Ocean.

Investigators from the CIA and the Philippines intelligence service would learn of another chilling element to the plot after questioning the man who set off the chemical fire in the sixth-floor flat. Abdul Hakim Murad, the son of a Pakistani crane operator, had returned to retrieve the computer and was caught trying to flee.

His accomplice, police later learned, was Ramzi Yousef, the British-educated brains behind the 1993 World Trade Center bombing and, at that time, the world's most wanted man with a $2 million bounty on his head. Yousef, who was KSM's nephew, was arrested the following year in Pakistan.

During intense 'tactical interrogations' at a military base on the outskirts of Manila, Murad revealed he had trained as a pilot in Texas, New York and North Carolina, totting up 275 hours of flying time to get a commercial pilot's licence on 8 June 1992.

According to a transcript of the interrogation, Murad confessed his pilot training was for a suicide mission in which he planned to buy a small Cessna aircraft, fill it with explosives and fly it into the CIA headquarters in Langley.

Worse, the terrorists also planned to fly commercial planes into the Pentagon, the White House, Congress and some US skyscrapers. All that was missing were more trained pilots.

Sources in the Philippines confirmed that both the FBI and the CIA had full access to all the evidence from Bojinka. Bearing in mind the US interest in the investigation, it is quite likely that the CIA was represented at Murad's interrogations.

'We told the Americans about the plans to turn planes into flying bombs as far back as 1995. Why didn't they pay attention?' General Avelino Razon, one of the lead Bojinka investigators would later complain to reporters.

Just one person died as a result of the plot when Yousef tested his bomb-making skills by planting an explosive aboard a Philippine Airlines flight. But while the Americans patted themselves on the back and moved on, KSM and bin

Laden, unbowed, set about perfecting their plans to exact the maximum amount of destruction on the United States from the air.

Yousef and Murad would be extradited to America and sentenced to life behind bars, and many of the lessons from Bojinka would be forgotten until 11 September 2001 when all the chickens would come home to roost in the most horrific way imaginable.

There is a sign on the wall of an airless, windowless room amid the labyrinth of offices at CIA headquarters that reads, 'Every Day Is September 12th'. Perhaps the agency would have fared better if it had set the clock back to before the attacks were allowed to happen.

~~TOP SECRET SPECIAL HANDLING NOFORN~~

THE JOINT CHIEFS OF STAFF
WASHINGTON 25, D.C.

UNCLASSIFIED

13 March 1962

MEMORANDUM FOR THE SECRETARY OF DEFENSE

Subject: Justification for US Military Intervention
in Cuba (TS)

1. The Joint Chiefs of Staff have considered the attached Memorandum for the Chief of Operations, Cuba Project, which responds to a request of that office for brief but precise description of pretexts which would provide justification for US military intervention in Cuba.

2. The Joint Chiefs of Staff recommend that the proposed memorandum be forwarded as a preliminary submission suitable for planning purposes. It is assumed that there will be similar submissions from other agencies and that these inputs will be used as a basis for developing a time-phased plan. Individual projects can then be considered on a case-by-case basis.

3. Further, it is assumed that a single agency will be given the primary responsibility for developing military and para-military aspects of the basic plan. It is recommended that this responsibility for both overt and covert military operations be assigned the Joint Chiefs of Staff.

For the Joint Chiefs of Staff:

SYSTEMATICALLY REVIEWED
BY JCS ON _____
CLASSIFICATION CONTINUED

L. L. LEMNITZER
Chairman
Joint Chiefs of Staff

1 Enclosure
Memo for Chief of Operations, Cuba Project   EXCLUDED FROM GDS

EXCLUDED FROM AUTOMATIC
REGRADING; DOD DIR 5200.10
DOES NOT APPLY

~~TOP SECRET SPECIAL HANDLING NOFORN~~

The Northwoods memorandum: the opening page of a top secret Department of Defense memo from 1962 suggesting a series of dirty tricks to discredit Castro's Communist regime in Cuba.

Chapter Twenty-Four

The Precedent

Washington DC, 13 March 1962

The 13 March 1962 memo was addressed to President John F. Kennedy's defence secretary, Robert McNamara, from the US Joint Chiefs of Staff and marked 'Top Secret Special Handling'.

Written at the height of the Cold War, a little under a year after the calamitous Bay of Pigs Invasion by 1,500 CIA-trained Cuban expats, its subject line read, 'Justification for US Military Intervention in Cuba', and it was signed by the then Chairman of the Joint Chiefs of Staff, Army General Lyman L. Lemnitzer.

It was as official as a memorandum with the full weight of the American military could get, but it reads like the script from a Quentin Tarantino movie, only less believable. The ensuing pages suggest hijacking planes, blowing up a US ship, killing Cuban refugees and orchestrating a domestic terror campaign – all so the Americans can blame Fidel Castro as a pretext to go to war with communist Cuba.

Operation Northwoods, the real-life government plan dreamed up under the administration of one of America's most admired and respected presidents, is quoted by conspiracy theorists as an example of how the most unlikely of scenarios can turn out to be true. If such a plan can be recommended by the military under JFK's leadership in 1962, why is it so unbelievable to think that the Bush White House was incapable of such a plot in 2001?

Of course, the two situations aren't linked; there's no connecting the dots here, and the ideas never left the planning table. But Northwoods does show just how crazy it can get.

'The desired resultant from the execution of this plan would be to place the United States in the apparent position of suffering defensible grievances from a rash and irresponsible government of Cuba and to develop an international image of a Cuban threat to peace in the western hemisphere.'

That was the aim. Here are some of the methods suggested to build opposition to Cuba as part of a 'cover and deception' plot.

In Cuba, 'friendly' Cubans would stage mock 'over-the-fence' attacks on the US base at Guantanamo Bay and start fake riots near the main gates. Saboteurs – again, friendly Cubans – would be arrested on the base. Ammunition dumps would be blown up, aircrafts set ablaze, mortar shells lobbed over the fences and ships would be sunk in the harbour. There would even be funerals for mock victims. All this would be fabricated.

That wasn't nearly enough for the Operation Northwoods planners. They were just getting started. As a US response to these make-believe attacks by Cuba, the American military could respond by one of two options. 'We could blow up a US ship in Guantanamo Bay and blame Cuba,' says the report.

Or there is option B: 'We could blow up a drone (unmanned) vessel anywhere in the Cuban waters. We could arrange to cause such incident in the vicinity of Havana or Santiago as a spectacular result of Cuban attack from the air or sea, or both.

The presence of Cuban planes or ships merely investigating the intent of the vessel could be fairly compelling evidence that the ship was taken under attack. The nearness to Havana or Santiago would add credibility, especially to those people that might have heard the blast or have seen the fire. The US could follow up with an air/sea rescue operation covered by US fighters to "evacuate" remaining members of the non-existent crew. Casualty lists in US newspapers would cause a helpful wave of national indignation.'

Not content with causing chaos around Cuba, the military planners suggest taking the (fake) terror to the mainland. 'We could develop a Communist Cuban terror campaign in the Miami area, in other Florida cities and even in Washington,' it recommends. 'We could sink a boatload of Cubans en route to Florida (real or simulated). We could foster attempts on lives of Cubans in the United States, even to the extent of wounding in instances to be widely publicised. Exploding a few plastic bombs in carefully chosen spots, the arrest of Cuban agents and the release of prepared documents substantiating Cuban involvement also would be helpful in projecting the idea of an irresponsible government.'

You really couldn't make this up. It continues: 'Use of (Soviet) MIG-type aircraft by US pilots could provide additional provocation. Harassment of civil air, attacks on surface shipping and destruction of US military drone aircraft by MIG-type planes would be useful as complementary actions. An F-86 properly painted would convince air passengers that they saw a Cuban MIG, especially if the pilot of the transport were to announce such fact. The primary drawback to this suggestion appears to be the security risk inherent in obtaining or modifying an aircraft. However, reasonable copies of the MIG could be produced from US resources in about three months.'

It is hard to believe that the US military would seriously consider a fake plane hijacking and, let's not forget, they didn't actually go forward with this plan. But they thought about it.

'Hijacking attempts against civil air and surface craft should appear to continue as harassing measures condoned by the government of Cuba. Concurrently, genuine defections of Cuban civil and military air and surface craft should be encouraged.

'It is possible to create an incident which will demonstrate convincingly that a Cuban aircraft has attacked and shot down a chartered civil airliner en route from the United States to Jamaica, Guatemala, Panama or Venezuela. The destination would be chosen only to cause the flight plan route to cross Cuba. The passengers could be a group of college students off on a holiday or any grouping of persons with a common interest to support chartering a non-scheduled flight.'

At this point, the plan shows some similarities to the more 'out there' 9/11 Truther claims.

Remember, this is an official document. It continues: 'An aircraft at Eglin AFB would be painted and numbered as an exact duplicate for a civil registered aircraft belonging to a CIA proprietary organisation in the Miami area. At a designated time, the duplicate would be substituted for the actual civil aircraft and would be loaded with the selected passengers, all boarded under carefully prepared aliases. The actual registered aircraft would be converted to a drone.

'Take off times of the drone aircraft and the actual aircraft will be scheduled to allow a rendezvous south of Florida. From the rendezvous point, the passenger-carrying aircraft will descend to a minimum altitude and go directly into an auxiliary field at Eglin AFB where arrangements will have been made to evacuate the passengers and returned the aircraft to its original status. The drone aircraft, meanwhile, will continue to fly the filed flight plan. When over Cuba the drone will be transmitting on the international distress frequency a 'MAY DAY' message stating he is under attack by Cuban MIG aircraft. The transmission will be interrupted by destruction of the aircraft, which will be triggered by radio signal. This will allow ICAO [International Civil Aviation Organisation] radio stations in the western hemisphere to tell the US what has happened to the aircraft instead of the US trying to "sell" the incident.'

The Northwoods planners also thought it was a good idea to make it look like the Cubans had shot down USAF planes in an unprovoked attack over international waters. After faking the incident and spreading aircraft parts and a parachute off the coast of Cuba, the real pilot would be spirited away, leaving the impression he was dead.

It's not like the Operation Northwoods memo was the only one of its kind. In a proposal codenamed Operation Dirty Trick, which was sent in a 2 February 1962 note to Air Force Brigadier General Edward G. Lansdale, the idea was to blame Cuba if astronaut John Glenn's space mission that month ended in tragedy.

The proposal was 'to provide irrevocable proof that, should the Mercury manned orbit flight fail, the fault lies with the Communists et al Cuba … by manufacturing various pieces of evidence which would prove electronic interference on the part of the Cubans.'

The plan was rendered moot because Glenn made it back to Earth safely, but the planners had another idea for the general in charge of fostering revolt in Cuba. Operation Good Times involved mocking up a photo of 'an obese Castro with two beauties in any situation desired' by 'a table brimming over with the most delectable Cuban food'.

'This should put even a Commie dictator in the proper perspective with the underlying masses,' said the memo.

The over-arching conspiracy spurring these bizarre plots was Operation Mongoose. Led by Lansdale, it was a secretive effort to look at more innovative methods of doing away with Castro. According to the *New York Times*, the CIA devised thirty-three different plans under Mongoose, quite apart from the military's madcap proposals. They included sending Castro a toxin-ridden wetsuit or a poison pen as a deadly gift, hiring a mafia hitman and destroying Cuba's sugar crops with biological weapons. Operation Free Ride involved US planes dropping one-way airline tickets to Mexico City and Caracas. Operation Raindrop would change the weather. The US would 'seed clouds off Cuba, which would produce heavy rains during cane harvesting season ... The state of the art will permit colouring the rain (red/green),' the unnamed author wrote.

It would be foolish to think that Kennedy and his attorney general brother Bobby were blind to all this stuff. Maybe some of the ideas may have even seen the light of day had JFK not been assassinated himself in Dallas in 1963.

As I have stated elsewhere in this book, I do not think Bush or anyone in his Cabinet, as hawkish as many of them were, would go so far as to be actively involved in orchestrating the 9/11 plot. I do, however, believe them capable of covering up the truth.

And the Pentagon's pocketbook thriller antics in the early 1960s, under one of the admired presidents in US history, show just how crazy governments and the military can get if left unchecked.

Chapter Twenty-Five

The (Military) Cover-Up

**US Senate, Capitol Hill, Washington DC,
21 September 2005**

Joe Biden was emphatic. He wanted answers. He wanted
to know why there was a cover-up. 'I mean, I don't get the
purpose of the cover-up,' he said. 'Is it to protect the Clinton
administration? The Bush administration? Is it to protect
something that was going on that was illegal under the law?
I mean, I don't get it. I don't understand why people aren't
just coming forward and saying, "Here is the deal. This is
what happened."'

This was long before his two terms as vice president and
his epic battle with Donald Trump for the top job. Biden was
asking the obvious questions at a Senate Judiciary Committee
hearing, called to investigate reports of yet another intelligence
failure before 9/11.

As if it wasn't enough that the CIA was aware that known
al-Qaeda killers Khalid al-Mihdhar and Nawaf al-Hazmi were
in the United States for eighteen months before the attacks
and intentionally kept that information from the FBI, it now
seemed that the US Defense Intelligence Agency, the military
equivalent of the CIA, had also identified Mihdhar and Hazmi,

as well as ringleader Mohamed Atta and Flight 175 pilot Marwan al-Shehhi back in the summer of 2000.

Once again, they had failed to pass on that crucial information to the FBI, the agency with responsibility for domestic criminal investigations, and once again, the 'wall' between the intelligence services was being blamed.

This time, the Pentagon spooks had also come up with an even more intriguing excuse for what appears on the surface to be every bit as damaging as the allegations made against the CIA, because it seemed to identify Atta, the leader of the American cells. Take him out of the equation and, in all possibility, the attacks may never have happened.

Apparently, the reason the Department of Defense lawyers gave for blocking the handover of information about the four al-Qaeda operatives was the Civil War Posse Comitatus Act. Dating all the way back to 1878, it was signed into law by President Rutherford B. Hayes as a means to prevent federal troops from being used to enforce domestic legislation. It was enacted after violent paramilitary groups were deputised in the American South to suppress African-American civil rights groups and was intended to put an end to the tradition of southern states turning to the US Army to help settle disputes (although it didn't prevent Donald Trump from using the National Guard to tackle civilian unrest in 2020). Like other presidents, including George W. Bush and three commander in chiefs in the 1960s civil rights era, Trump invoked an even older law, the 1807 Insurrection Act, that was originally supposed to allow a president to bring in a militia to guard against 'hostile incursions of the Indians').

Judiciary Committee Chairman Arlen Specter had called a hearing in September 2005 to find out the truth of the allegations that the US military had also dropped the ball after identifying

Atta and his fellow al-Qaeda plotters. If he thought he would get any real answers, he was quickly set straight. Five key witnesses, some from the military, some civilian, but all working at the Pentagon, were ordered not to testify by their Langley bosses and any documents that may have had any bearing had been destroyed, again by order of the Defense Department.

Specter's hearing and questions that it raised would soon be swept under the carpet, along with every other inconvenient truth about 9/11. But on this day at least, it sounded like Biden and the judiciary wanted an open airing about a secret operation that veered dangerously close to an issue that was just beginning to unsettle Americans, and, indeed, people around the world: just how vulnerable was their privacy on the Internet?

Project Able Danger was a data-mining project set up by the US Special Operations Command and the Defense Intelligence Agency – with the authorisation of the chairman of the Joint Chiefs of Staff – around 1999 to 2000 to plough through the gargantuan amount of information available online to target international terrorists, with particular emphasis on al-Qaeda, and try to get a handle on their activities. The small team of five operatives plumbed open data and paired it up to classified knowledge to which only they had access and tried to find patterns of behaviour and, even more importantly, tried to identify individuals who could be dangerous.

By all accounts, they were better at this than even they realised at the time. One data analyst even had a photo of Atta pinned to a chart on the wall of his office at Andrews Air Force Base in Maryland in 2000 (before the Department of Defense investigators removed and destroyed it).

The chart, and as many as twenty others like it, followed the movements of al-Qaeda operatives around the world, using information gleaned from known incidents such as the 1993 World Trade Center bombing and the attacks on USS *Cole* and the African embassies, and from known al-Qaeda members and supporters, such as the Blind Sheik, Sheikh Omar Abdel-Rahman.

The names associated with these events were plugged into open-source data systems to see what connections the computer would find. Forget 'six degrees of Kevin Bacon', the committee was told, a reference to the infamously broad base of the Hollywood actor's connections, this was 'six degrees of Sheik Rahman'.

Rahman, a preacher who had been blind since childhood, was jailed for life in the US in 1995 after being convicted of masterminding a series of terrorist plots and was branded the 'Godfather' of extremist Islamic terror groups. Several followers were imprisoned following the 1993 World Trade Center attack, but Rahman was arrested on a broader conspiracy, which included a plot to bomb the bridges and tunnels around New York City and the FBI headquarters in Manhattan. His name just kept cropping up in counterterrorism investigations. Rahman died behind bars in North Carolina in 2017. He was described by bin Laden biographer Peter Bergen as 'the spiritual guide of 9/11'.

Some of the Able Danger associations meant nothing. Others, as it turned out, were spot on. Five al-Qaeda cells were identified – one of them, Atta's Brooklyn crew. Clicking on each name of the chart would bring up a wealth of supporting information. The chart, said data analysts, showed that al-Qaeda had 'a surprisingly significant presence within the United States'.

Specter's committee was told that the amount of Able Danger data destroyed in May to June 2000 was up to 2.5 terabytes

– the equivalent of one-quarter of all the written material in America's hallowed Library of Congress.

The chart was an enormous al-Qaeda library in itself but, instead of being used to help pursue the monsters responsible, it was all destroyed to prevent the Pentagon from a little embarrassment.

According to an FBI agent who was contacted by members of the Able Danger programme, she arranged three meetings between Lieutenant-Colonel Tony Shaffer, one of the project's leaders, and the bureau's Washington Field Office in September 2000 so that key information about Atta and his Brooklyn al-Qaeda cell could be handed over and trigger the possible launch of a criminal investigation. On each occasion, the meetings were called off at the last minute by Defense Department officials. The reason? Pentagon lawyers believed Atta was in the US on a green card and that if anything went wrong, it could backfire with the military being blamed for an operation that violated the privacy of a civilian who was in the country legally.

'We didn't know that Atta's name was significant' at the time, Schaffer told the *New York Times*. 'We just knew there were these linkages between him and these other individuals who were in this loose configuration' of terror suspects linked what appeared to be an al-Qaeda cell in America.

It will come as no surprise that the 9/11 Commission wasn't interested in the Able Danger foul-up, rejecting requests from Congressman Curt Weldon, one of the lawmakers campaigning for the facts to come out into the open, to meet with investigators and ignoring the failure completely in its final report, ruling it 'historically insignificant'.

The lack of transparency, Weldon told the committee, was 'unacceptable to the families and friends of the victims of

9/11 and flies in the face of every ideal upon which this country was founded.'

Again unsurprisingly, the DOJ's office of the deputy inspector general came up with a report in 2006 that whitewashed the Able Danger scandal. Mohamed Atta wasn't identified, there was no bar on sharing information with the FBI and the destruction of all that al-Qaeda intelligence was 'appropriate'. So much for transparency.

We would have known much more about this sorry saga through the first-hand testimony of Lieutenant-Colonel Schaffer, the project's liaison between the data boffins and the Defense Intelligence Agency, who wrote a book about his experiences called *Operation Dark Heart*. But the Department of Defense clearly thought the public wasn't ready for the truth; they bought up all 10,000 copies at a cost of $47,000 and destroyed them all.

From terminating terabytes to burning books, it's not a good look for the land of the free.

Chapter Twenty-Six

The Figurehead: Wanted Dead (Not Alive)

Abbottabad, Pakistan,
1 a.m., 2 May 2011

Less than a year after 9/11, Interpol's office in Washington DC appeared to be the only place in the world where they didn't know who Osama bin Laden was. A lawyer's request for a copy of bin Laden's arrest warrant on 8 August 2002 was met with an impossible request from an official at the Interpol, US National Central Bureau, at the Department of Justice.

'You must submit an authorization (privacy waiver) signed by Usama bin Laden consenting to the USNCB's release to you of any record that it may have pertaining to him … After the USNCB receives a completed form, signed by him, we will search our systems of records for his name.'

It was a tall order by any stretch of the imagination, as America had been searching unsuccessfully for the al-Qaeda leader since the previous September and before. It wouldn't be until 2 May 2011 that anyone in the West knew for certain where he was – and by then, it was too late to get him to sign any forms.

As with almost everything connected to 9/11, the death of

Osama bin Laden still raises many questions. Coming as it did at the tail end of Barack Obama's first term, it inevitably played a part in his re-election the following year. There was rejoicing in the streets of America following the president's White House announcement that the world's most wanted man had finally been hunted down and killed. Once again, we were expected to believe, with little verification, the narrative fed to the media in the hours and days that followed.

We were asked to believe that bin Laden was hiding in plain sight in a sprawling fortress compound near a Pakistani military base in Abbottabad, just sixty miles from the bustling metropolis of Islamabad with its million-plus population.

Bin Laden had swapped the remote, barren mountains on Afghanistan's inhospitable border for a comfortable mansion in one of Pakistan's most picturesque and affluent cities. Abbottabad – named after James Abbott, the Indian Army officer who founded the town in 1853 – has such a pleasant climate that it has long been a major hub for tourists visiting the region. A military base offered added security in the city that was the former home of the Gurkhas.

Behind the walls of his hideaway, bin Laden had every reason to believe he was way beyond the searching eyes of the Americans he had taunted for so long, or at least that was how his last living arrangements were portrayed by the jubilant US administration. His family was with him and a parade of couriers would bring him everything he needed from the outside world. The huge three-storey house he was living in was eight times larger than most other homes in the area, hardly a low-profile hideaway for the al-Qaeda leader with a multi-million-dollar bounty on his head.

Yet, according to US intelligence sources, bin Laden was taken completely by surprise by the US special forces who left with the hunting trophy they had spent the best part of a decade stalking.

He had survived two wars launched with the aim of capturing him and his followers. The last time the Americans and the British got as close was just a few months after the hijacked airliner attacks on New York and Washington, when bin Laden managed to elude them on horseback through the caves and gullies in the White Mountains of eastern Afghanistan. For most of the next decade, bin Laden lived up to the nickname of 'Elvis', which he had been given by the CIA because there had been so many bogus and fanciful sightings.

The story that came out after the hit was that Obama was told in an intelligence briefing that there was a possible lead that bin Laden was hiding in plain sight in Abbottabad the preceding August and that it took eight months for US and Pakistani agents to confirm for certain that the information was accurate. Obama and his national security chiefs supposedly wanted to be absolutely sure, because the tip seemed so implausible. After so many dead-end enquiries, it was hard to believe that the elusive terror chief would be so brazen to live in a town favoured as a retirement spot for Pakistan's military and society elite. The ten-foot walls and heavy security surrounding the compound made verification all the more difficult.

The administration suggested that just one week before the Navy SEALs raid, Obama was finally given concrete photographic proof that bin Laden was there and gave his authorisation for Operation Neptune Spear to target the West's terrorist bogeyman.

US special operations forces were handed down one explicit instruction for the mission – get Osama bin Laden, dead or alive. The raid on the compound, which was just 100 yards from a Pakistani military academy, was launched at about 1.15 a.m. on Sunday, 2 May 2011.

Bin Laden's guards opened fire from the roof and one of the four helicopters used by the US anti-terror forces crashed. During the operation, which took just forty minutes from start to finish, bin Laden was shot in the head in a firefight as he tried to evade capture.

Three of his men were also killed, along with a woman they supposedly tried to use as a human shield. One of bin Laden's eleven sons, Khalid, was among the dead. There were differing accounts of the details of bin Laden's last moments, but he was with a number of his wives and was unarmed when he was shot in his bedroom fifteen minutes into the raid.

SEAL Team Six member Robert O'Neill, using a pseudonym, went public with his claim that he was the one who shot bin Laden, saying he killed him with a bullet in the forehead. Another SEAL, Matt Bissonnette, followed up with another version in which the al-Qaeda leader was already injured by an initial volley of bullets from the SEAL on point before he and O'Neill burst into the bedroom to finish him off. Bissonnette faced a federal investigation after failing to submit his account of the raid, the number-one bestseller *No Easy Day*, to the US Department of Defense for prepublication review.

No Americans were hurt in the mission, but it didn't go without a hitch. One helicopter they used to breach the mansion walls suffered a mechanical breakdown and couldn't fly some of the soldiers out. The SEALs burned the wrecked helicopter and used another one to ferry bin Laden's body back to the Ghazi air base in northwest Pakistan. He was buried at sea within twenty-four hours of his death, complying with Islamic tradition. No photograph of the body nor any DNA evidence confirming identification was ever made public in spite of Freedom of Information requests from a number of media outlets.

Amnesty International was among the human rights organisations unhappy with the information provided concerning the circumstances of bin Laden's death. 'Given that he was not armed, it is not clear how he resisted arrest and whether an attempt was made to capture him rather than kill him,' said Amnesty International Director Claudio Cordone. 'Amnesty International believes that US forces should have attempted to capture Osama bin Laden alive in order to bring him to trial if he was unarmed and posing no immediate threat,' she added.

It was an ignominious ending for bin Laden after one of history's biggest manhunts. After he had evaded capture in mid-December 1991, there were precious few credible leads of his whereabouts. But the background story leaked by US intelligence was that around 2008, CIA agents managed to identify one of bin Laden's most trusted couriers, after a detainee at Guantanamo Bay gave them his nickname. It took another two years for them to discover the area where the courier and his brother were operating.

By January of 2011, they found out that the courier and his brother were living in a mansion that appeared to be much larger than anything they could afford. Suspicions were raised further by the thick walls around the compound. While other homes in the area put rubbish out to be collected, the residence's trash was burned in the grounds of the mansion, which did not have phone or Internet service.

By February 2011, US intelligence officials were said to be confident that bin Laden and his family were living inside the walls of the courier's home and, by March, Obama was convening top secret meetings with his senior security staff and CIA agents had rented a house in Abbottabad to spy on the mansion.

Just as with the events of 11 September, the official version of bin Laden's death has largely been accepted, despite the hazy explanations of America's involvement with our old friends from ISI, the Pakistani Inter-Services Intelligence.

Many CIA officials with a keen knowledge of the region, who were not involved in the bin Laden hit, had a deep mistrust of ISI because of the agency's traditional ties with the Pashtuns of Waziristan, who were believed to have harboured bin Laden for some of his years on the run.

That didn't mean that the CIA didn't have a strong working relationship with the Pakistani spy service. Quite the contrary. As we have already seen, despite their philosophical and operational differences, the two agencies often form an unhealthy and secretive alliance.

While Operation Enduring Freedom was successful in liberating Afghanistan from Taliban control after 9/11, there was no doubt that the real prize was bin Laden himself. First for Bush and, later, for Obama, the longer bin Laden remained at large, the greater the threat to their legacies. If they couldn't touch the hijackers, they should, at the very least, get the figurehead.

But for successive administrations, that was easier said than done. The al-Qaeda chief had chosen his first redoubt with care. For several years before 2001, he had developed an intricate network of caves and dwellings 14,000 feet up in the settlement known as Tora Bora. The impenetrable mountains not only made it difficult for anybody to track him, but they were also just a few miles from Pakistan, allowing him to easily escape as Western troops moved in.

For many years before he settled in Abbottabad, the CIA

believed bin Laden moved from village to village in Waziristan. He communicated only about once a month and never used a telephone. When he reached a village with his bodyguards, he would request a meeting with the local tribal leader and a substantial bribe would be paid. Bin Laden would then be the guest of the village, where under Pashtun custom, he must be protected.

The main obstacle in finding him was that even if someone wanted to betray him and collect the $25 million reward, there was no one to turn to. The local police would know bin Laden was there, and if anyone tried to report his presence, they would quite likely be killed. One local mullah from Waziristan agreed to send information about bin Laden's movements; his beheaded body was found several weeks later with a message that his was the fate of spies.

The commander of one top-secret US military force told the *60 Minutes* TV news show how soldiers under his command found bin Laden but had let him slip through their fingers. The Delta Force commander, calling himself Dalton Fury, expressed his frustration at having known where bin Laden was, but feeling powerless to do anything. At one point, he said, his forces were closing in on bin Laden's men, but he decided to abort the mission because he did not have support from Afghan troops.

In another incident, Delta Force troops actually saw a tall man dressed in camouflage that they believed was bin Laden, only to have the al-Qaeda leader escape their bombing campaign in the mountains.

Fury talked about a book he has written entitled *Kill Bin Laden*, which detailed his memories of the campaign in Tora Bora in 2001. 'Our job was to go find him, capture or kill him, and we knew the writing on the wall was to kill him, because nobody wanted to bring Osama bin Laden back to stand trial in the United States somewhere,' the mission commander told his interviewer.

He said the administration's strategy was to let Afghans do most of the fighting, however. Using radio intercepts and other intelligence, he said, the CIA pinpointed bin Laden's location in the Tora Bora mountains near Pakistan.

Fury's Delta team joined the CIA and Afghan fighters and piled into pickup trucks. He claimed their orders were to kill bin Laden and leave the body with the Afghans, keeping an Afghan face to the war. However, an audacious plan to come at bin Laden from the back door was vetoed by a higher-up. Fury claimed he was never sure who it was. A second plan to drop hundreds of landmines over any escape route into Pakistan was also vetoed, with Fury claiming he had no idea why.

The only option left was a frontal assault. Fury said he had fifty men in Delta Force up against bin Laden's 1,000 fighters, so support from the Afghan forces was needed. But, he claimed, many of the Afghan soldiers were not on board – seeing bin Laden as a hero. One night, alone without his Afghan allies, Fury said he was told bin Laden was a mere two kilometres away. He had to make a decision, and faced with overwhelming odds, he elected to stay away.

The decision always nagged him. He wrote in his book: 'My decision to abort that effort to kill or capture bin Laden when we might have been with 2,000 metres of him, about 2,000 yards, still bothers me. It leaves me with a feeling of somehow letting down our nation at a critical time.' But, he added, it wasn't worth the risk.

Fury had a second chance. Later, a Delta Force squad nicknamed Jackal radioed that they had bin Laden in sight. He wrote: 'The Operation Jackal team observed fifty men moving into a cave that they hadn't seen before. The mujahideen said they saw an individual, a taller fellow, wearing a camouflage jacket. Everybody put two and two together: "OK, that's got to be Osama bin Laden egressing from the battlefield."

'They called up every available bomb in the air, took control of the airspace. And they dropped several hours of bombs on the cave he went into. We believe, it was our opinion at the time, that he died inside that cave.' Later, however, Fury was proven wrong, when American forces were unable to find bin Laden's body and the al-Qaeda leader began releasing radio and video footage again.

Fury told *60 Minutes* that he believes he knows what happened. He said bin Laden was wounded in the shoulder by shrapnel from an American bomb and was then hidden in a town next to the al-Qaeda cemetery.

'We believe a gentleman brought him in; a gentleman, him and his family were supporting al-Qaeda during the battle. They were providing food, ammo, water. We think he went to that house, received medical attention for a few days, and then we believe they put him in a vehicle [and] moved him back across the pass,' he was quoted as saying.

What appears indisputable is that bin Laden needed – and got – help to remain beyond America's clutches. But was the dramatic raid in Abbottabad really an elaborate charade designed to hide the truth about his demise and make it more palatable to the world?

The lack of any photographs of bin Laden's body – unlike when Libya's Muammar Gaddafi was killed – has only served to fuel the conspiracy theories.

According to Pulitzer Prize-winning investigative journalist Seymour Hersh, there was no great mystery about bin Laden's hiding place. He claimed bin Laden had been a prisoner of the ISI inside the Abbottabad compound since 2006 and that Pakistan's two most senior military officers, General Ashfaq Parvez Kayani, chief of the army staff, and General Ahmed Shuja Pasha, director general of the ISI, not only knew about the US mission but welcomed the SEAL helicopters with open arms by ensuring they weren't intercepted.

Hersh, who famously revealed the truth about the My Lai massacre in Vietnam and the Abu Ghraib prison abuses by US soldiers, claims the courier story was faked by the US and that the tip-off came in 2010 from a former Pakistani intelligence agent in return for a lion's share of the $25 million ransom offered for information about bin Laden's location. Writing in the *London Review of Books* in an article that has received more than 2 million page views, Hersh said the agent was relocated to Washington DC, where he worked as a consultant with the CIA.

Sources told Hersh that bin Laden had been betrayed to the ISI by tribesmen, and that the Pakistanis had been holding him in reserve as a pawn, potentially to be used in negotiations with the US. The feared terror firebrand was reported to be 'an invalid' living in a house with barred windows and armed guards around the clock.

When the Americans finally told the Pakistanis that they knew where bin Laden was being held, wrote Hersh, a deal was struck involving military aid and some 'under-the-counter' incentives to permit the kill-or-capture operation. The raid, he says, was staged so the Americans could claim bin Laden from the ISI and assassinate him.

It will come as no surprise that there was an alleged complication involving Saudi Arabia. Hersh claimed the Saudis had been financing bin Laden's upkeep in Abbottabad the entire time.

'The Saudis didn't want bin Laden's presence revealed to us because he was a Saudi, and so they told the Pakistanis to keep him out of the picture,' Hersh quoted a retired senior US intelligence official as saying. 'The Saudis feared if we knew we would pressure the Pakistanis to let bin Laden start talking to us about what the Saudis had been doing with al-Qaeda. And they were dropping money – lots of it. The Pakistanis, in turn, were concerned that the Saudis might spill the beans about their control of bin Laden. The fear was that if the US found out about bin Laden from Riyadh, all hell would break out. The Americans learning about bin Laden's imprisonment from a walk-in was not the worst thing.'

He claimed the ISI agents guarding bin Laden at the compound around the clock were ordered to make themselves scarce as soon as they heard the rotor blades of the American helicopters arriving overhead. There was no way the ailing terror boss was getting out alive.

'They knew where the target was – third floor, second door on the right,' the former intelligence official told Hersh. '[They were ordered to] go straight there. Osama was cowering and retreated into the bedroom. Two shooters followed him and opened up. Very simple, very straightforward, very professional hit.'

In the days and weeks after the raid, the White House gradually walked back their claims that bin Laden was armed and that he used his wives as shields. The idea that the SEALs could have captured bin Laden alive and that there was no firefight, or any real opposition, have been conveniently brushed under the carpet.

After Obama's dramatic announcement revealing bin Laden's death, Hersh claims the Pakistanis felt the Americans had 'sold them down the river'.

It should be said that Hersh's sources remain anonymous and his version has been dismissed both by the authorities and by highly respected authors such as Mark Bowden, who wrote the 2012 book about bin Laden's demise called *The Finish*.

Nevertheless, the Americans have gone to great lengths over the years to insist bin Laden could have been taken alive. White House and Pentagon officials are adamant the SEAL Team Six was given the option to take him as a prisoner. But they are empty words.

The most obvious argument against taking him captive was that, behind bars at Guantanamo Bay or anywhere else the Americans held him, the al-Qaeda boss would be seen as a martyr to the Islamic cause. There was also the possibility that if he did decide to talk, he could reveal some uncomfortable truths about the three countries most closely linked to 9/11 – the US, Pakistan and Saudi Arabia. The risk was simply not worth taking.

During the final run-up to the 2020 US presidential election, an even more bizarre scenario played out in the world's media. QAnon, a far-right group of conspiracy theorists with a considerable online following, had posted a tweet suggesting that bin Laden was still alive and that the SEALs actually killed his body double – and were then wiped out themselves.

While the tweet may have fed the group's hunger for conspiracies, it would never have crossed over into the mainstream media had Donald Trump not retweeted it to his 87.2 million followers.

The president's apparent support for the group – and for the bin Laden theory – was raised at a televised Town Hall debate by NBC moderator Savannah Guthrie, who asked Trump to disavow QAnon, something he was determined not to do.

'That was a retweet,' insisted Trump. 'I'll put it out there. People can decide for themselves. I won't take a position.'

'I don't get that, you're the president,' Guthrie hit back. 'You're not like someone's crazy uncle who can just retweet whatever.'

'Let's waste a whole show,' Trump snapped at Guthrie when she pressed him on QAnon and their theory that Democrats in America were a 'Satanic paedophile ring'.

'I know nothing about it,' he replied. 'I know they are very much against paedophilia, they fight it very hard. But I know nothing about it.'

O'Neill, the Team Six triggerman, stuck by his story. 'Very brave men said goodbye to their kids to go kill Osama bin Laden,' he tweeted. 'We were given the order by President Obama. It was not a body double. Thank you, Mr President. I know who I killed, homie. Every time.'

Nothing remains of the Abbottabad hideaway; it was reduced to rubble after the raid. It is much harder to erase the feeling that we still do not know all the facts about the death of Osama bin Laden.

FBI TEN MOST WANTED FUGITIVE

Murder of U.S. Nationals Outside the United States; Conspiracy to Murder U.S.
Nationals Outside the United States; Attack on a Federal Facility Resulting in Death

USAMA BIN LADEN

Deceased

Date of Photograph
Unknown

Aliases:
Usama Bin Muhammad Bin Ladin, Shaykh Usama Bin Ladin, the Prince, the Emir, Abu Abdallah, Mujahid Shaykh, Hajj,
the Director

DESCRIPTION

Date(s) of Birth Used:	1957	Hair:	Brown
Place of Birth:	Saudi Arabia	Eyes:	Brown
Height:	6' 4" to 6' 6"	Complexion:	Olive
Weight:	Approximately 160 pounds	Sex:	Male
Build:	Thin	Nationality:	Saudi Arabian
Occupation:	Unknown		

Scars and Marks: None known
Remarks: Bin Laden is the leader of a terrorist organization known as Al-Qaeda, "The Base". He is
left-handed and walks with a cane.

CAUTION

Usama Bin Laden is wanted in connection with the August 7, 1998, bombings of the United States Embassies in Dar es
Salaam, Tanzania, and Nairobi, Kenya. These attacks killed over 200 people. In addition, Bin Laden is a suspect in other
terrorist attacks throughout the world.

REWARD

The Rewards For Justice Program, United States Department of State, is offering a reward of up to $25 million for
information leading directly to the apprehension or conviction of Usama Bin Laden. An additional $2 million is being
offered through a program developed and funded by the Airline Pilots Association and the Air Transport Association.

CONSIDERED ARMED AND EXTREMELY DANGEROUS

If you have any information concerning this person, please contact your local FBI office or the nearest American Embassy
or Consulate.
June 1999 Poster Revised November 2001

MOST WANTED: the FBI wanted poster for Osama (Usama) bin Laden, updated
to show that he is 'deceased'.

Chapter Twenty-Seven

The Trial

**Guantanamo Bay, Cuba,
20 January 2010**

The wizened defendant, his grey beard streaked with red dye, sits waiting in the dock for what will be the fortieth series of pre-trial hearings in the case against him as the alleged planner of the 9/11 attacks nearly two decades earlier.

Khalid Sheikh Mohammed looks like Gandalf on his last legs; he is fifty-five but looks more like eighty-five. He will be lucky if he lives to face the military commission and the death sentence that awaits him if he is found guilty. The trial date had been set for January 2021 but was again delayed because of the coronavirus pandemic that prevented anyone, including defence lawyers, from travelling to the US military base, Guantanamo Bay, in Cuba that has been KSM's heavily fortified home since 2007.

There is little doubt about his guilt. The evidence against him is considerable and, as we have learned, he is also believed to have killed *Wall Street Journal* journalist Daniel Pearl and almost certainly orchestrated the thwarted Bojinka Plot, the precursor to 9/11. Just as the 9/11 families have pleaded for the full facts behind what happened in the run-up to the attacks, so have they waited desperately to hear that at least one perpetrator of the atrocity would be brought to justice.

The great scandal is that the US has thrown down one obstacle after another to prevent the trial from starting, and even when it does, eventually, much of the evidence against KSM and his four co-conspirators has been ruled inadmissible.

The delaying tactics, spearheaded by the CIA with the tacit support of the military, have already stalled the legal proceedings for so long that most people without a vested interest have no clue that the case is still hobbling along. Some of the motivation for the continuing delays and the snail's pace of the prosecution is explained by concern over what the 9/11 mastermind may say in open court about the hijackers, especially Mihdhar and Hazmi and their time in America.

But torture is the real shadow hanging over the case.

After KSM was captured in Rawalpindi, Pakistan, on 1 March 2003 and handed over to the Americans, he and the other accused – Walid bin Attash, Ramzi bin al-Shibh, Ammar al-Baluchi and Mustafa al-Hawsawi – were secreted away to a number of different CIA 'black sites' in Afghanistan, Romania and Poland. KSM was transferred to Guantanamo Bay in December 2006.

While he was held in Poland, KSM was waterboarded 183 times, kept awake for weeks at a time standing up, slammed repeatedly against a wall, had water hosed into his backside and was interrogated while naked by female agents. According to CIA cables, the torture was pretty ineffective, with doubts over the veracity of much of the information given, and was eventually halted amid fears KSM was suffering lasting physical and mental damage. It was only after the treatments ended that he started talking, perhaps grateful that his jailers had stopped the punishments.

KSM and the others were kept away from the court system for years through delaying tactics by the CIA, which was insistent that isolation was imperative to prevent any future attacks, fearing publicity over the case could stir up anti-American sentiment. A plan by the Obama administration to try them in a federal court in Manhattan was met by a massive public backlash and eventually blocked by Congress, meaning that the only place willing to take on the cases was a purpose-built military courtroom at Guantanamo Bay, about as remote as any trial could be. But before any realistic prosecution could be mounted, there needed to be evidence untainted by torture.

Fearing KSM's confessions to the CIA would not hold up in court, the FBI quizzed him formally once he was in Cuba in 2007, but defence lawyers have argued that those interviews were also tarnished by the 'enhanced' interrogation techniques that were legal under Bush but later outlawed by Obama. Put simply, it's a mess that the CIA and the US administration would rather bury under a mountain of bureaucracy than risk being trawled through in a court of law.

For years, the men were denied lawyers and it was June 2008 before formal charges were brought against them. Even before COVID-19 put the world in a tailspin, the logistics of the trial meant progress was excruciatingly slow.

Each month or so, a plane would take off from Washington DC bound for Cuba with most of those involved in the case on board, including prosecution and defence lawyers, but not, of course, the defendants, for a new round of hearings. They would often be cancelled for any of a number of reasons, including hurricanes, flight delays or, on several occasions, changing faces, including three different senior military officers who quit as judges presiding over the complex and time-consuming proceedings. Every time someone dropped from the case, their replacement would need to get the necessary security clearance. There are, incidentally, more than 30,000 pages of pre-trial transcripts.

Coronavirus brought a new set of problems, with lawyers prevented from travel to Guantanamo Bay and phone calls and zoom meetings banned. With face-to-face interviews impossible, all contact was confined to emails that were censured to ensure no classified materials were shared.

The five al-Qaeda defendants were part of a shrinking group of forty detainees in Cuba, down from a high of 677 in 2003. The cost per prisoner, according to the *New York Times*, is $13 million a year, making it the most expensive prison in the world.

Defence lawyers have already argued, with some success, that any confessions or information gained under torture was worthless. Their contention that the FBI's follow-up interviews were similarly stained by the spectre of torture was agreed by one judge and then refuted by another.

Once again, the CIA's priorities, whatever you think of them, are working against the interests of the 9/11 families. The CIA had no interest in prosecuting KSM and the others; it only cared about the intelligence they could extract from them. Intelligence agents will argue to this day that the information was useful in preventing further attacks and in providing a deeper insight into the terror group. The Bush administration, which gave the CIA the power to use the torture techniques, would argue the same.

But legal experts say the case against the 9/11 mastermind was straightforward. If not for the torture complications, the case would likely have been dealt with long ago and KSM would have felt the full weight of the law. The families would have found some measure of justice and an element of closure, albeit not nearly enough. Instead, they wait, frustrated and angry, for the US to win its first conviction of an al-Qaeda terrorist directly involved in 9/11.

One key reason for the delaying tactics is that both KSM and, indeed, the Senate Intelligence Committee investigation led by Senator Dianne Feinstein insisted that much of the evidence he gave up during and after the torture sessions was fabricated. That presents an additional problem for the government narrative enshrined in the 9/11 Commission Report, which is essentially an official version of KSM's account of events.

If that is the case, the government's report on 9/11 is based on a foundation of lies.

'So, you have the 9/11 Commission Report, which is supposed to be the official narrative of what happened and why it happened, and it's completely based on a term called "bunk",' says Kristen Breitweiser, one of the Jersey Girls responsible for forcing through the appointment of the commission by President Bush. 'It's all bullshit. It's all based on Khalid Sheikh Mohammed. Did you ever see the movie, *The Usual Suspects*? It's like Keyser Söze – Philip Zelikow decided to write it all down and sold it to the American public.

'Khalid Sheikh Mohammed's version of what happened was testimony from torture. It's not credible and no one talks about that. They based the report on how and why something happened that killed 3,000 people on tortured testimony that Dianne Feinstein said was not credible at all. Everybody assumes that what KSM said and the 9/11 Commission used is the gospel and it's not.'

It is part of the official narrative that enhanced interrogation techniques – torture to you and me – were effective in breaking KSM and his cohorts. The CIA and intelligence chiefs from the Bush era will continue to claim credit for the secrets the detainees spilled during their long captivity.

The reality is that torture forces a victim into compliance, and that's a very different thing to the truth. They will say what they believe the interrogator wants to hear. It is worth little in a court of law and, worse, it could well be a pack of lies.

So, where does that leave the 9/11 Commission Report? On the rack.

Chapter Twenty-Eight

The Insider

Jamal Khashoggi never made any secret of his old friendship with Osama bin Laden. After the al-Qaeda leader was killed in Pakistan in 2011, Khashoggi wrote on Twitter, using bin Laden's nickname: 'I collapsed crying a while ago, heartbroken for you Abu Abdullah. You were beautiful and brave in those beautiful days in Afghanistan, before you surrendered to hatred and passion.'

The *Washington Post* columnist had long since distanced himself from his old contemporary's violent extremism, but the connection, fostered through interviews and long, intimate conversations at the jihadist stronghold in the caves of Tora Bora in Afghanistan and in Sudan, meant he was one of the very few people with the knowledge to piece together the puzzle of what really happened on 11 September 2001.

For Khashoggi had always been more than he seemed. He was a journalist reporting on Afghanistan's guerilla war with the Soviets and an unapologetic champion of the mujahideen's cause; he was a spokesman for the House of Saud and its most outspoken critic; and he was working both for Saudi Arabia's intelligence services and the CIA.

He had left his homeland a year earlier and settled in Washington DC because he dared challenge Mohammed bin Salman and the new Desert Kingdom regime that was both reforming and restraining in equal measure.

But it was not what Khashoggi said that put him in such jeopardy; it was what he kept to himself. And now he was being asked to say what he knew.

Khashoggi was under no illusions that by agreeing to meet with former FBI agent Catherine Hunt on 26 October 2017, he was venturing onto dangerous ground. As a counterintelligence expert with foreign postings in Egypt and Iraq, where she was awarded the FBI Campaign Support Medal for her work under fire, Hunt was no lightweight herself.

She was employed as an investigator by lawyers representing the families of many of the 2,977 victims murdered in al-Qaeda's hijacked plane assault on the World Trade Center and the Pentagon. Their lawsuit targeted Saudi Arabia but many of the questions could just as well have been directed at the United States government, which had obfuscated the truth about the worst terrorist attack in the nation's history since day one.

Hunt knew of Khashoggi's friendship with bin Laden, just as she knew that his connections within the Saudi royal family gave him unique access to its intelligence secrets. What she really wanted him to tell her was what he knew about 9/11.

It was only a 'preliminary meeting', Hunt would say later, but Khashoggi did agree to meet with her boss, New York lawyer Jim Kreindler, giving the families hope that they may finally get some answers.

That same day – 26 October 2017 – Khashoggi texted

Khalid bin Salman, the Crown Prince's younger brother who was then Saudi ambassador to the United States. The contents of the message have never been revealed, but less than a year later, on 2 October 2018, Khashoggi was brutally murdered inside the Saudi consulate in Istanbul. He was suffocated and his body was dismembered by a fifteen-member gang of state assassins, some of them closely associated to Mohammed bin Salman, Saudi's de facto ruler. Despite the kingdom's strong denials, the CIA concluded the Crown Prince was behind the assassination.

The lawyer for the 9/11 families, Jim Kreindler, is convinced that it was Catherine Hunt's meeting with Khashoggi and the possibility that he could spill the secrets behind the hijack plot that sent alarm bells ringing in Riyadh.

'Khashoggi was part of the intelligence community and we knew he knew a lot about the Saudi government's involvement in 9/11,' said Kreindler. 'I'm sure that as soon as she left, he called KBS [Khalid bin Salman] and said, "Look, the 9/11 lawyers are on to me. They know that I know what you guys did and I didn't give them anything, but you're holding my kid in Saudi Arabia, and if you harm him, I will."'

'So, my belief is that Khashoggi was killed not because he was a dissident, there are lots of dissidents, but because he was holding this axe over the Saudis' heads.'

The connection between Khashoggi and 9/11 is outlined in court documents in a March 2020 letter written to US Magistrate Judge Sarah Netburn by lawyers representing the families who also alleged that other witnesses were facing intimidation.

Kreindler & Kreindler lawyer Andrew Maloney told the court: 'Mr Khashoggi had previously been a government official for Saudi Arabia. In fact, I think he worked for Prince Turki, who was former head of Saudi intelligence. Mr Khashoggi knew Osama bin Laden, knew of other supporters of al-Qaeda. He had valuable information.'

The 9/11 lawyers claimed 'the Kingdom's actions in the murder of *Washington Post* journalist Jamal Khashoggi interfered' with their efforts to obtain evidence.

'Mr Khashoggi was himself a potential witness in this case, and was interviewed by Plaintiffs' investigator on October 26, 2017,' says the letter to Judge Netburn. 'Mr Khashoggi sent a text to senior Saudi officials that same day, and less than a year later on a trip outside the US he was brutally murdered and dismembered by the Kingdom inside its consulate in Istanbul, Turkey.

'A United Nations investigation confirmed the responsibility of the Saudi government, including the most senior Saudi officials, in the murder of Jamal Khashoggi.

'After committing the murder,' it continues, 'Saudi officials engaged in extensive efforts to conceal the grisly crime and obstruct official international investigations. For instance, the Kingdom issued an official press statement that Mr Khashoggi had "visited the consulate to request paperwork related to his marital status and exited shortly thereafter". In fact, Saudi officials arranged in advance for a "look-alike" – a Saudi "General" described as a "High Ranking Intelligence Officer employed at the Royal Palace" who resembled Mr Khashoggi – to walk out of the Consulate wearing the murdered man's own clothes past video cameras, to support the Kingdom's false story that Mr Khashoggi had actually left the Consulate.

'At the same time, the Saudi government issued blanket denials of responsibility. Saudi Prince Khalid bin Salman thereafter stridently denied all allegations of the Saudi government's involvement in Mr Khashoggi's disappearance, "I assure you that the reports that suggest that Jamal Khashoggi went missing in the Consulate in Istanbul or that the Kingdom's authorities have detained him or killed him are absolutely false, and baseless."

'Investigators later concluded that at the same time the Kingdom was publicly denying responsibility, it had actively employed teams of Saudi government officials to methodically destroy a variety of evidence of Mr Khashoggi's murder. To this day, Saudi Arabia is still hiding the location of Mr Khashoggi's body.

'In resisting appropriate protections for witnesses, the Kingdom conspicuously ignores proof that the concerns the witnesses have raised are well founded and grounded in the Kingdom's own misconduct. As more than 100 journalists and activists emphasized in a letter to the United Nations shortly thereafter, the murder of Jamal Khashoggi "constitute[d] nothing less than an act of state terror intended to intimidate journalists, dissidents, and exiled critics the world over".'

Unsurprisingly, the Saudis continue to claim that neither Crown Prince Mohammad bin Salman Al Saud, the country's de facto ruler, nor the royal family had anything to do with it.

However, if we are to believe that Khashoggi's death was connected to his inside knowledge about the Saudi role in 9/11, should we then be surprised at the CIA breaking ranks and pointing the finger of blame at the kingdom for the murder?

Probably not, would be the answer. The murder made headlines around the world and the US would have stuck out like a sore thumb if it had kept quiet.

It was all talk anyway. The Saudis carried on as if nothing had happened and eighteen months later Trump was tweeting about his 'friend' MBS and how they were working with Russian President Vladimir Putin to boost the oil industry.

Whether it was the death of 3,000 innocent people or one

well-connected journalist, America and Saudi Arabia were going to put their interests over the truth. Every time.

Chapter Twenty-Nine

The Betrayal

9/11 Repository, 180 Greenwich Street, New York City, 11 September 2021

Beneath the 1,776-foot-tall Freedom Tower and behind the walls of the National September 11 Memorial and Museum, a world away from the noisy hustle and bustle of tourists and workers outside on the streets of New York, is the silent resting place of the 9/11 dead.

Astonishingly, of the 2,753 people killed at the Twin Towers site, the remains of 1,113 people are still unidentified. Just 293 bodies were recovered intact, a tragic mercy to those families able to give them a conventional funeral. The great majority of the victims were obliterated by the plane crashes, the fires or the collapses of the towers – 21,905 pieces were eventually collected from the ruins, many of them as small as a nail or an inch of skin. Of those pieces, 7,204 have not been tied into a victim.

Most of us who lived through the tragedy remember the heartbreaking images of tearful relatives and friends at the scene in the days after the attacks, posting photos and messages appealing for help in locating loved ones.

Doctors and nurses stood in readiness at hospitals across

New York, expecting a deluge of patients from the towers that never came. Oblivion had come so absolutely that thousands of lives were extinguished in moments, leaving nothing behind. It was as if they never existed. Only memories remained.

As the days turned into weeks and hopes of a miracle faded, many had to accept the fact that the missing were dead, without ever finding any proof. Even now, despite more than $80 million being spent on the most expensive forensic operation in US history, only 60 per cent of the victims have been formally identified.

The unidentified remains are held in a private climate-controlled underground repository behind the museum, awaiting the DNA technology that may one day pair them to the names of the dead. Forensic scientists have returned to the same body fragments more than a dozen times, hoping to pass the 85 per cent threshold to guarantee an accurate ID. The last body part to be positively identified in the painstaking work by the New York Medical Examiner's office was in June 2019. Before that, it was March 2015.

There's no blame here. The Twin Tower attacks were unprecedented, and if the ensuing mass gathering of biological fragments by the police in the aftermath was haphazard, that was only to be expected. Nothing had prepared them to deal with a disaster on this kind of scale.

But what this repository of heartache does illustrate is the agony that continues to this day for the 9/11 families. For so many of them, it has meant that a funeral left an emptiness that cannot be filled. They will never know the end of the story. There were countless examples of bravery from the first responders who gave their lives for others, the office workers who helped their colleagues to safety, and then went back to help some more, and the multitude of unheralded acts of sacrifice we will never get to know. So many died in such a short time that it is impossible to piece together those final minutes.

Some, like Geoff Campbell's family, took solace in the fact that his remains showed he wasn't caught in the terrible fires that consumed the towers. Kristen Breitweiser wears Ronald's wedding ring on her right hand as an ever-present reminder of what she has lost. She chooses to believe that her voice, professing her undying love for him, was the last he heard. Many others don't even have that much to go on.

And the tragic legacy of 9/11 goes way beyond the families who lost someone that day. The list of those losing their lives as a result of the Twin Tower attacks continues, and most people don't have a clue it is happening.

Thousands of people are sick and dying of lung cancer because New York City and Christine Todd Whitman, who was head of the Environmental Protection Agency in the Bush administration from 2001 to 2003, said the air quality in downtown Manhattan in the wake of the attacks was safe. They let thousands of people – children and families – breathe that air, and now, years later, they're dying of horrific cancers. The whole area was a death chamber and it should have been evacuated.

Do most people know that? No, they don't. They just think that the poor 9/11 rescue workers are sick. Well, they're sick because the government didn't take care of them.

That's the aftermath. What about the events you have read about in this book that allowed 9/11 to happen? It is no longer enough to pay lip service to these broken families as presidents and politicians have done up until now.

The families have been repeatedly lied to about the events leading up to the 11 September attacks for twenty years. And why? To save the jobs and reputations of a small squad of intelligence agents who thought they knew better than the law? To save the administration of a newly elected president, who faked facts about the involvement of Iraq to go to war and was more worried about his relationship with oil-rich Saudi Arabia than being transparent about America's shortcomings to the people, his people, who lost everything?

The lies from the spies have been compounded by the administrations of Obama and Trump. Obama tried to thwart the efforts of the families to get their own answers by vetoing (unsuccessfully) a change in the law that allowed them to sue a foreign government. Trump pledged his help and reneged the very next day. The two presidents may share little in common, but they are complicit in this.

The great tragedy of 9/11 is that so many of the families feel badly let down by their own leaders. They have not been given the answers they have been asking for, not even close. What began as an aching suspicion that the US authorities were not being upfront and transparent about what happened has become an aching sore, compounded by the fact that two huge lawsuits against Saudi Arabia, by literally thousands of 9/11 plaintiffs, are being sabotaged by their own government.

Saudi Arabia has been targeted in the legal actions that Obama sought to prevent, not because of any vendettas against the kingdom or even because of its vast wealth, but because the facts as presented up until now simply do not add up.

The 9/11 families just want to know what really happened. They hoped the 9/11 Commission would stay true to its mission and connect the dots. The result was a costly public-relations exercise to obscure the lines ever further. By their own admission, attempts by Congress to get to the truth were foiled at every turn by the Machiavellian scheming of the FBI and the intelligence services.

The idea that the 9/11 attacks could have been prevented had the FBI been alerted about the presence in America of Mihdhar and Hazmi does not come from some crackpot conspiracy theorists. It is supported by former FBI agent Mark Rossini and former White House antiterrorism chief Richard Clarke. They are not outsiders. They were there.

The Jersey Girls still want to know why they are being ignored while the people they believe were to blame for the intelligence failures were rewarded with promotions and awards.

'The CIA purposely withheld information that should have been shared,' said Kristen Breitweiser. 'They purposely and knowingly did it and 3,000 people are dead because of it – and that's not a conspiracy, that's a fact, and we've never received any legitimate answer with regard to that or accountability. [Former CIA Director] George Tenet was given a Medal of Freedom. How the hell are you given a Medal of Freedom when you did not give the truth to the 9/11 Commission, did not give the truth to the Joint Inquiry of Congress and did not give the truth to the American public and the world?

'They are never going to tell the whole truth. The whole truth is just too bad. So, they're going to do what I would call limited hangout. And the limited hangout is, you'll blame a small group of people. You'll call them horribly bad people and you'll get your accountability for that group of bad people. And we'll all move on. Meanwhile, everyone else who had their fingers in it walk away smiling. I'd love nothing better for it to really just be the failure of a few CIA guys to report something. But I know too much about the story and the CIA doesn't control NORAD and they don't control oversight of banking and they don't control to some extent the borders and the issuance of passports.'

The biggest betrayal is the 9/11 families' treatment at the

hands of the people who are supposed to represent them. Even after twenty years, that's still hard to swallow.

'It's bad enough to be a victim of terrorism, but the terrorists owed me no duty. I didn't elect a terrorist to protect me. In that sense, what they did to my husband is expected,' said Kristen. 'But my own government with elected officials, they're supposed to look out for me. They're supposed to protect me. They're supposed to represent me. They have a sworn duty to do that. And the fact that they don't do that, particularly given my status as a victim, is kind of inconceivable, because it's not like I'm a victim through no fault of their own. I'm a victim because of their failures and that's proven – Tom Kean and Lee Hamilton made that very clear in the 9/11 Commission Report. But there were also several things that could have happened, and the attacks would never have taken place.

'We're not stupid. We caught on to what was going on early on. Our view is that if you screw it up, if you made mistakes, had failures, throw it on the table. Let's examine it. Let's learn from it. Let's make sure it never happens again. The only way you can help us at this point is making sure no one ever walks in our shoes. The only way you can do that is by examining where you screwed up and making sure things are put in place so nothing like that ever gets repeated.

'But there just wasn't a drive for that. There was just cover-up, cover-up, cover-up. And you don't learn lessons from that. If anything, the people that made the mistakes are emboldened because that's what happened with 9/11. Everyone who made a mistake, got promoted. Everyone got an award. They got rewarded and they got promoted to be shut up.'

Dig deep in the 9/11 Commission Report, the sanitised official account of the attacks, and you will find a hint at the truth it hides. A staff statement, prepared for the commission's public hearings and included in the report, suggests that putting Mihdhar and Hazmi on a no-fly watchlist before the attacks would probably not have prevented them from boarding a domestic flight inside the US.

Instead, the 9/11 investigators saw it as an 'intelligence story'. Without actually saying the terrorists were allowed to stay free so their movements could be watched and followed, they certainly made a case that would be an avenue worth pursuing.

'The intelligence mission was why the suspects were tracked in Malaysia rather than being detained and deported,' says staff statement number two. 'If the FBI had been given the opportunity to monitor Hazmi and Mihdhar in California and had been patient for nine months, or a year, then some larger results might have been possible, even after Mihdhar left. The universe of possibilities expands after Hani Hanjour joined Hazmi in December 2000, after which the two of them lived in Phoenix for several months before driving across the country and linking up with other future hijackers in northern Virginia. Up to this point all of these hijackers named so far were involved in the hijacking of American Airlines 77, which hit the Pentagon. But in northern Virginia they linked up with a hijacker who would join the team assigned to United 175, thus creating a possible opportunity to penetrate the other teams associated with the "Hamburg cell" as well.

'These are difficult "what ifs". It is possible that the Intelligence Community might have judged that the risks of conducting such a prolonged intelligence operation were too high – the risk of losing track of potential terrorists, for example. It is possible that the pre-9/11 FBI would not have been judged capable of conducting such an operation. But surely the Intelligence Community would have preferred to have the chance to make these choices. That is why we see this as an intelligence story – and a challenge for Intelligence Community management.'

In the contest for the 2020 Democrat presidential nomination won eventually by Joe Biden, one of his rivals, Tulsi Gabbard, was sufficiently concerned to raise the issue, suggesting the US was actively covering up Saudi Arabia's role in 9/11. 'We are eighteen years removed from this terrible crime, and the victims of this crime, the families who are here today, the American people, deserve all of the evidence to fully come to light,' the Hawaii congresswoman said on the campaign trail in New York City in October 2019. She added that the victims' families 'want the truth, and they deserve the truth'.

It is easy to espouse conspiracy theories hiding behind a social media handle, speaking on a radio show or writing from the safety of a desk, just as the search for the truth can be confused with a cry for attention.

But there are also some so-called conspiracy theories that require more scrutiny. Time allows us to look at history from a new perspective. The narrative in the weeks and months that followed 11 September seemed relatively straightforward. The attacks were masterminded by an embittered terrorist with an abiding hatred of the West and an army of Islamic militants willing to give their lives to strike a blow into the very heart of the capitalist beast. Families of the victims buried their dead. Previous generations may have gone away to war in Europe and Korea and Vietnam, but now a war few understood had come home to their shores. Revenge was demanded and duly delivered with wars in Afghanistan and Iraq.

By the tenth anniversary of 9/11 it was clear that while there may have been many reasons for the West wanting to go to war with Iraq, the terror attacks on New York and Washington should not have been among them. By the twentieth anniversary, many 9/11 families were left wondering whether the attacks should have happened at all. You have read the background to this alternative narrative. You can make up your own mind.

The harder you look at the circumstances of that terrible day, the more questions there are.

How did World Trade Center Building 7 – which was 370 feet from the Twin Towers and not hit by a plane – collapse so quickly and symmetrically? How could two planes down three towers?

Why would hundreds of engineers and architects feel the official version of how the towers fell was so wrong and so damaging to their professions that they formed a group called the Architects and Engineers for 9/11 Truth to lobby for a new inquiry? They are still calling for that inquiry and their numbers are growing.

You may not think the Bush White House would stoop so low as to aid the terrorists by instructing the military to stand down and not engage the hijacked airliners in the pursuit of supremacy – and oil – in the Middle East, but an estimated 100 million people have viewed *Loose Change*, a conspiracy theory documentary by 'Truther' director Dylan Avery suggesting precisely that.

These are not all just conspiracy theories dreamed up by a nutty minority. A 2016 study from Chapman University in California found more than half of Americans believe their government is concealing information about the 9/11 attacks. Sections of the official US 9/11 Commission Report were redacted for years – and much of it remains classified.

The danger in the obsessive secrecy of the US authorities and the government's two-decades-long campaign of deception is that it feeds the wackos and their crazier theories.

The inquests into the nearly 3,000 deaths were peremptory, the inquiries demeaning and the investigations self-serving.

There is no transparency. It simply cannot be right that the 9/11 families continue to be pitted against their own government when all they are seeking is the truth about one of history's most tragic and troubling episodes.

We are too used to Hollywood endings where the spy overcomes all odds to save the world, just in time. The reality is way messier. The line dividing right and wrong is often so thin as to be invisible and the truth is often simply the most convenient lie.

The one similarity is that in life, as in cinema, if the audiences don't like the ending, the people in power tear up the script and rework it until they do.

The deaths of nearly 3,000 people shocked the world and dominated the headlines for a while, and then the world moved on, leaving the families who lost everything to pick up the pieces themselves. They find themselves the forgotten dupes of the biggest cover-up in modern history and the people who perpetrated it get off scot-free, their reputations enhanced.

An independent inquiry, backed by the full force of the US law, is the only way to right this wrong. The investigators must have full access to every official document connected to the 9/11 attacks and the legal weight to demand what is not volunteered. Every document, every page, should be made public. Enough time has passed; the sell-by date on secrecy has long run out. The inquiry should not be answerable to the White House or Congress or any political party. It should be answerable to the American public.

Only then can America's leaders look the 9/11 families in the eye and say that everything possible has been done to assuage their pain.

Only then can the innocent victims of the attacks finally rest in peace …

Sources

Chapter 1

Archives.gov: Summary of Khan's Allegations to the FBI [Federal Bureau of Investigation] in 2000, c. 2003 (declassified 8 July 2015).

The Guardian: 'UK spymasters shrugged off al-Qaeda recruit's warning' (6 June 2004).

Niaz Khan Video Deposition, Motley Rice.

Document: FBI. From Michael Jacobson to Front Office re Niaz Khan (declassified 8 July 2015)

Document: Plaintiffs v. Kingdom of Saudi Arabia, United States District Court, Southern District of New York (filed 20 March 2017)

Chapter 2

New York Times: 'THREATS AND RESPONSES': Excerpts from Statement by Sept. 11 Commission Staff (17 June 2004)

Document: Office of the Inspector General: A Review of the FBI's Handling of Intelligence Information Prior to the September 11 Attacks (November 2004).

The New Yorker, 'THE AGENT: Did the C.I.A. stop an F.B.I. detective from preventing 9/11?', Lawrence Wright (3 July 2006).

The Public Broadcasting Service: 'What If', Jim Gilmore (3 October 2002)

Document: Interview of former FBI asset.

Chapter 3

Washington Times: 'FBI had human source in contact with bin Laden as far back as 1993', Guy Taylor and John Solomon (25 February 2014).

Document: Omar Al Bayoumi Rental Agreement.

Yahoo News: 'In court filing, FBI accidentally reveals name of Saudi official suspected of directing support for 9/11 hijackers,' Michael Isikoff (12 May 2020).

ProPublica/*New York* Magazine: 'The Saudi Connection: Inside the 9/11 Case that Divided the F.B.I.', Tim Golden and Sebastian Rotella (23 January 2020)

New York Times: 'Did the Saudis Play a Role in 9/11? Here's What We Found', Daniel Victor (25 January 2020).

ProPublica/*New York Times* Magazine: 'Operation Encore and the Saudi Connection: A Secret History of the 9/11 Investigation', Tim Golden and Sebastian Rotella (23 January 2020).

Document: 2012 FBI Summary Report (5 October 2012).

Document: Deposition Stephen Moore, ex-FBI. US District Court, Southern District of New York (15 September 2017).

Document: Deposition Catherine Mannherz Hunt, ex-FBI. US District Court, Southern District of New York (26 September 2018).

Document: Unredacted copy of 2012 FBI Summary Report.

Chapter 4

Interview with former FBI Special Agent Mark Rossini (17 August 2020 and follow-ups)

Newsweek: 'The Inside Information that Could Have Stopped 9/11', Jeff Stein (14 January 2015)

Chapter 5

The National Security Archive: The Anwar al-Awlaki File, compiled Scott Shane. (15 September 2015).

The Guardian: 'Anwar al-Awlaki's life of extremism' (30 September 2011).

New York Times: 'Imam's Path from Condemning Terror to Preaching Jihad' (8 May 2010).

The Hill: 'Rep. Peter King investigating links between Anwar al-Awlaki, 9/11 hijackers', Jordy Yager (16 August 2011).

Documentary: *The Roads to Terror*, French TV documentary series (*Les routes de la terreur*) first broadcast 2011

Chapter 6

The Atlantic: 'Anwar Al-Awlaki's Links to the September 11 Hijackers', J. M. Berger (9 September 2011).

Document: The People of the State of California v. Anwar Aulaqi (unclassified 4 December 2012).

Document: FBI case notes on Anwar al-Awlaki (unclassified 10 January 2013).

911 Commission Report.

Document: United States v. Ali al-Timimi (filed 18 August 2020).

New York Times: 'F.B.I. Chief Admits 9/11 Might Have Been Detectable', Neil A. Lewis (30 May 2002).

Document: Robert Mueller Memo – Anwar Aulaqi; IT-UBL/Al-Qaeda.

Document: FBI Memo: Anwar Nasser Aulaqi, IT-UBL/AlQaeda, OO:WFO

Chapter 7

Document: FBI 'Phoenix Memo' (10 July 2001)

Die Zeit: 'Deadly Mistakes', Oliver Schröm (2 October 2002).

Historycommons.org

28Pages.org: 'FBI Told Former Agent Not to Help 9/11 Victims Build Case Against Saudi Arabia', (1 August 2018).

Document: Review of the FBI's Handling of Intelligence Information Related to the September 11 Attacks (released publicly, June 2006).

Chapter 8

New York Post: 'How the FBI is whitewashing the Saudi connection to 9/11', Paul Sperry (April 12, 2015)

Document: Freedom of Information / FBI documents released to Broward Bulldog detailing allegations of Sarasota links to 9/11 hijackers.

The Investigative Project on Terrorism.

Sun Sentinel: 'FBI should stop hiding what happened in Sarasota before 9/11' (10 September 2019)

Sun Sentinel: 'Sarasota 9/11 connection remains cloaked in government secrecy, breeding suspicion of Saudi role in terror attacks', Bob Graham (17 May 2019).

Herald Tribune: 'Judge rules FBI must release details of 9/11 Sarasota investigation' (27 August 2019).

Chapter 9

Document: White House Briefing Note: 'Bin Laden Determined to Strike Within the United States' (6 August 2001).

Interview with former FBI Special Agent Mark Rossini (17 August 2020 and follow-ups).

Document: FBI email from Washington DC HQ to New York Field Office (29 August 2001).

Document: FBI Interview of Sibel Edmonds, former translator, Federal Bureau of Investigation (declassified 8 July 2015).

Chapter 10

India Today: 'Omar Sheikh, a tale of terror trail, to walk free in Pakistan in Daniel Pearl case', Prabhash K. Dutta (2 April 2020).

9/11 Timeline: Sept. 11's Smoking Gun: The Many Faces of Saeed Sheikh

The Telegraph, India: 'Omar Sheikh: if not Daniel Pearl, a trail with links to ISI, 9/11 mastermind and bin Laden' (16 April 2020).

The Guardian: 'The Pakistan Connection', Michael Meacher (21 July 2004).

The Australian: 'CIA Paid Pakistan for Terror Suspects', by Daniel McGrory (26 September 2006).

The Scotsman: 'The English Islamic Terrorist', Stephen McGinty (16 July 2002).

Dateline DC: 'Did Pearl Die Because Pakistan Deceived the CIA?' (3 March 2002)

The Week, India: 'Daniel Pearl murder: Omar Sheikh, three others rearrested after acquittal', Mandira Nayar (4 April 2020).

Chapter 11

Homeland Security Digital Library: 9/11-NORAD (North American Aerospace Defense Command): full audio transcript.

Chapter 12

Interview with Matt Campbell (10 June 2020 and follow-ups).

Daily Mirror: 'This War is a Farce', John Pilger (29 October 2001).

West Sussex County Times: '9/11 controversy in Horsham court' (27 February 2013).

Daily Mail: 'TV licence evader refused to pay because the "BBC covered up facts about 9/11 and claimed tower fell 20 minutes before it did"', Mark Duell (25 February 2013).

Chapter 13

National Fallen Firefighters Foundation: Scott Matthew Davidson

All That's Interesting: 'The Story Behind the 9/11 Photo of a Doomed Fire Truck Heading Toward the Twin Towers', Hannah McKennett (16 December 2019).

9/11 Always Remember: Scott Matthew Davidson – WTC (521) – Firefighter.

Variety: 'How Pete Davidson Found His Voice on "Saturday Night Live"', Ramin Setoodeh (28 August 2018).

New York Times: 'Pete Davidson Nuzzles Up to the Prickly Joke', Jon Caramanica (1 October 2015).

Hollywood Reporter: 'Charlie Sheen on His Surprising New "9/11" Movie and Those Truther Comments', Ryan Parker (8 September 2017).

New York Times: 'The September 11 Records / oral histories' (made public 12 August 2005).

Document: Federal Emergency Management Agency (FEMA) Report (published May 2002).

Document: National Institute of Standards and Technology (NIST) Report (published September 2005).

Chapter 14

Interview with Richard Gage, Founder and CEO, Architects and Engineers for 9/11 Truth (October 2020 and follow-ups).

Seattle Times: 'Twin Towers Engineered to Withstand Jet Collision', Eric Nalder (27 February 1993).

Documentary: PBS: *America Rebuilds: A Year at Ground Zero*, US TV documentary first broadcast September 2002.

Document: University of Alaska Fairbanks (UAF): 'A Structural Reevaluation of the Collapse of World Trade Center 7' (published 2019).

Chapter 15

Interview with Tim Frolich, World Trade Center survivor (April 2020 and follow-ups).

Interview with Jim Kreindler, Partner, Kreindler & Kreindler (April 2020).

Dartmouth College Speech: 'Saudi Arabia's Role in 9/11 and Why the U.S. Government has Kept it Hidden', James Kreindler (2 January 2020).

Attorney website: Kreindler Files 9/11 Terror Lawsuit Against Saudi Arabia (full complaint).

Document: Justice Against Sponsors of Terrorism Act (JASTA), 2016.

Document: Motley Rice Lawsuit: Plaintiffs v. Kingdom of Saudi Arabia (filed 17 March 2017).

Document: Kreindler & Kreindler Lawsuit: Plaintiffs v. Kingdom of Saudi Arabia (filed 20 March 2017).

Website: https://passjasta.org/

Yahoo: 'In court filing, FBI accidentally reveals name of Saudi official suspected of directing support for 9/11 hijackers', Michael Isikoff (12 May 2020).

Chapter 16

Popular Mechanics: 'Debunking the Myths About the 9/11 Attack on the Pentagon' (9 September 2020).

Documentary: *Loose Change 9/11: An American Coup* (released on video September 2009; written and directed by Dylan Avery).

Document: Robert Mueller statement to Joint Intelligence Committee Inquiry (September 2002).

Chapter 17

Document: United Airlines Flight 93 cockpit voice-recorder transcript.

Chapter 18

Donald Trump interview with WWOR (11 September 2001).

CBS News: 'Profiting from Disaster' (19 September 2001).

Associated Press: 'Options exchange probing reports of unusual trading before attacks' (19 September 2001).

Interview with Richard Gage, Founder and CEO, Architects and Engineers for 9/11 Truth (October 2020 and follow-ups).

Chapter 19

FBI source (name withheld)

Document: Judicial Watch v. Federal Bureau of Investigation

Document: FBI Files / Saudi flight manifest

New York Times: 'The Great Escape', Craig Unger (1 June 2004).

Los Angeles Times: 'After 9/11: the Saudis Who Slipped Away', Craig Unger (11 April 2004).

Chapter 20

The Guardian: 'Living with 9/11: the anti-terror chief', Paul Harris (5 September 2011).

The Daily Show with Jon Stewart (2008).

ABC News: 'Behind the 28 Pages: Questions About an Alleged Saudi Spy and the CIA', Richard Clarke (19 July 2016).

Vimeo: Richard Clarke at Fordham Law Conference (26 April 2016).

Document: Former CIA Director George Tenet's statement to Congress (29 January 2003).

Chapter 21

Interviews with Kristen Breitweiser, 9/11 widow and one of the 'Jersey Girls' (17 August 2020 and follow-ups).

Chapter 22

Interviews with Kristen Breitweiser, 9/11 widow and one of the 'Jersey Girls' (17 August 2020 and follow-ups).

The 9/11 Commission Report (published 22 July 2004).

The Cipher Brief: '9/11 Commission Director: No Evidence that CIA Sought to Recruit Hijackers', Philip Zelikow (3 November 2017).

Chapter 23

Los Angeles Times: 'The Plot', Terry McDermott (1 September 2002).

Chapter 24

Document: Justification for US Military Intervention in Cuba. Chairman of the Joint Chiefs of Staff, US Army General Lyman L. Lemnitzer (dated 13 March 1962).

Chapter 25

Document: Minutes of September 2005 meeting of Senate Judiciary Committee.

Document: Project Able Danger.

New York Times: 'Officer Says Pentagon Barred Sharing Pre-9/11 Qaeda Data With F.B.I.', Philip Shenon (16 August 2005).

Document: Account of FBI Interview with Dina Corsi, Intelligence Operations Analyst re: Hamzi and Midhar (4 November 2002).

Chapter 26

Document: Memo to Interpol, Washington DC (8 August 2002).

London Review of Books: 'The Killing of Osama Bin Laden', Seymour M. Hersh (21 May 2015).

Document: OSAMA BIN LADIN & AL QAEDA Documents Captured at Abbottabad Compound, BACM Research.

Chapter 28

Interview with Jim Kreindler, partner, Kreindler & Kreindler (April 2020).

Document: Letter to US Magistrate Judge Sarah Netburn from Plaintiffs' Executive Committees (March 2020).

Courthouse News Services: '9/11 Families Detail Meeting With Slain Reporter Khashoggi', Adam Klasfeld (4 March 2020).

Chapter 29

Document: Staff Statements I and II, The 9/11 Commission Report (22 July 2004).

Associated Press: 'Tulsi Gabbard: Release documents related to Saudis and 9/11', Karen Matthews (29 October 2019).

Chapman University, California: 'What Aren't They Telling Us?' Chapman University Survey of American Fears (11 October 2016)'

Select Bibliography

Bowden, Mark, *The Finish: The Killing of Osama bin Laden*, Grove Press, London, 2012

Clarke, Richard, *Against All Enemies: Inside America's War on Terror*, Free Press, New York, 2004

Duffy, John and Nowosielski, Ray, *The Watchdogs Didn't Bark: The CIA, NSA, and the Crimes of the War on Terror*, Hot Books, New York, 2018

Edmonds, Sibel, *Classified Woman: The Sibel Edmonds Story*, Sibel Edmonds, Alexandria, Va, 2012

Fury, Dalton, *Kill Bin Laden: A Delta Force Commander's Account of the Hunt for the World's Most Wanted Man*, St Martin's Press, New York, 2008

Hamilton, Lee H. and Kean, Thomas H., *The 9/11 Commission Report: Final Report of the National Commission on Terrorist Attacks Upon the United States*, W. W. Norton & Company, New York, 2004

Meyssan Thierry, *9/11: The Big Lie*, Carnot Publishing, London, 2002

Owen, Mark and Maurer, Kevin, *No Easy Day: The Only First-hand Account of the Navy Seal Mission that Killed Osama bin Laden*, Penguin Books, London, 2013

Tenet, George, *At the Center of the Storm: My Years at the CIA*, Harper Collins, New York, 2006

Unger, Craig, *House of Bush, House of Saud: The Birth of Modern Terrorism*, Gibson Square Books, London, 2019

Woodward, Bob, *Bush at War*, Simon & Schuster, New York, 2002

Wright, Lawrence, *The Looming Tower: Al-Qaeda's Road to 9/11*, Penguin, London, 2007

Zuckoff, Mitchell, *Fall and Rise: The Story of 9/11*, Harper Collins, New York, 2019

Index